BEYOND CARBON NEUTRAL

BEYOND CARBON NEUTRAL

HOW WE FIX
THE CLIMATE CRISIS *NOW*

SAMUEL M. GOODMAN, PHD

NEW DEGREE PRESS

BEYOND CARBON NEUTRAL

How We Fix the Climate Crisis Now

ISBN   978-1-63676-823-6   *Paperback*

          978-1-63730-219-4   *Kindle Ebook*

          978-1-63730-267-5   *Ebook*

This book is dedicated to my wife, Ashley, whose love and support made the entire project possible.

TABLE OF CONTENTS

———

AUTHOR'S NOTE

As of the publication of this book, we are in the midst of the coronavirus pandemic that is raging across the world. This disaster will profoundly impact society for years to come beyond the short-term impacts to human health and the lives lost. With millions out of work, facing eviction, or experiencing a rapid decline in their material conditions, it is extremely likely that we are facing an economic situation unrivaled in severity since the Great Depression. The recovery will need to take the same form now as it did then: massive investments to put people back to work.

The programs of yesteryear built infrastructure across the country, leading us out of the Depression and providing a foundation for future prosperity. We can and should do the same now for climate change. Doing so would mitigate both crises, making the country more stable after the pandemic and ensuring stability by safeguarding the future. In addition to those benefits, making climate change-mitigating investments will provide a renewed sense of shared purpose. Achieving a successful energy transition will inject trillions of dollars into the economy and put millions back to work, for there is certainly much work to be done. We need only make the decision to begin.

INTRODUCTION

The world burned in 2019. First, there was Brazil, where tens of thousands of human-made fires spread out of control in the usually nonflammable Amazon Rainforest, pushing it closer to an irreversible collapse.[1] Australia then ignited from June into the next year. Bushfires ravaged a cumulative area larger than Missouri and spread smoke halfway across the world.[2] California also joined the scene that summer, settling into the new normal of wildfire seasons destroying large swaths of the state.[3] And each year forward is likely to get worse. Siberia started burning in 2020, releasing greenhouse gasses from the permafrost in addition to smoke and ash from the fires.[4]

Each of these conflagrations started with a different spark, but the cause was the same. The world is burning because

---

1 Borunda, "See How Much of the Amazon," August 29, 2019; Woodward, "The Amazon Rainforest Is Burning," August 24, 2019; Irfan, "The Amazon Rainforest's Worst-Case Scenario," August 27, 2019.

2 BBC News, "Australia Fires," January 31, 2020.

3 Cosgrove, "These Are the Largest Wildfires," October 9, 2019.

4 Machemer, "The Far-Reaching Consequences," July 9, 2020. A *greenhouse gas* is any chemical in the atmosphere that traps heat.

of climate change. Australia was in the middle of a historic drought that made the landscape a tinderbox.[5] The same conditions happened throughout Brazil. An ongoing heatwave in Siberia made conditions possible for forest fires.[6] Periodic burning in California is normal, but every degree of warming makes the conflagrations more intense, more widespread, and more difficult to control.[7] In each case, the root cause was the same: rising heat, drought, and changing weather patterns.

Climate change causes more disruptions than just drought- and heat-driven fires. Nonetheless, at least these devastating fires drew massive attention while they were ongoing. People will only ignore scientific truths for so long, and personal experience with deadly heatwaves and watching your home ignite tends to burn away the blinders of denial so much quicker.[8] With daily images across the media, perhaps, finally, some correction would happen.

And then, nothing happened.

Denialism remains strong. The global response to climate change was basically unchanged, and the justification for inaction followed familiar patterns. Brazil's government doesn't publicly recognize the contributions of climate change at all, labeling it an insidious plot from a left-wing cabal.[9] Russia now acknowledges climate change exists and

---

5   Hannam, "How Bad is this Drought," November 4, 2019; Thompson, "Yes, Climate Change Did Influence," March 4, 2020.

6   Stone, "A Heat Wave Thawed Siberia's Tundra," July 6, 2020.

7   Borunda, "Climate Change is Contributing," October 25, 2019.

8   Funk and Kennedy, "How Americans See Climate Change," April 21, 2020.

9   Tharoor, "Bolsonaro, Trump and the Nationalists," August 23, 2019; Reuters Staff, "Brazil Foreign Minister Says," September 11, 2019.

is a threat but claims its underlying causes are still mysterious.[10] The Australian government, elected before the fires on a climate change-skeptical platform, has downplayed links between their fires and greenhouse gas emissions.[11] If the first step toward solving a problem is admitting one exists, too many still haven't started the journey.

Even acknowledging a problem exists does not guarantee a solution. Instead, we move into a more abstract realm to justify inaction: cost. Those who wish to preserve the status quo on climate policy, regardless of their incentives, have largely turned to a monetary argument. A substantial portion of the proposed Green New Deal response was centered on the predicted cost.[12] While sometimes conceding the reality of climate change, this framework buries the absolute imperative of the crisis. The implication is that there are scenarios in which the costs outweigh the probable or even possible benefits of taking action.

Once the discussion turns to loans, taxes, and spreadsheets, it is easy for people to lose focus and disengage from the issue. It also provides a smokescreen so those in power can provide the illusion they are reasonable about the problem but only dedicated to *common-sense* solutions. The result is no different than denying climate change whole cloth—nothing happens. Most frustratingly, inaction is wholly unjustified when considering a fair cost-benefit analysis of our predicament. Nature does not care about markets. Physics does not care about financial institutions. If you truly

---

10   Isachenkov, "Putin Acknowledges Threats," December 19, 2019.

11   Reuters Staff, "Australia's Leaders Unmoved," January 7, 2020.

12   For example: Dorman, "House GOP Resolution Blasts," May 22, 2019; Loris, "The Green New Dealt," May 29, 2019; Gleckman, "The Green New Deal would Cost," February 7, 2019.

want an accurate cost-benefit analysis, here is the bottom line: you either reverse climate change or you lose everything.

THE COST OF INACTION

Please, say these words out loud: I am dead; my children are dead; my grandchildren are dead; everyone I have ever known or have yet to meet is dead. We are dead because of climate change.

That is the cost of inaction. Our bodies may still be moving, but we are presently dead because nothing we do carries any meaning so long as climate change is allowed to drive us toward the abyss. We can take pride in our homes and the objects we've filled them with, but they will be swept away. The wildfires that are already commonplace on continent-wide scales will only become more frequent and devastating, consuming our possessions and driving people from their property.[13] In a morbidly comical balance, the seas will rise elsewhere and drag homes and livelihoods beneath the waves.[14] Nowhere will be safe from more frequent and more dangerous weather. Storms and floods will inundate the interior, while what's left of the coasts will be increasingly ravaged by hurricanes and storm surge.[15] The years spent being fiscally responsible will have been made pointless, as any gains are wiped from existence in mere moments.

As a people, we can extol the virtues of the things we've built, feats we've achieved, and the secrets of the universe we've unlocked. When civilization collapses, it will be as if

---

13 Lieberman, "Wildfires and Climate Change," July 2, 2019; Westerling et al., "Briefing: Climate and Wildfire," 2014.

14 To see how your area would fare, see: NOAA, "Sea Level Rise Viewer," accessed August 6, 2020; Treat et al., "What the World," September 2013.

15 NASEM, "Global warming," accessed August 6, 2020.

these accomplishments never happened. It won't matter that we've landed on the moon if only a scramble for survival occupies our thoughts. Curing diseases won't do any lasting good if the entire system falls under the weight of resource shortages and long-forgotten pathogens emerging from the permafrost.[16] The monuments we've built for ourselves will crumble once there's no one who can maintain them.[17] It will be as though climate change has erased our entire history. You may seek joy in raising your family, finding comfort knowing a part of you will live on after you are gone. However, your descendants are unlikely to survive for long. A changing climate means more drought and famine, more crop-eating insects during longer and hotter summers, and floods that wipe away plantings.[18] It means acidified oceans that no longer yield enough fish.[19] The future created by climate change is one where access to basic necessities are precious and fought over, whether on a personal scale or through wars to control what resources remain.[20] A world subject to climate change is a hostile place that cannot support eight billion people.

Climate change will wipe away all traces of our existence, and we must internalize this realization before any progress

16   Goudarzi, "As Earth Warms," November 1, 2016.

17   The world would start to look like the Chernobyl Exclusion Zone: Allan, "Chernobyl," May 28, 2019; Barras, "The Chernobyl Exclusion Zone," April 22, 2016.

18   Gray, "Earth's Freshwater Future," June 13, 2019; Deutsch, "Increase in Crop Losses," 916.

19   NOAA, "Ocean Acidification," updated April 2020; Rojas-Rocha, "Worsening Ocean," July 29, 2014.

20   Sova, "The First," November 30, 2017; Klare, "If the US Military," November 12, 2019; Aton, "Once Again," June 9, 2017.

can happen. That is the only way we can truly make reversing it our overriding priority. It won't matter if we reform any other part of our society in the meantime. If we don't solve climate change, literally nothing else will matter. This understanding is neither natural nor comfortable to confront, but it must be if we are to reverse the inaction, apathy, and deception that have plagued our response for decades. Our only hope of reclaiming our lives is to do something about climate change.

HOPE

Climate change is a vast, all-encompassing threat that humans innately lack the ability to grapple with it. Our lack of comprehension is one of the reasons why we have not yet been able to mount a response in proportion to the threat. Consider the amount of carbon dioxide, the primary driver of climate change, humans add to the atmosphere. We emit around thirty-seven *billion* tons every *year*.[21] That amount of gas collected together occupies the volume of a cube seventeen miles wide, seventeen miles long, and seventeen miles tall.[22] We can do the math and measurements, but those numbers are not fully intelligible, not to an individual.

One of my guiding purposes for going to graduate school was to contribute to solving climate change. I thought, as a scientist, I would be able to make some single-handed advancement that would make the difference. It's what guided my decision-making when choosing a program, an advisor, and a research project. However, if my time in the laboratory taught me anything, it is that such thinking is

---

21   Harvey, "CO_2 Emissions," December 6, 2018.

22   See appendix for calculation details.

counterproductive. One person confronted with 4,965 cubic miles of carbon dioxide is ultimately powerless, no matter how intelligent, resourceful, or compassionate they might be. No amount of individual action, recycling, or cutting back will make a dent in climate change. That is a depressing thought for an individualistic society. We are raised to believe that we are solely in control of our own destiny, but that is not true in this instance. It is bigger than any one person, be they a scientist or senator. We must make peace with the fact we are, each of us, very small pieces in an enormous system that requires an overhaul. Yet, it is not bigger than all of us. There is still time to keep the door from closing on our future.

The impetus behind this book is to prove that statement is correct. It was partially born of frustration, as I have seen the same dead-end ideas endlessly repeating themselves within the discourse. If you have been watching progress on climate change, I am willing to bet you are similarly frustrated at the lack of concrete action. If you are new to the arena, it can be overwhelming to navigate a treacherous sea of technical information, half-truths, and inertia. The rest of the book aims to find solid ground and yield a comprehensive and actionable approach, a strategy. Its assembly shows how we can use the tools available to us now to fix climate change. The discussion is centered around the United States, but conditions elsewhere will be variations on the same themes.

This book is structured to answer the overarching question of climate change in three movements. The first covers how we can stop the problem from getting worse by cutting our emissions through a rapid shift to renewable power sources. Our ultimate objective needs to be to return the climate to its stable preindustrial condition, which is the subject of the second part. However, neither of those objectives will happen unless we marshal societal institutions—business, the government, and the people—to accomplish them, as is laid out in part three. Each is dependent on the others, and isolated success in one area will not yield the results we need. We must pursue them all simultaneously.

Most importantly, the book is written to push back against despair. That is our true enemy, the idea of surrender in the face of an overwhelming problem. Being a scientist means following the data, and decades of minimal activity does not portend a positive future. At least not without major forcing functions to change the status quo. And this is the moment when that must happen. We have precious little time, less than a decade, to begin work in earnest before we have missed our last opportunity to make a survivable climate for our descendants.[23] Success requires we focus only on the goal ahead, and despair will only slow us down. There is no time to waste, so let's begin.

---

23   IPCC, "Summary for Policymakers," 2018, 13.

CHAPTER 1

THE FOUNDATION

Our hope to reverse climate change rests on acting together, acting decisively, and—most importantly—acting quickly. This cannot be an ad hoc affair if we mean to effectively marshal the necessary resources. We need a coordinated approach that is more than a plan and certainly more than a vision. We need a strategy. Our strategy will need to be actionable and comprehensive, which means we need to start by laying a firm foundation. The cornerstone of a successful strategy is an accurate diagnosis of the problem.[1] Without one, you will not solve the core issue. Climate change is a large and complex problem and, to mitigate it, we must begin by understanding its root cause.

Carbon dioxide traps heat in the atmosphere. That much is a fact of physics. Trapped heat raises temperatures, which alters the climate in myriad ways. There are natural fluctuations in carbon dioxide content throughout the year. Plants absorb carbon dioxide to grow and release it as they decompose. More accumulates in winter when fewer plants are absorbing it, which is drawn down when snow

---

1   For an introduction to strategies, see: Rumelt, *Good Strategy Bad Strategy*.

melts and spring covers more of the Earth. This is the natural carbon cycle that life depends upon. However, humans are releasing vast quantities of carbon dioxide to power our homes, cars, and businesses, far beyond the ability of nature to incorporate within the existing system. Since nature cannot absorb what we are emitting, more carbon dioxide enters the atmosphere, trapping more heat. Thus, we are causing climate change.

With such a clear diagnosis, the solution seems like it should be obvious: we just need to stop emitting carbon dioxide. That is, we need to decarbonize. This is easier said than done. There are many ways we could potentially reduce emissions, and not all of them will be equally effective. Since time is of the essence, we need to focus on actions that will create the most benefit. Narrowing down our choices will rely on the next step of strategy building, setting the guiding policies that define our suite of potential solutions.

Just as blueprints define the structure of a house, guiding policies shape a strategy. They aren't solutions to climate change themselves, but they will lead us to the solutions. Our guiding policies will reflect the rules we will use to evaluate different approaches to solving climate change, and they reflect the overall philosophy that will guide our choices. Absent guiding policies, we run the risk of taking actions that work against each other, or we may become so bogged down in the number of available options we lose the ability to act decisively. While careful consideration of each option is necessary, we can't afford to fall into such traps.

GUIDING POLICY 1: FINDING A TARGET SECTOR
Our first task is to narrow our focus to the sectors contributing the most to climate change and whose emissions can

be most thoroughly reduced. Looking at the data, we can broadly focus our decarbonization efforts on transportation, buildings, industry, and electricity generation.[2] Each would be a fine target on its own, given they all emit millions of tons of carbon dioxide per year. Due to time and resource constraints, it would be better to narrow down the options and find overlap wherever possible.

Let's start with transportation since there's been a big push lately for electric vehicles. The thinking goes like this: if we stop using gasoline and diesel fuel to power cars and trucks, we can substantially reduce greenhouse gas emissions across the economy. In total, switching to electric vehicles would prevent about 1.6 billion tons of carbon dioxide, about 30 percent of total US emissions, from entering the atmosphere every year—not a bad start.[3] The technology is viable. Otherwise, we wouldn't see year-over-year growth in this sector. All we need to do is build more electric cars, install more charging stations, and call it a day.

The problem is the power for a vehicle still needs to come from somewhere, whether from the fuel in the engine or a power plant miles away. If you are charging your car in the United States, there's a good chance the electricity is generated by burning fossil fuels. Unless you're pulling solely from renewable sources, the amount of transportation emissions savings by switching to electric vehicles would be offset by a similar increase in emissions from electricity generation, so decarbonizing the transportation sector is impossible in isolation.

---

2   USEPA, "Sources of Greenhouse Gas," accessed August 1, 2020.

3   USEIA. "How Much Carbon Dioxide," May 20, 2020.

Buildings are a less obvious but nonetheless important contributor to climate change. You can find several sources of carbon emissions in your own home, like a stove, furnace, or water heater that runs on natural gas. You may not be able to see the emissions, but every time you cook a meal, turn up the heat, or take a shower, more carbon dioxide adds to the atmosphere. The obvious solution is to replace those appliances with electric units, much like replacing existing cars with electric vehicles. However, the problem is the same: electricity has to come from somewhere, and if you're burning fossil fuels to supply this added electricity demand, you will see little benefit.

Manufacturing is another potent area we could focus on for reducing emissions. Take the chemical industry as an example. It's one of the largest energy users, where huge quantities of heat are required to drive reactions, run distillation columns, and generate steam. Most of that heat is provided by burning fossil fuels, like your home's furnace on a much larger scale. The goal here would be to replace those boilers and heating systems with electrical units. Now we're back to the same issue we had with the cars and buildings: without a decarbonized power grid, electrifying industry won't fundamentally make a difference.

Analyzing our targets reveals a singular conclusion. Decarbonizing other sectors will not be successful without a renewable power grid. While electrification will be an important piece for complete decarbonization, it is not the current rate-limiting step for our transition.[4] Thus, our first guiding policy is this:

---

4   Roberts, "The Key," updated October 27, 2017.

(1) Transitioning to renewable electricity generation is the priority for reducing carbon emissions.

GUIDING POLICY 2: USING EXISTING TECHNOLOGIES

We need to address the elephant in the room before considering how to best replace the existing power generation capacity. There's always talk whenever you bring up renewable technologies about the need for research and development.[5] A focus on research has been used in proposals like the Green *Real* Deal (not to be confused with the Green *New* Deal).[6] An innovation-dependent approach implies the technology either doesn't exist or is currently too expensive to be fully implemented. These claims, however, are excuses for not taking action, and their effects would be to slow the transition to a renewable grid and maintain the fossil fuel status quo.[7] That's why they're often put forward by those benefiting from the current system.[8]

Let's start with the idea innovation is the fundamental bottleneck for action. In a recent report, the International Energy Agency rated renewable power generation technologies by their maturity.[9] Essentially, they estimated how much

---

5   For example: Roberts, "We Have to Accelerate," September 16, 2020.

6   For example: Colman, "Gaetz Drafting," March 3, 2019.

7   Lamb, "How 'Discourses of Delay,'" July 6, 2020.

8   For example, the U.S. Chamber of Commerce, which has historically advocated on behalf of fossil fuel interests, is a proponent of an innovation-based approach to climate change. Harbert, "Clean Power Plan," October 29, 2017; Kelly, "After Calling for Climate Action," September 29, 2020; Hackbarth, "Here's a Chart Showing," June 12, 2015.

9   IEA, "Energy Technology Perspectives 2020," July 2020, 71; Roberts, "Many Technologies Needed," July 14, 2020.

more innovation is required to bring each one to its full potential. Only a few were rated as "mature" and require negligible additional innovation before they can be implemented, including geothermal. Geothermal is extremely useful for a clean energy transition, as we will discuss in chapter six. Yet, with no innovation barrier, we're presently not investing much in it. That will be the same for every other technology, regardless of how advanced they are, because innovation is not the problem: our will to use them is.

Next, there's the idea technology needs to be improved before it's implemented. This is superficially true, as there's always room for improvement with any technology. The continual improvement in solar cell efficiency since the 1970s is evidence of that. However, research is never truly finished, and you never know when you're going to achieve a certain breakthrough. If you're waiting for technology innovation to be *complete*, you will be waiting forever. To borrow a phrase from President Truman, "imperfect action is better than perfect inaction." That is, eventually, good enough must be good enough.

Finally, there is the cost argument. Innovation, it is supposed, will bring down costs and incentivize a renewable transition without further direct action. Another way to bring down the costs of manufacturing is by scaling up production. Making more renewable energy sources will naturally bring costs down if we start to build massive amounts, which is more certain than the progress of innovation. Even if the implementation is *expensive* on some arbitrary scale, it also makes no sense to quibble about prices when the alternative is the collapse of civilization.

There will never be a single magic bullet for solving climate change. If a new technology arrives, we will certainly evaluate its utility and incorporate it into the strategy. We just can't afford to sit on our hands waiting for any specific approach to exit development. For that reason, our second guiding policy is this:

(2) The strategy will only rely on technology that currently exists.

GUIDING POLICY 3: REVERSING THE DAMAGE

The billions of tons of carbon we've pumped into the atmosphere won't be going anywhere unless we do something about it. Until then, all the problems associated with the warming we've experienced thus far will continue to make life difficult. One of our overall goals must be to remove that excess carbon dioxide and return to the climate conditions that allowed civilization to develop.

Releasing carbon dioxide into the atmosphere is easy and cheap while taking it out is difficult and expensive. It is akin to un-baking a cake. There hasn't been any economic incentive to do so yet, as the atmosphere is treated as a free, unlimited dumping ground for carbon dioxide under the current system. As a silver lining, because there has been no groundwork laid to this point, we have the flexibility to approach the problem directly and efficiently, without having to work with or replace existing capital. Our focus in part two is putting together our approach for drawing down atmospheric carbon dioxide.

Timing considerations will temper our plans to return balance to the carbon cycle. It does not make sense to invest effort and materials into removing carbon dioxide while we are still emitting vast quantities of it. It would be like trying to drain a bathtub while the faucet is still running. Doing so would also only decrease the imperative for taking fossil fuels offline by creating a false pause in our present trajectory. Because emissions are the ultimate source of our problems, all the activities for drawing down atmospheric carbon have to take second position to decarbonizing the power grid. Thus, enter guiding policy 3:

(3) Pulling carbon dioxide out of the atmosphere will occur only after fossil fuel emissions have ceased.

GUIDING POLICY 4: TAKING NONIDEAL ACTION

Our decision to prioritize the grid will not prevent continued warming by the carbon dioxide that's already in the atmosphere. It will take decades for the climate to recover while the strategy is being implemented. A best-case scenario implies significant disruption of society and a massive wave of extinctions throughout every ecosystem. The only way to mitigate those problems is to act as quickly as possible to reach a stable end state.

You can think of this as triage. In a medical setting, triage happens when more patients require medical attention than caregivers are equipped to handle. It means sorting who gets what treatment depending on the extent of their injuries. For our purposes, triage means making trade-offs that we normally wouldn't want to make, like eliminating certain jobs or disrupting a habitat in favor of fixing the overall climate problem.

We must consciously make such changes because we can't delay taking action until a perfect solution presents itself. Each subsequent chapter ends with a discussion of a disquieting choice, a sacrifice we must face if we are to fully implement a strategy that reverses climate change. So long as humans exist on this planet, we will alter its ecosystems, and those alterations will reflect in our society. At this point, we need to mitigate the worst of the damage. The fourth guiding policy summarizes this:

(4) Action must be taken even if the result is not ideal.

GUIDING POLICY 5: RETHINKING INSTITUTIONS

The next aspect we need to consider is the structural framework through which we will accomplish our actions. Essentially, we must decide who is going to be doing what. We can't just hand wave away responsibility and assume someone will take up the mantle for implementing these policies. Just as a verb without a subject is a sentence fragment, giving directions to no one is an incomplete strategy.

Engrained in this part of our strategy is the understanding things cannot continue as they have. If they could, climate change would never have been an issue in the first place. The problem with the radical shifts we must make is they will disrupt the current status quo. Even though it will lead to a better end state, any change in our lifestyles will naturally create discomfort and resistance. Humans are, after all, creatures of habit. Fully confronting climate change means challenging our own senses of comfort and familiarity.

Part three of this book analyzes which power structures are best suited for achieving our goals. That analysis includes the recognition that just because an institution or a way of thinking has worked in the past doesn't mean that it will be useful for solving this problem. We must be willing to question the utility of those aspects of our society. Otherwise, we will miss critical insights into how the same forces that have created our current predicament might impede our strategy.

That is a major risk. All our planning and design may be for naught if countervailing incentives are not removed. Thus, we have our next guiding policy:

> (5) Institutions or philosophies that impede progress must be changed.

GUIDING POLICY 6: AVOIDING TEMPORARY SOLUTIONS

Prioritizing speed is necessary for fully combating climate change. However, we must be careful as the desire to move quickly may lead us to incorrectly evaluate some solutions as being more viable than they really are. A final test of any proposed action must be the expected longevity of the benefit. If a carbon neutral power source is available but would be quickly depleted, that would not be a good addition to the strategy. We would be forced to make multiple investments to ultimately solve the problem when we could have utilized a more permanent option at the outset. We will always need power, so it only makes sense to invest in options that will provide us energy over the longest possible time. We also want to be able to solve climate change forever, so an action that takes carbon out of the atmosphere but does not lock it away permanently would not be a wise target either.

The philosophy of this approach is familiar to any other purchase decision we make. We can purchase a cheap garment that wears out quickly, or we can spend more on one of quality that lasts a long time. We need to recognize it is most efficient to free ourselves from the shackles of climate change once and then be done with it. This concept is summarized as our sixth and final guiding policy:

> (6) Temporary solutions to climate change are not viable.

ACTIONS

Now that we have our diagnosis and guiding policies, the real work begins. All strategies are only so much vision statement, motto, and fluff until they have a set of coherent actions to implement. To be coherent, all of our actions must work together toward solving climate change and not against each other. The rest of the book is dedicated to detailing those actions. Each chapter discusses how a class of technology or policy can contribute to solving climate change and how they can best be applied.

PART ONE

INFRASTRUCTURE

CHAPTER 2

THE FIRE

—

I always used to spend holidays at my grandparents' farm. Beyond the staple foods and football, one common event was my uncles and my dad heading out to the workshop to talk about cars. I would tag along but could not contribute because I simply lacked the knowledge. Cars are complicated pieces of machinery, and there is a unique subset of language used to talk about them that I was not privy to. There is no shame in that. I just needed time and experience to learn what I didn't know.

The complexity of the power grid is not unlike that of a car. It is a deeply technical subject with myriad moving parts and connections that appear to be a jumbled mess until you begin to comprehend it. Some understanding is required if we're going to make headway on our strategy. Applying our guiding policies will require knowledge of what we are going to be changing. If we don't have a reasonable picture of the status quo, we won't be able to make adequate and effective decisions. Building some foundational comprehension of the grid will help put the current fossil-fuel-based system in context and explain why only renewable options can replace our current energy system.

ENERGY, POWER, AND SCALE

The concepts of energy and power are central to understanding the electrical grid and the infrastructure enabling it. Energy quantifies our ability to do something, and it can take many different forms. Operating a pump (mechanical energy), heating some water (thermal energy), or turning on a light bulb (electrical energy) are all examples of energy being used to perform some kind of useful work. The concept of power is derived from energy, and it is defined as the amount of energy used over a given time. An old incandescent lightbulb provides a familiar example: common sizes were rated at 60 watts (W) of power, meaning they draw 60 joules of electrical energy per second (J/s).

Electrical generators are usually rated in terms of the power they can output during normal operation, which can provide a useful frame of reference. A typical solar panel produces about 300 W (that is, 300 joules of energy every second), which is enough to power a laptop or several small appliances. The water heater in your house requires an order of magnitude more powerful than that, drawing several thousand watts, or kilowatts (kW), when it is in use.

Grid-scale generators supply several thousand times more power than even the largest household devices can consume. A typical wind turbine produces multiple megawatts (MW) of power during normal operation.[1] Fossil fuel and nuclear power plants are the largest installations we currently have, whose output is measured in either the hundreds of MW or single gigawatts (GW).[2] Presently, the entirety of the US

---

1   The prefix *mega* represents million.

2   The prefix *giga* represents billion. USEIA, "How Much Electricity," updated December 30, 2019.

power grid exceeds that scale by another factor of a thousand, with a capacity of about 1.1 terawatts (TW) in total.[3]

Even though electrical generators are rated in terms of power, we'll primarily be using energy throughout the book because it is more useful for tabulating the total needs and production over the course of a year. For perspective, an American house will draw several kilowatts at any one time, which translates to the yearly energy consumption of about 38 gigajoules (GJ).[4] Every major power source we'll be talking about starts on the terajoule (TJ) scale, such as a wind turbine that produces about 18 TJ over the course of a year. Talking about the energy needs of a state pushes our scale up several more notches. California consumed about 700 petajoules (PJ) of energy per month in 2018.[5] The entirety of the United States is several steps above that. We consumed 106 exajoules (EJ) of energy across all sectors and forms in 2019, enough to meet the needs of 2.8 *billion* homes.[6] To help visualize the magnitude we're talking about, if every joule we consume is represented by one drop of water, 106 EJ would be equivalent to Lake Michigan. This final scale of energy is the true target that our strategy is seeking to replace.

A final consideration for our power sources is whether or not they are dispatchable. A dispatchable power source can be brought online to provide the energy you need when you need it. Not all power sources are dispatchable. Solar panels

---

3   The prefix *tera* represents trillion. USEIA, "Electricity Explained," updated March 19, 2020.

4   USEIA, "How Much Electricity," updated October 9, 2020.

5   The prefix *peta* represents quadrillion. USEIA, "California State Energy Profile," updated January 16, 2020.

6   The prefix *exa* represents quintillion. USEIA, "U.S. Energy Facts Explained," updated May 7, 2020.

produce power from sunlight, but the sunlight we receive is not controllable, making it a nondispatchable source. The most flexible dispatchable sources are referred to as peaker plants because they can be brought online in minutes to balance the grid during peak demand. All fossil fuel power sources are dispatchable, and they constitute the majority of peakers, which is one of the reasons why they are the current backbone of our power grid.

FOSSIL FUELS

The bulk of our electricity presently comes from two fossil fuels. Coal and natural gas combined account for 62 percent of consumption. In contrast, all renewable sources together only total 17 percent.[7] Those statistics demonstrate the magnitude of the work the strategy has to accomplish. They represent the hundreds of power plants spread across every state, all of which we will have to replace. While a problem for us now, there are legitimate reasons why our grid was designed this way, mostly because of how easily we can convert fossil fuels into useful energy.

All power plants based on fossil fuels work on the same general principles. The fuel is burned in a furnace to heat water. The water boils to become high-pressure steam. The steam then spins a turbine to generate electricity, which is sent to the grid. The water is cooled and recycled back to the furnace, where the cycle is repeated. The main product of burning the fuel is carbon dioxide gas, which is released into the atmosphere and creates the problems this strategy aims to solve. The specifics of the process will vary depending on the physical properties of each fuel.

---

7   USEIA, "Electricity Explained," updated March 19, 2020.

Coal is essentially a flammable rock made of carbon. Being a solid allows coal to be easily mined, handled, and transported, and it was the first fossil fuel to see large-scale exploitation. Unfortunately, coal is rarely a pure material, often bearing impurities that lower its energy density and harm the environment or human health. Coal is often contaminated with sulfur that causes acid rain or toxic heavy metals like mercury.[8] As such, the power plants based on coal are usually older, less efficient, and dirtier than their natural gas cousins.

Natural gas is primarily composed of the simplest hydrocarbon, methane. This fuel only became a staple of the energy grid further into the twentieth century, once we installed the necessary infrastructure for capturing and distributing it. Using natural gas in a power plant carries several advantages over coal. For one, it has a higher energy density, so natural gas will produce more power than an equivalent weight of coal. There is still a contamination issue, but impurities can be removed from natural gas before it is burned, something that is next to impossible for coal. As a large-scale fuel, natural gas is also cheaper and easier to extract than coal due to advances in hydraulic fracturing (fracking) which have since made the United States energy independent.[9]

Coal plants are being retired, and new ones are no longer being built, thanks to the advantages of using natural gas. That is unfortunate for our strategy since we would much prefer those resources go to building power sources that don't emit carbon dioxide instead. The choice to use natural gas is a consequence of society's historical reliance on fossil fuels.

---

8   UCS, "Coal Power Impacts," updated July 9, 2019.

9   IER, "The United States Was Energy Independent," March 11, 2020.

It is simply easier and cheaper to integrate new fossil fuels into the existing scheme because they operate in the same way as the coal they're replacing. Since all fossil fuels are dispatchable power sources, there is no need to account for daily or seasonal fluctuations. You can just set the dial at whatever output you need. These factors create the inertia our strategy will have to overcome.

Fortunately, the future is on our side. Fossil fuels are fundamentally finite. There is only so much coal, oil, and natural gas buried below our feet. Even if our strategy and transition never existed, we would eventually run out of them and have to rebuild the power grid anyway. Whether it happens in a decade or a hundred years, that day will come. Thus, our requirement for permanent solutions necessitates that none of our actions can rely on the continued use of fossil fuels because they are fundamentally nonviable in the long-term.

NUCLEAR POWER

Nuclear energy has very similar qualities to fossil fuels. The internals of the power plant are conceptually the same: a heat source boils water to produce steam to turn a turbine and generate electricity. That heat source is also dependent on a finite fuel, currently uranium, mined from within the Earth.[10] Since those reserves will eventually be depleted, the same reasoning precluding fossil fuel use applies to proliferating nuclear power as well.

That is, in many respects, unfortunate. Nuclear energy is carbon neutral since it doesn't eject carbon dioxide into the atmosphere as it generates electricity. It is also incredibly

---

10 Depending on the technology, we may have several centuries worth of nuclear fuel reserves.

energy dense, capable of outputting tremendous amounts of power from individual facilities.[11] Those two factors mean nuclear sources will have to be part of our energy mix for the time being, even if we don't build any new ones. The United States generates about a fifth of its yearly energy from nuclear reactors.[12] Shutting them down would require replacement power sources to compensate for that change instead of decommissioning fossil fuels. Doing so only makes our job more difficult and would unnecessarily delay the transition.

Germany and Japan offer examples of what to avoid. Both countries started mothballing their infrastructure after the reactor meltdowns at the Fukushima nuclear facility in 2011. Japan previously generated about 30 percent of its electricity from nuclear power before that incident, and replacing it required increased gas and coal consumption.[13] Germany took a similar path and has replaced some of its nuclear capacity with coal.[14] Even with government policy favoring renewables, the wake left behind by the nuclear shutdown has largely preserved the old fossil fuel baseload.[15] Thus, our objective is clear: keep our nuclear sources running for as long and efficiently as possible to speed the transition.

The United States' nuclear fleet is not very efficient from a fuel standpoint. Only a fraction of its potential energy is

---

11 USEIA, "What is the Status," updated April 15, 2020.

12 USEIA, "What is U.S. Electricity," updated February 27, 2020.

13 World Nuclear Association, "Nuclear Power in Japan," updated March 2020; Buchholz, "How Fukushima Changed," March 10, 2020; Rooney, "Eight Years after Fukushima," December 11, 2019; IEA, "Japan," accessed August 28, 2020; McCurry, "Japan Should Scrap," September 12, 2019.

14 Oberhaus, "Germany Rejected Nuclear Power," January 23, 2020.

15 Appunn, Haas, and Wettengel, "Germany's Energy Consumption," August 21, 2020.

extracted before it has to be taken out and replaced with fresh uranium. The old material is ultimately consigned to nuclear waste storage, but it could be put to better use through recycling. France is able to get 70 percent of its electricity from nuclear plants because their spent fuel is reprocessed and reused in reactors, drastically cutting down the need to mine and refine additional material.[16] Nothing is preventing us from doing the same thing, only a Carter-era ban on the practice.[17] Reversing that policy and building reprocessing capabilities would be a relatively easy way to keep using nuclear power for the time being while not spending additional resources on mining and extracting raw materials while simultaneously helping keep down the level of nuclear waste we have on hand.

Building new nuclear reactors would mean more nuclear waste. Dealing with it is another global-scale challenge, just not so acute as climate change. The 80,000 tons the United States has produced will continue emitting dangerous levels of radiation for ten thousand years.[18] Fighting climate change by building more traditional reactors would only increase the scale of that problem. Fortunately, some alternatives could solve both problems at once. Breeder reactors, for example, are capable of using a wider variety of fuels, including some existing nuclear waste. They also break down the fuel into products that are dangerous for much shorter periods of time,

---

16   Planete Energies, "France's Overall Energy Mix," August 27, 2018; Krikorian, "France's Efficiency," September 4, 2019.

17   The stated reason was to prevent the nuclear proliferation. Andrews, "Nuclear Fuel Reprocessing," March 27, 2008, 3.

18   USGAO, "Disposal of High-Level Nuclear Waste," accessed August 1, 2020.

decades instead of millennia.[19] Unfortunately, none of those options are quite ready, running afoul of our requirement that we only use proven technology.

The conclusion is we won't be building more nuclear power, at least for the time being. Even though nuclear energy is not fundamentally sustainable, it could be capable of providing a great deal of carbon neutral power that helps us get over the hump of our grid transition. We may need to replace newly developed reactors in a hundred years, but it is a small price for bending our rule to only use permanent solutions. Until those better technologies are fully proven, our existing nuclear facilities will continue operation and provide carbon-free electricity to the grid during our transition, and we'll reprocess our spent fuel to prolong their operation. Therefore, the rest of our new grid will need to be built using the other carbon neutral options available to us: renewables.

RENEWABLES

The fundamental difference between nuclear and other carbon neutral options is that solar, wind, hydropower, and geothermal do not rely on a finite fuel source. Hence, the name renewables. We can tap into them for as long as we need because their energy ultimately originates from the sun. While a star like ours has a definite energy output and lifespan, the billions of years before the sun burns out allows us to treat it as an infinite power source.

Renewable power sources are substantially more varied in type but mostly operate on the same turbine-spinning principles as a fossil fuel or nuclear plant. Photovoltaic power

---

19   For more information, see: Martin, *Super Fuel.*

is the only exception, being able to directly convert sunlight to electricity. The sun's energy can also be captured as heat to generate steam and turn a turbine into a solar thermal facility. We can use the wind to turn a turbine directly, cutting steam out of the equation. The same is true for hydropower, only swapping air and steam for liquid water. Geothermal is more of a one-to-one process equivalent to current fossil fuels. Only the Earth's internal heat is used to generate steam, not coal or natural gas.

Connecting renewables to the grid has to be done in the knowledge that they are, except for geothermal, nondispatchable power sources. Simply building more of them leads to a duck curve, shown in the accompanying figure. During the day when the sun is shining or when there is a lot of wind, a large portion of the grid becomes energized with that renewable power instead of fossil fuels. Conversely, at night, when it's cloudy or when the wind isn't blowing, baseload needs to ramp up to meet the gap in renewable output, which currently means fossil fuels. Unless we can replace that baseload, our strategy will be incomplete.

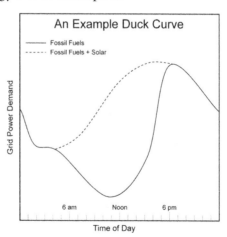

Multiple localities have already run into this limitation, to the point where it doesn't make sense to add more renewable capacity. For example, in South Australia, the available solar resources can provide over 90 percent of the electricity demand during the day.[20] However, as soon as the sun goes down, natural gas plants kick into gear to make up the difference. The grid needs to have built-in accommodations for this variability. Energy storage infrastructure allows us to do this. Multiple technologies can take excess energy when it is available, hold onto it, and release it when needed.

There are many more caveats to each form of renewable power generation, and each subsequent chapter in part one is dedicated to exploring them further. Each has its own strengths and weaknesses for the strategy. It is difficult to fully replace the flexibility and reliability of a fossil fuel source with any one renewable technology. If they weren't both finite and changing our climate, it would be easy to rely on coal and natural gas forever. Unfortunately, that isn't the world we live in.

SACRIFICE: ISOLATION

Venezuela used to be a highly prosperous country. For decades, the economy was expanding, and the average standard of living was among the best in South America.[21] That progress seems a far cry from the current turmoil, but both situations can be attributed to Venezuela betting everything on its oil industry. At its peak, the extraction and export of oil and petroleum products made up a quarter of the country's

---

20   Parkinson, "Solar Meets 100 per cent," October 12, 2020.

21   Kiger, "How Venezuela Fell," May 9, 2019.

total economic output.[22] That is fine when prices for those commodities are high, but a collapse in oil prices during 2014 meant the government could no longer satisfy its obligations. The resulting political unrest and civil turmoil are natural risks for an oil-centric economy.

The situation in Venezuela is a symptom of the resource curse. This concept describes how countries focused on extracting abundant raw materials—like oil, coal, minerals, or timber—tend to be less wealthy and less developed than the countries using those resources to manufacture finished goods. Changes and downturns hit these countries especially hard. During a recession or market shift, economies built around one resource suddenly find themselves facing collapsing prices that cause havoc across their entire system. Lost revenue drives down employment, which drives down spending, causing a negative feedback loop as the problem spirals out of control. The moral of the story is that a homogenous economy is dangerous, and Venezuela isn't the only nation at risk.

The energy transition required by the strategy will ultimately render economies based on extracting fossil fuels obsolete. This will cause problems for those countries. Forty-six nations have fossil fuel exports accounting for at least 5 percent of their gross domestic product (GDP).[23] That includes both developing countries like South Sudan and highly developed nations like Norway. Some will be diversified enough to weather the storm, but many countries across

---

22   Depersio, "How Does the Price of Oil," updated June 25, 2019.

23   Trade data from: Observatory of Economic Complexity for Harmonized Schedule subheadings 2701, 2707, 2709, 2710, 2711, and 2901, accessed August 28, 2020. GDP data from: Worldometer, "GDP by Country," accessed August 28, 2020.

the developing world will be in dire straits after a renewable transition. It will be devastating for their economies and standard of living.

Those nations and their people won't just fade away because they are left behind after fossil fuels are phased out. Economic disruption typically precedes political upheaval and violence, meaning existing tensions and instabilities across the world will only magnify. Experience also shows such conflicts are unlikely to respect existing borders. Surrounding nations would likely be drawn into expanding regional conflicts. That may lead to the notion that we need to delay the transition to help shore up stability across much of the developing world, but that would be just as dangerous.

Climate change is already having destabilizing effects, and they will only worsen under a status quo approach.[24] An example happening right now is the Syrian Civil War that, even with the collapse of ISIS, still smolders. Despite the political movements and religious facets controlling the narrative in media, the igniting spark can be traced back to a changing climate. A prolonged drought starting in 2006 displaced a substantial number of people from rural areas where farming was becoming difficult and drove them into the cities to look for work.[25] Poor economic and political conditions combined with a higher concentration of unsatisfied people created the first demonstrations and protests. The government's response did the rest. Each person made

---

24 The U.S. national security sector acknowledges the risks by climate change, per: USDOD, "National Security Implications," July 23, 2015; EESI, "The National Security Impacts of Climate Change," December 2017.

25 This is referred to as a climate migration. Welch, "Climate Change Helped Spark," March 2, 2015.

choices for their own reasons, but the climatic conditions made certain outcomes more likely.

All nations will become one stray ember closer to igniting so long as the climate continues to shift. If the events in Syria are any indication, the remainder of the twenty-first century will see increasing conflict over resources, like water at the heart of the Darfur conflict and mass movements of people fleeing scarcity and violence in the global South. People will have to begin leaving the Ganges basin and the Persian Gulf in the summer as those regions become uninhabitable before the end of the century, while increased heat will drive people north from Central America.[26] As governments use more and more resources to deal with these issues, there will be less for us to use to decarbonize, creating a vicious cycle.

This reality leaves the strategy with no choice but to continue pressing on at full speed to replace our dependence on fossil fuels. A runaway greenhouse effect will deteriorate everything forever, while moving quickly gives us a better chance at recovery for all, eventually. However, that doesn't mean we shouldn't do everything we can to make the transition easier for everyone, regardless of their country's level of development.

The countries cursed with abundant fossil fuels aren't condemned to failure because of the transition. Every region holds some advantages for generating renewable power or making use of that power. Whether they are countries like South Sudan near the equator that can become solar powerhouses or those like Peru that can build massive amounts of offshore wind, every nation can be a beneficiary of a

---

26 Ghoshal, "Heatwaves could Turn Parts," August 10, 2017; Gubash, "Searing Heat could Make," August 12, 2018; Beaubien, "Whatever Happened to," August 26, 2019.

decarbonized power grid. Plentiful renewable energy can also make these countries better able to host higher value economic activity, as it would lower the costs of electricity. Most countries' main issue is finding the resources to make that transition happen, even if their commitments to international agreements show that they want to.

Nations like the United States were able to develop their economies and standards of living thanks to the availability of cheap fossil fuels. In fact, building an industrial base using fossil fuels is what will enable the transition away from them since you gain the ability to invest in more advanced technologies with cheaper energy. Large developing nations like China and India have certainly taken this tactic to heart, and they are now some of the largest emitters in the developing world.[27] While they are taking steps to slow down fossil fuel use, that priority is always balanced with the goal for further economic development.

A reasonable argument is that asking developing countries to transition away from fossil fuels prematurely will effectively kick away the ladder they could climb to reach a better standard of living. As a corollary, since developed countries are responsible for the majority of historic carbon emissions, you can argue the burden for decarbonization should primarily fall on them.[28] The forceful imposition of new requirements for developing countries also sounds like a new form of imperialism, undoubtedly an unfavorable situation for formerly colonized peoples. There is truth to that thinking, but the reality of the situation makes investing in further fossil fuels an untenable proposition.

---

27 UCS, "Each Country's Share," updated August 12, 2020.

28 UN, "Adoption of the Paris Agreement," 2015.

Carving out lowered goals for that group will not do them any good in the long run because it's an impermanent investment. Fossil fuels are fundamentally exhaustible and, by delaying the transition, they will end up paying twice—once to develop and once to switch to a renewable grid. It only makes sense to build and transition their grids now. Thus, there is an impasse. The only remedy for both increasing the standard of living in the developing world and curbing emissions is for developed countries not to kick away the ladder but to offer a hand up.

Offering aid to other nations is not a universally supported political position in the United States.[29] However, sending money to help transition from fossil fuels is not altruistic. We only account for 15 percent of emissions, so even if the domestic grid became fully decarbonized, the problem would persist. We have to sacrifice the notion that one nation can fix this problem alone because this is not an isolated problem. Every country and every person has a stake. If richer nations want to avoid the global upheavals of climate change, they will have to provide support to those without the means to undertake a transition themselves.

Massive reconstruction of foreign infrastructure is not without precedent. The United States rebuilt much of Western Europe after World War II with the Marshall Plan. A similar endeavor for energy across the world would provide security for developed nations by mitigating climate change and improving security abroad by stabilizing and improving the lot of people in developing countries. That would be more effective for preserving national security than the billions

---

29   Bateman, "U.S. Public Opinion," April 18, 2018.

of dollars in military aid doled out every year.[30] Instead of giving countries money to buy munitions to fire during future resource wars, efforts would be better spent removing the causes of those wars in the first place. We just have to sacrifice the idea that we should only invest to exclusively benefit ourselves.

30 About a third of U.S. foreign aid is military assistance. McBride, "How Does the U.S. Spend," October 1, 2018.

CHAPTER 3

THE SUN

Many polytheistic religions have a sun god in their pantheon. Some, like the ancient Egyptians, even made it the king of the gods. It's not completely illogical to have respect for the sun, regardless of your beliefs. Looking at it for too long will blind you, and simply being exposed for too long burns your skin; attributes certainly warranting caution. More positively, it is the source of all life on the surface of the Earth. No sun would mean no photosynthesis, no plants, and no people. The only living creatures would be clustered around hydrothermal vents in the ocean, surviving off the heat and chemicals emanating from deeper within the planet, at least until the Earth cooled and became as lifeless as Mars.

The sun is also a boon to our quest for renewable energy. It releases the equivalent energy of about four *trillion* atomic bombs every second of every day.[1] The only reason we don't fry is that the ninety-three million miles between us and the sun protect us from 99.9999999 percent of that radiation. The energy that does reach us is still enormous, such that the Earth receives the same amount of energy from the sun in

---

1   UTIA, "The Sun's Energy," accessed July 21, 2020.

a half-hour as the entirety of human civilization produces in a year.[2] That makes the sun a virtually unlimited and inexhaustible resource for our strategy, but only if we tap into it properly.

Every form of solar power fundamentally does the same thing: the energy contained in sunlight is converted into electricity. There are two primary ways of doing that. We can either directly convert light into electric power with photovoltaic materials or capture the energy as heat. Each approach has its own strengths and limitations but will ultimately compete with each other for the strategy's resources. Let's begin by looking at each, in turn, to determine exactly how we'll use the sun as a renewable power source.

PHOTOVOLTAICS

Photovoltaic cells are what we typically recognize as solar power. They're the rectangular modules that populate roofs and fields. Solar cells are a bit unique among power sources because they can directly convert sunlight into electricity. When light hits the solar cell, electrons become excited and, since electricity is simply the movement of electrons, those excited electrons can immediately provide electric power. Compare that to your typical natural gas power plant: you have to burn the gas to make heat, the heat is used to generate steam, and the steam is used to turn a turbine that finally produces electricity.

The scale of a solar panel installation can be as large or as small as it needs to be. It is only limited by how much space and materials are available. Individual panels can fit on a roof top or thousands of them can stretch across the landscape in

---

2   USEIA, "EIA Projects," September 24, 2019.

neat rows facing the sun. No matter the quantity installed, the production of usable power will occur so long as there is enough sunlight available. Over their lifetime, solar cells produce twenty to fifty times the energy needed to build them, meaning it is absolutely possible to build a self-sustaining photovoltaic system.

There are myriad ways to make a photovoltaic cell. The National Renewable Energy Laboratory (NREL) maintains a chart tracking the status of dozens of options.[3] One of my first research projects as a graduate student was on alternative solar cell materials, falling under the quantum dot category that NREL tracks.[4] Our idea was to bind nanoparticles together with DNA to assemble them into rational patterns and improve electrical conduction. The results were, shall we say, underwhelming. We never got close to making a new record in solar cell efficiency, but we did explore some interesting new physics.[5]

While any number of materials that did make the NREL chart could be useful in theory, only two satisfy our requirements to use technology that is ready and can be deployed quickly—cadmium telluride and silicon. Silicon is by far the current leader, taking up 95 percent of the market.[6] It has benefited from decades of research to improve its efficiency at converting light into electricity and is manufactured en masse through a mature supply chain. Cadmium telluride is almost as efficient and is also produced in massive quantities.

3   NREL, "Best Research-Cell Efficiency Chart," accessed August 3, 2020.

4   Noh et al. "Direct Conjugation," January 2014.

5   Goodman et al. "Multiple Energy," October 2014.

6   Philipps and Warmuth, "Photovoltaics Report," updated September 16, 2020.

One of the largest solar cell producers in the world exclusively manufactures cadmium telluride solar cells.[7]

Both silicon and cadmium telluride could theoretically do the job, but only if they're able to scale quickly enough to rebuild the grid. The potential for silicon is basically infinite. Its primary raw material is sand. In contrast, cadmium telluride relies on much rarer elements. Tellurium only exists in low concentrations within certain ores, and less than 500 tons are produced per year across the entire world.[8] That means it cannot be a workhorse for the strategy, but it can fill a niche.

Tellurium is a byproduct of copper refining that would otherwise go to waste. Even the small amounts produced can be used to manufacture substantial photovoltaic capacity every year. The Topaz Solar Farm in California, for example, was built with nine million cadmium telluride modules.[9] These panels are also designed for recyclability, so any new capacity we build will continuously regenerate.[10] Thus, we can make use of a small but otherwise unused resource to help speed the transition while primarily relying on inexhaustible silicon.

With silicon as our primary photovoltaic material, we can start to estimate just how much of the country we'd have to blanket in solar cells to make a dent in our energy needs. While we'll never build a grid using only one power source or technology, doing the calculations as if we would, helps to frame our constraints. Let's assume we're going to build

---

7   First Solar, "First Solar Becomes," October 24, 2019.

8   USGS, "Tellurium," January 2020.

9   First Solar, "Topaz Solar Farm," April 15, 2011.

10   Field, "First Solar Breaks Down," December 4, 2018.

enough solar panels to provide all the energy the country needs and that there is enough energy storage available to even out any variability. The next step is to determine how much land we'd need to cover in solar panels.

While we could use the theoretical performance of solar cells to perform the calculation, it is more accurate to look at the output of real-world installations. Doing so factors in construction limitations, changing weather and seasons, and land-use constraints. Using some of the largest installations spread across the country as a basis yields a value of 330 terajoules of electrical energy per square kilometer (TJ/km²).[11] That means, we can power about 9,000 homes with every square kilometer we cover in solar panels.[12]

The total US energy demand is substantially larger than that. In 2018, the sum total of our energy needs was about 106 exajoules (EJ), that is, 106 million TJ.[13] Meeting that demand would require a countrywide solar farm encompassing 317,000 km². That number seems large because it is. For perspective, that's three-quarters of California, 100 Rhode Islands, or 3 percent of the entire country. With 130,000 modules per square kilometer, we'd need almost forty-two *billion* individual units. However, it's important to remember that we already dedicate massive areas of land and resources to energy production that is much less efficient.

---

11   See appendix for calculation details. Sunpower, "Solar Star Projects," 2016; Shugar, "Mount Signal 3," December 9, 2018; 8minute Solar Energy, "8minute Renewables," November 12, 2012; Misbrener, "8minutenergy Completes," July 11, 2018; Cassell, "Sempra Working," June 4, 2015; USEIA, "Electricity Data Browser," accessed December 24, 2020.

12   A square kilometer is about one-third of a square mile.

13   USEIA, "In 2018," April 16, 2019.

Consider ethanol. It's used as a gasoline additive, the E in E85, to the tune of 54.5 billion liters per year. All of that ethanol comes from corn, which is grown on 141,000 km² of farmland. Burning all that ethanol produces, at most, 1 EJ of energy, which is less than 1 percent of our yearly energy needs. Normalizing that energy output by the total acreage means that growing corn is about two hundred times *less* land efficient for generating power than solar cells. If we can dedicate that many resources to ethanol, we certainly can do it for solar power.

SOLAR THERMAL

Our second method of harvesting sunlight is solar thermal.[14] We're still converting sunlight into energy, but instead of going directly to electricity, we're first generating steam to turn a turbine. A solar thermal plant is mostly composed of massive mirrors. These mirrors reflect sunlight onto a central point, concentrating the light that would normally spread over a large area onto a tiny target. It's similar in principle to how you start fires with a magnifying glass. With all that energy hitting one spot, you can generate very high temperatures, up to several thousand degrees. That heat is moved using a high-temperature heat transfer fluid, which runs through a heat exchanger to generate the steam that turns a turbine to generate electricity.

There are three main options for heat transfer fluids that have either been investigated or are currently in use. The first is water. A solar thermal design based on water can generate steam directly without going through an intermediate heat exchange step, simplifying the mechanics somewhat.

---

14   Also known as concentrated solar power.

Options two and three are to use either a synthetic oil or molten salt (a salt heated past its melting point) and keep the steam-generating step separate. The advantage of these two is that you can natively use them for energy storage. Instead of generating steam, excess oil or molten salts can be directed to insulated storage tanks. Their heat is then kept on hand until needed, such as at night when the mirrors can no longer capture sunlight. In that scenario, fluid from the tanks would be directed back into the steam generating system, allowing the plant to provide energy for more of the day and help eliminate our reliance on fossil fuel peaker plants. This configuration doesn't work for a solar thermal plant that generates steam directly since you can't keep it on hand overnight. As energy storage increases the flexibility of the grid, water thus won't be a viable heat transfer fluid option for our strategy.

Oil and molten salts do not have the same potential when it comes to thermal energy storage. The molten salt mixture most commonly used is made of different nitrate chemicals that can operate from 290–585°C. Operating below this temperature range risks having the salt solidify in the system while operating above it risks decomposing the salt.[15] Thermal oils typically have an upper-temperature limit of 300–400°C before they risk breaking down, and their lower limits typically range from 200–250°C. Those values create a disparity between oil and salts, such that salts are able to store about 10 percent more energy per pound, allowing molten salts to edge out the win.[16]

---

15   Reddy, "Molten Salts," July 2011; Gomez-Vidal and Kruizenga, "Technology Pathway Molten Salt," February 1, 2017; Glatzmaier, "Summary Report," August 2011.

16   See appendix for calculation details.

There are two configurations of solar thermal with energy storage used on the utility-scale. The first uses a grid of parabolic mirrors to reflect sunlight onto a pipe containing the heat transfer fluid. The other option uses a circle of mirrors to surround a pillar (called a solar power tower) and reflect light onto the top segment where the heat transfer fluid circulates. This latter configuration is more recognizable since the tall tower and ring of mirrors are prominent and visually striking.

Both options are in use at multiple plants across the world, so the first question is to decide which kind we'd like to invest in. There are more of the first, and they yield about 303 TJ/km^2 on average, not too far from solar cells.[17] Towers, in contrast, only average about 218 TJ/km^2, meaning more land would be required for the same benefit.[18] The numbers for parabolic mirrors would seem to make our choice clear. However, molten salt-based solar thermal projects are typically in the tower configuration, while parabolic mirrors equipped for storage use oil to collect the heat and transfer it to a molten salt at a later step.[19] Either will ultimately perform the same function, but parabolic mirrors would require extra equipment for the added heat transfer step.

---

17 Values were averaged for the following facilities: Solana Generating Station (Arizona), Mojave Solar Project (California), and Genesis Solar Energy Project (California). Peltier, "Top Plant," December 1, 2014; California Energy Commission, "Mojave Solar Project," accessed December 24, 2020; NREL, "Genesis Solar," April 25, 2014; USEIA, "Electricity Data Browser," accessed December 24, 2020.

18 Cited values are for the Ouarzazate Solar Power Station Noor III (Morocco) and Ivanpah Solar Power Facility (California). African Development Bank, "Ouarzazate Solar Complex," November 2014, 9; Strauss, "Take a Look," November 2012; USEIA, "Electricity Data Browser," accessed December 24, 2020.

19 Dieterich, "24-Hour Solar Energy," January 16, 2018.

Towers have an additional advantage over parabolic mirrors since they are better able to generate higher temperatures. With all the mirrors pointed at one spot, the temperature of the tower can easily exceed 1,000°C, which is more difficult to achieve with parabolic mirrors. Higher temperatures are potentially more useful as they allow you more options for using the energy. Since molten salts have a higher maximum temperature, any high-temperature application will have to rely on the tower configuration.

We can use molten salts in this way to help decarbonize sectors outside of electricity generation, including reducing fossil fuel use in manufacturing. You could, for instance, use the molten salts to provide heat for a large-scale chemical process like fertilizer manufacturing. Making fertilizer starts by pulling nitrogen out of the air and converting it into ammonia, which requires temperatures between 400–500°C, well within molten salts' operating range but outside of thermal oils. This example also provides a tidy loop, as fertilizer production is the starting point for manufacturing the salts themselves.

Unfortunately, not every process present is so amenable. Many require far higher temperatures, such as steel and hydrogen production, requiring temperatures exceeding 1,000°C, which would completely decompose the salt mixtures we have available. There are ongoing investigations into new salts with higher temperature ranges, but these have not progressed enough to fully satisfy our requirement to use existing technology.[20] Until they do, we can still take a good chunk of fossil fuel consumption offline by investing

---

20   Perret, "Solar Thermochemical Hydrogen," May 2011; Hydrogen Europe, "Project HYDROSOL-PLANT," August 28, 2020.

in industrial solar thermal, so long as doing so fits in with the rest of the strategy.

SOLAR PRIORITIZATION

We have two proven technologies—photovoltaic cells and solar thermal—to choose from for our solar investments. And we will have to make choices because our resources are limited. The problem with solar is not every building site is created equal. The amount of energy you can get from a given facility is entirely dependent on the intensity of sunlight that reaches it over the course of a day and year. You obviously can't collect sunlight at night, but even during the day, your power output will be less than optimal if inclement weather clouds the sky. Even in the same climate, moving north will decrease your solar potential because the days are shorter and the sun is less directly overhead.

Fortunately, the scientists at the US Department of Energy have already calculated the solar potential of the entire country. Using that information, we can prioritize different regions of the country for solar investment. The figure shown here is a map with regions labeled A–D, where A has the best solar potential and is more attractive for investment.[21] The best locations in the Southwest desert states reflect the superiority of locations that are dry and close to the equator. For comparison, a solar panel in Phoenix will generate almost twice the power of one in Seattle or Boston. This is the prime real estate for the strategy and where we will want to first focus our efforts.

---

21 Regions prioritized based on the data presented in: NREL, "Solar Resource Data," accessed January 14, 2021. Map created using public domain image: Codomo, "File:PNGedUSoutline.png," May 20, 2006.

Solar Regions of the Contental United States

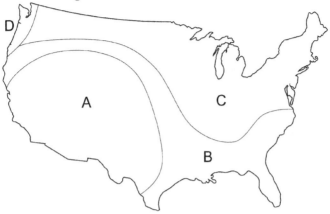

SOLAR FARMS

The land in the Southwest is not infinite, and not every patch of land that receives the most powerful sunlight is amenable for construction. A solar farm requires a swath of flat land with minimal obstruction between the collectors and the sun. That situation isn't as common as we might like in a region dominated by mountain ranges. It means we also have to be thoughtful about the type of solar collectors we use to make best use of the space we have.

The large installations in the desert will have to be solar thermal plants to the exclusion of photovoltaics. At their best, they can provide the same energy density as photovoltaics, but, more importantly, the energy storage capabilities enable us to receive energy during the day and night. That has to be of paramount importance because every bit of storage we can build as part of our energy generation infrastructure, the less we will have to invest in elsewhere. Photovoltaics can feed into other forms of grid storage, but that is extra infrastructure we would have to build in addition to the solar farm.

Doing both at once with solar thermal is simply more efficient. To that end, we'll exclusively use molten salts to maximize our energy storage capacity. The choice of building a tower for direct energy storage versus parabolic mirrors for indirect energy storage will depend on the local geography and conditions. Power towers will be generally preferable since they can make full use of the molten salt's temperature range and don't need an intermediary heat transfer step for energy storage.

There is one impediment to using the desert we will have to get around. Undeliverable power will do us no good. Germany has already run into this problem, where it can't get all of the renewable energy from the North down to where it's needed in the South of the country.[22] Avoiding this problem means building more transmission infrastructure—large towers supporting power lines that bring electricity long distances across the country. Expanding this capacity will add to the land and resource requirements of new power plants, never mind additional pushback from people who don't want high-transmission lines running near their homes. Requirements for additional infrastructure will have to be a factor as we evaluate each site and prioritize our resources.

We can help lower our power transmission requirements by decarbonizing some industries with adjacent solar thermal. It doesn't make sense to move all our manufacturing to the desert, so we'll go to them, starting with the Gulf Coast. A lot of heavy industry is already there, especially for chemical manufacturing that routinely requires high temperatures. We'd simply be replacing nonrenewable heat sources with an adjacent solar thermal collector. Installing a solar farm at

---

22 Deign, "Germany's Maxed-Out Grid," March 31, 2020.

each plant won't be feasible, but doing it where possible will increase the speed of our decarbonization by directly taking fossil fuels out of the mix. Building solar thermal in other parts of the country doesn't make as much sense and won't be a priority. There simply isn't enough consistent sunlight in other regions to justify that scale of investment. Most importantly, we'll need undeveloped land to absorb carbon and reverse climate change, and solar farms just require too much space. Empty space is easy to find in the desert, but less so around areas with a high population density like cities, towns, and suburbs. We'd have to spread out into undeveloped areas, but that's where photovoltaics can start to play a role.

DISTRIBUTED SOLAR

We don't always need a condensed solar farm to make use of sunlight. While solar thermal requires concentrated infrastructure to be useful, photovoltaic cells can be used as small, distributed installations. Distributed means instead of a single farm containing thousands or millions of collectors, we'll spread individual solar panels over a large area to generate the same amount of power. We can even do so without having to develop new land since the panels are light enough to be placed on buildings.

Most commercial buildings are already good candidates for photovoltaic arrays since they have large, flat, rectangular roofs. There are also enough of them to make a substantial dent in our energy needs. Let's use Costco as an example. A typical store has a roof area of 0.013 km² (144,500 square feet).[23] Multiply that number by the number of Costco stores

---

23   Latham, "Costco by the Numbers," September 25, 2017.

across the country, and we have an area that could generate around 3,400 TJ of electricity and power 90,000 homes every year if we covered those roofs with solar panels.[24] Thus, our goal will be to install them on every business, school, warehouse, library, and parking garage that can host them.[25]

One primary benefit of installing on businesses and other larger buildings is using the energy directly. Those users currently consume a substantial fraction of our yearly energy, both from electricity and fuels.[26] Keeping the power generation on-site means those consumers won't have to rely as much on the broader grid, and we won't have to expand distribution infrastructure as much to supply them. At the peak of the day, they'd be able to pull from their own capacity and allow other power sources to feed into grid-scale storage or supply consumers who can't host an array of panels.

Prioritizing larger distributed installations means the strategy won't be focused on houses at the outset. Doing so does make sense in the long-term, once the low-hanging fruit has been dealt with. Houses represent the majority of buildings in this country, so they offer the greatest collective distributed solar resource. However, houses are also mostly unoccupied and draw less power during the peak parts of the day, so the electricity they generate would have to be transmitted elsewhere to be used instead of being consumed locally. We'll cover them eventually, but they won't be the highest priority.

***

---

24   See appendix for calculation details.

25   Only about 1 percent of the total commercial roof photovoltaic capacity is currently utilized. Hoen, Rand, and Elmallah, "Commercial PV," October 2019.

26   USEIA, "Use of Energy Explained," updated September 28, 2018.

The first part of our strategy is thus complete. We'll use vast quantities of solar collectors to help power our new renewable grid. In the Southwest, large solar thermal farms will collect the intense desert sun, keeping enough energy on hand with thermal storage to provide power through the night. The rest of the country will start fitting roofs with photovoltaic panels. We'll start in areas A and B on the prioritization map, working through the most amenable regions first.

SACRIFICE: A TORTOISE

So far, we've discussed three of our six guiding policies in this chapter. We need to talk for a minute about number four, triage, and explore it with a real-world example.

Let's assume there's a large solar farm being planned in the desert. It will provide power to a nearby metropolitan area and help close the fossil fuel plants in the region. Unfortunately, it would share land that's also inhabited by an endangered species of tortoise.[27] Building the facility will disturb the habitat, and the fences around the plant will prevent tortoises from finding adequate food or a mate. Through building the solar farm, we would be increasing the likelihood the species goes extinct by "chipping away at the biodiversity that's out there in these deserts."[28]

To lose any species to human activity is a tragedy. We have been responsible for multiple extinctions over the years, like the dodo bird and passenger pigeon. We know better now the harm that arises when we damage an ecosystem. Every lost species is an irreplaceable source of both knowledge and

27 Nevada Fish and Wildlife Office, "Threats to Desert Tortoises," April 16, 2014.

28 Quote attributed to Laura Cunningham of Basin and Range Watch from: Price, "Massive Solar Farm Clears," January 30, 2020.

support for the broader biosphere. On top of that, climate change itself is already poised to be a great reckoning for many animals, probably leading to the first mass extinction due to unnatural causes. It would seem unconscionable to take action that risks purposefully ending a species when biodiversity is already so threatened.

There's really only one way to approach this in the context of triage. Not building that solar farm would mean less renewable power will be available and that more fossil fuels will have to be burned. That will only make climate change worse, and the afflicted tortoise might instead go extinct anyway. From a purely utilitarian perspective, not building the power capacity because of one species' potential extinction increases the risk that many others will die off across the globe. In the words of Mr. Spock, "the needs of the many outweigh the needs of the few." Thus, we should go ahead and build the solar farm regardless of the tortoise.

A cold calculus like that will probably not sit well with many people. While it answers the question of how to minimize the overall damage, it doesn't speak to the moral tradeoff of willingly sacrificing the tortoise. The tortoise is, in a sense, innocent. It did not cause the problem that needs fixing, yet demands are being placed upon it to create the solution. This seems unfair in the cosmic sense. It claws at an inner sense of justice most people have, that you should not dole out an undeserved punishment.

It's important to remember that all human activity has an impact on the natural world. Building a house displaces habitat. Building a highway disrupts migration patterns.[29]

---

29 Unless you plan around it and install animal crossings: Stewart, "Bridges for Animals," February 9, 2017.

Fields of monoculture crops displace complex ecosystems. Buildings kill birds.[30] Ocean shipping interferes with whale communications.[31] The bottom line is there is no action we can take to build a civilization that will not negatively impact nature. The loss of a tortoise is only one aspect of that tradeoff.

The only fundamental choice we have to make is how much of an environmental impact we can tolerate. At one extreme, we fully exploit the natural world, and it collapses. On the other, we chose not to disrupt nature at all, and humanity no longer exists in its current form. The key is finding balance. Species will go extinct regardless of what we do, as they have without our input for billions of years. We should focus on saving as many as we can while having the courage to knowingly make those tradeoffs.

Part of that calculus might mean sacrificing more of our resources to protect the environment. There are efforts underway for aiding the tortoise population, for example, by designing fences with periodic spaces to allow them through. With the proper resources, solar farms could be made more compatible with the native wildlife.[32] But not every solution to a sacrifice is so easy, and the ecological disruption caused by new power plants sometimes can't be mitigated. We just have to decide the end goal is worth the cost, either sacrificing resources to protect nature or making sacrifices to preserve the planet.

---

30   Aratani, "Buildings Are Killing," April 7, 2019.

31   Sommer, "Whales Get a Break," July 20, 2020.

32   Kerlin, "Can Solar Energy," September 9, 2018.

CHAPTER 4

THE WIND

My family always seemed to take vacations out West. While we could have just as easily taken another path out of Wisconsin, it seems we always took the westward interstates toward the Plains and Rockies. Part of the reason was dad didn't like driving in cities. The one time we went through Toronto in rush hour was proof of that. We were left to take in the repetitive scenery of cornfields preceding the mountains of Wyoming and Colorado. There is surely no expanse of land greater in distance than I-80 through Iowa and Nebraska.

The straight highways flanked by straight rows of straight corn stalks have changed since then. You can now see lines and clusters of wind turbines off in the distance, slowly turning thanks to the persistent breeze permeating the open Plains. They started off as a rarity, something new and remarkable to comment on as we drove by. By the time I moved out to Colorado for graduate school, they seemed ubiquitous and ordinary. The spinning blades of the wind turbines have become a marker signifying what our new normal will look like.

Wind turbines are on par with solar panels in the general consciousness when one thinks of renewable energy. They're certainly hard to miss. A wind turbine operates much like a fossil fuel generator: a mechanical object spins a magnet to generate electricity. Instead of requiring the intermediate production of steam, the motion of the air is sufficient. They can also be placed where they're most useful in any quantity we need, much like photovoltaic solar cells.

Wind turbines also share the critical downsides of photovoltaic power. Most importantly, they are nondispatchable sources. That is, we can't guarantee they will produce power exactly when we need it. Solar panels provide nothing when it is dark and cloudy, and wind turbines lie fallow when there is no wind. No turbine will spin 100 percent of the time. Data from California shows intermittent performance on both day-to-day and season-to-season bases.[1] For our strategy, there are two caveats with the wind. It will have to be accompanied by some sort of storage to balance things out, just like solar, and we will have to prioritize where we're going to put them to maximize our resources.

We can determine the best locations for building our wind infrastructure by constructing a map. The one below prioritizes different regions based on data gathered by scientists at the US Department of Energy.[2] The regions marked A will be our top priority, followed by B and C. Unlike the solar map, we've got two classes of wind turbine regions to discuss: onshore and offshore, each with its own caveats and

---

1   California Energy Commission, "Visualization of Seasonal Variation," accessed October 17, 2020.

2   USEIA, "Where Wind Power is Harnessed," updated March 24, 2020; USEIA, "DOE provides," January 30, 2012; NREL, "Wind Resource Data," accessed July 6, 2020. Map created using public domain image: Codomo, "File:PNGedUSoutline.png," May 20, 2006.

conditions. We'll need to go through them both, in turn, to properly utilize our available wind resources.

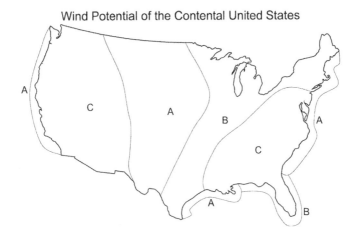

Wind Potential of the Contental United States

ONSHORE WIND FARMS

The first region worth discussing is the Great Plains. Relatively fast and consistent winds have already made this an attractive area for investment. The key to increasing performance in those areas depends on the size of the wind turbine itself. The wind is more constant when you're further up off the ground, and bigger blades and turbines can convert that energy more efficiently.

Here's where we run into our first issue. Federal and state regulations determine how tall you can build a turbine, often limiting them below 500 feet. While technically feasible, we will have difficulty building the most efficient turbines on land, at least not without additional regulatory procedures.[3] Another hurdle is the states in region A are, for the most

---

3   FAA, "FAA Updates," December 8, 2015; Zipp, "To be precise," April 6, 2012.

part, sparsely populated. With some exceptions, like the front range of Colorado, we'd have to significantly invest in new transmission infrastructure to bring that power to other areas. While solar in the desert suffers the same problem, the opportunity for inbuilt storage improves that calculus, but wind power doesn't have that option.

Both of those downsides limit the absolute utility of onshore wind. It will still play a role, and it would be helpful to figure out the scale of investment we're looking at. We can estimate the number of onshore turbines we'd need to power our entire grid using the same procedure as in the solar chapter. The average wind turbine yields about 18 terajoules (TJ) of energy every year in the United States.[4] To meet our annual energy needs of 106 million TJ, we would need about six million wind turbines spread across the country.

Millions of units seems like an incredibly large amount, and it is. It's also a bit worrying when you see how large of an area existing wind farms take up. Each turbine needs to be separated from its nearest neighbors by several times the length of its blades to maximize efficiency, meaning you can't pack the most efficient models very close together. As a result, you often see a couple of hundred turbines spread over tens of square kilometers. Entire landscapes across the country would have to be dedicated to this purpose to make a substantial dent in our energy needs.

---

4   See appendix for calculation details. Power Technology, "Alta," accessed December 24, 2020; Minnesota Power, "Bison Wind," accessed December 24, 2020; Neville, "Top Plants," December 1, 2009; Caithness Energy, "Project Overview," accessed December 24, 2020; The Wind Power, "Wind Farms," accessed December 24, 2020; USEIA, "Electricity Data Browser," accessed December 24, 2020.

Fortunately, the vast majority of that land will still be available for other purposes. The tower itself is only several meters in diameter, meaning the vast majority of the wind farm is unused and available for other purposes. Contrast that situation with a solar facility, where all of the land has to be dedicated to panels or mirrors. This situation allows synergy with other forms of land use. They can be placed in a field of crops with minimal disruption to agricultural operations, and the farmers can collect another source of income by leasing the land. This is a nontechnical reason why they have proliferated so much throughout the plains.[5]

Efficient, multipurpose land use allows us to expand wind turbines beyond the top priority areas more easily. For solar panels, the strategy focuses on deploying on rooftops since the land is already developed and we don't have to cut into more nature-filled areas. The same logic applies to the wind as well. Farmland is already developed, somewhat, with means of ingress for heavy equipment and is usually adjacent to roads hosting power lines. Therefore, that will be our first target across priority regions instead of clearing additional land to build new turbines.

OFFSHORE WIND FARMS

An offshore wind farm looks pretty similar to the one you would see in the middle of a field or prairie. The towers and blades have the same shape, and they're arranged in lines spread out over a large area. Some are built fairly close to shore, though most are several kilometers away.[6] The towers are attached to the seafloor, which requires firm underlying

---

5   AWEA, "Agriculture," accessed July 6, 2020.

6   Fraunhofer, "Distance to Shore," accessed July 20, 2020.

geology to anchor to. There are limits to the water depth they can be built in, but the engineering has continually improved, and turbines continue to be placed in deeper and deeper water. The overall operation of offshore units follows the same principles as their land-based cousins, although with unique advantages.

The conditions offshore help make wind farms more productive, regardless of turbine size. The wind is much more consistent out at sea, so they're able to provide more even power throughout the day and between seasons. The largest wind turbines are designed to be operated offshore to make use of these quality conditions. General Electric recently developed a gargantuan beast with a 12-megawatt turbine, about four to six times the nameplate output of your typical land-based unit.[7] European countries have been making substantial investments in offshore wind given these bona fides. There are now over 5,000 wind turbines in the waters off of Europe.[8] The London Array, for example, consists of 175 turbines, each putting out circa 51 TJ.[9] Repeating our calculation from earlier, we would only need two million of these offshore turbines to meet our needs, compared to six million onshore.

Investments overseas continue to accelerate, with hundreds of more turbines coming online annually. That success provides a good model for us to follow. Most of the US coast is highly amenable to wind power, falling in our priority region A. That's helpful due to the large number of

---

7   GE Renewable Energy, "Haliade-X," accessed July 6, 2020.

8   For more information on the European wind market, see: Wind Europe, "Offshore Wind in Europe," February 6, 2020.

9   Weston, "London Array," January 8, 2016.

people who live in coastal states who could use that power without additional large-scale transmission infrastructure. It would also be able to power regions like the Northeast and Pacific Northwest regions, where solar and onshore wind are less efficient.

***

There are not as many choices to make with wind power as solar since all the options fundamentally do the same thing. They generate nondispatchable electricity. It's just a matter of prioritization. This means going offshore is a top priority for the strategy given the lack of space limitations, high performance, and proximity to metropolitan areas. The United States is much less developed compared to Europe in this regard. There's only one offshore wind farm off the coast of Rhode Island, so we are starting with a blank slate to build an efficient system.[10] Inland construction is a lower priority, but it will still be important for diversifying the grid. That means not limiting ourselves to the Western plains but expanding out across the Midwest and South as well. Doing so will provide better resilience to mitigate daily and seasonal fluctuations over a larger area.

SACRIFICE: THE VIEW
What does Ted Kennedy, former Democratic senator from Massachusetts, and Donald Trump, the former Republican president of the United States, have in common? They both don't like wind turbines, or at least looking at them.[11]

---

10   McKenna, "America's First Offshore," May 1, 2017.
11   Schoetz, "Wind Farm," August 12, 2008.

Mr. Trump spent years fighting the Scottish Government, which was trying to build a wind farm offshore from his golf course in Aberdeen.[12] The initial installation planned to include a string of turbines several kilometers off the coast visible from the shore. Mr. Trump filed legal objections to the proposed project and its approval process. The challenge failed in 2015 when the United Kingdom's Supreme Court ruled unanimously for the government, and subsequently, construction began. The dispute involving the Kennedys, however, had the opposite outcome, and it deserves some attention.

The issue started in the mid-2000s when a developer sought to build a wind farm off the coast of Cape Cod. It would have largely powered the area and removed the need for several fossil fuel power plants. The project enjoyed widespread public support, almost 80 percent approval across the state, and everything had been permitted and approved.[13] However, the farm would never actually be built. Despite a decade of trying, the developer gave up on the project, and there are presently no offshore wind turbines in Massachusetts. All because a wealthy few had the funds to sustain legal opposition until the other side gave up.[14] Let me reiterate that: a broadly popular public works project that would have brought jobs and clean energy was scuttled because some rich people decided they didn't like it. Their arguments are telling, such as Robert F. Kennedy Jr claiming he supports wind energy in general, but just not there, implying the view

---

12   BBC, "Donald Trump," December 16, 2015.

13   Conte, "Cape Wind," September 1, 2006.

14   Doyle, "Koch's New Fight," September 21, 2006.

from his house has the same cultural value as Yosemite National Park.[15]

The Massachusetts situation raises several important concerns for our strategy. The first realization we have to make is that we cannot rely on certain elites to get this done. If they work to block everything inconveniencing them in the slightest regard using their disproportionate influence, they are, at best, unreliable allies. The necessary corollary is that we cannot allow people to use their power and wealth to override the needs and will of everyone else. The strategy would build those wind turbines off the coast of their estates, relying on the public in a democratic society to affect the change all of us are relying upon.

That class of people has additional, more insidious tools at its disposal, beyond the ability to launch dozens of lawsuits over a decade against a single wind farm. You might have seen news reports over the past several years about people complaining that wind turbines near them are causing any number of health issues. There is some truth to this, as the turbines are large machines that can produce disturbing sound if they're built too close to where people live.[16] However, like all good snake oil or panoptic ailments, that one accurate concern can be stretched until anything can be attributed to them. Looking into these claims reveals a couple of interesting things. Reports of illnesses usually appear once people believe they will, proving once again the placebo effect is a real thing.[17] The second observation is the

---

15   Kennedy, "An Ill Wind," December 16, 2005.

16   NRC, *Environmental Impacts of Wind-Energy Projects*, 157–160.

17   Rubin, Burns, and Wessely, "Possible Psychological Mechanisms," May 2014.

"consumer advocacy" groups and organizations pushing this narrative often have ties to the fossil fuel industry.[18]

Beyond targeting the general public, that industry also has more direct impacts on policy through its influence over elected officials. This is exhibited by legislatures in states like Ohio, who provided relief to struggling coal plants that actually cause health problems for surrounding communities.[19] This last example fits in nicely with the one from Massachusetts. A small group of people took control the situation to benefit a moneyed interest.

There is no such concentrated wealth or power behind a switch to clean energy. Fossil fuels have had a century and a half to accumulate financial resources and capital that dwarfs what little investment has been made in renewable energy thus far. That wealth gives them overwhelming control on an uneven playing field, such that any action opposing their interests with money alone will always find themselves overpowered. The only option we have to implement a strategy such as this and build a better future is to rely on a broader base of support, one able to wield power with democratic legitimacy.

Fossil fuel interests would continue the status quo regardless of the impact of societal well-being without a countervailing force from the people. That's why in countries with representational governments, they've tried so hard to confuse the issue and build popular support against renewables. Even in wind-friendly Europe, there is now a populist movement against further expansion in multiple countries.[20]

---

18   Anderson, "Trump's False Claim," April 17, 2019.

19   Pelzer, "Nuclear Bailout Bill," updated July 23, 2019.

20   Waters, "Anti-Wind Farm Activism," October 9, 2018.

Democracy can be frustrating when dealing with a problem like climate change, especially in the face of such blatant failures. Its debates and slow consensus-building appear to constantly stymie progress, especially when small interest groups can so easily derail what little progress we've made. Yet, the answer is more democracy is our only option for legitimate change. The will of the people needs to be strong enough to override the narrow interests of the few. That will mean negotiating with the not-in-my-backyard group from an overwhelming position of strength, such that they have no choice but to be willing to sacrifice their ocean view.

CHAPTER 5

THE WATER

———

One of my family's excursions out West took us to Las Vegas, Nevada. I was eight at the time, so I received a fairly sanitized picture of such a sinful city. The most uncouth experience was the bus ride to Hoover Dam, wherein the driver kept making dam-based puns, such as referring to the *dam* bus and encouraging us to visit the *dam* gift shop. The entire facility is an engineering marvel, especially considering how old it is. The turbines alone are the size of busses. The most memorable part of the trip was walking along the top. On one side was a relatively placid lake, and on the other, a several hundred-foot drop punctuated by a torrent of raging water.

Tapping into water's energy as it flows from the mountains to the sea allows us to build some of the world's most massive power plants. The Three Gorges Dam in China is the largest hydroelectric facility in the world in terms of capacity, capable of continuously outputting 22 gigawatts of power. For context, that's ten times what the Hoover Dam can provide and 1,800 times greater than the largest offshore wind turbine.[1] It is so large that the force of forty billion tons

---

[1]   USDOI, "What is the Biggest Dam," updated March 12, 2015.

of water accumulating in its reservoir literally slowed our planet's rotational speed.[2] That demonstrates the tremendous power of water. It levels mountains, carves canyons, and, when controlled properly, can provide a significant chunk of our electricity needs.

Water is as ubiquitous as the sun and wind. So long as there is weather and tides, we will be able to derive renewable energy from it. Like sunlight, there is theoretically enough waterpower to meet all of our needs, but only if we are able to tap into it properly.[3] The same procedure as in the previous chapters is required here. We need to determine the focus of our resources to provide the most benefit. The different approaches available to us can be neatly split like in the wind power chapter, and we will consider what we can do inland with fresh water and on the coasts with salt water.

FRESH WATER

A good place to start when evaluating our inland hydropower resources are dams since they already power a substantial portion of our grid. These stations work by using the flow of water to turn a turbine that spins a generator to make electricity. The energy you can extract from that water depends on how much you push through the turbines and how fast it's moving. You get more water through your dam by building it on a larger waterway, and you can give the water more energy by building a taller reservoir. The Hoover Dam is so tall because every extra foot adds additional energy to the water coming out of the bottom, thanks to gravity. It's

---

2   Trosper, "How an Infamous," October 1, 2013.

3   The total tidal power of the Earth is circa three terawatts. Selin, "Tidal Power," accessed September 14, 2020.

the same principle as dropping a ball from the second story instead of an inch off the ground. In short, the bigger your dam is, the more useful it will be.

The amount of energy you get from a dam can be enormous. The largest one in the United States, the Grand Coulee in Washington, delivers 76,000 terajoules (TJ) of electricity per year. To help visualize the scale, the quantity of water flowing through the dam is equivalent to eleven Olympic-size swimming pools every second of every day. The numbers are equally impressive on a renewable energy front, with the energy output being on par with 227 square kilometers of solar panels or 4,200 onshore wind turbines. And this is from just one dam. With all the rivers in the country, it seems like a natural thing to simply build more of them.

The amount of energy we can get out of a single dam is impressive, but we do need to acknowledge hydropower's limitations, starting with its variability. While water is always flowing through the dam, that flowrate and resulting power fluctuate throughout the year.[4] The output is typically higher in the spring, and early summer as the winter snows melt and swell the rivers that feed the dam. The power we get today is dependent on the weather a year ago because less snow one year leads to less hydropower in the next. That will only worsen as climate change alters rainfall, increasing hydropower potential in some areas and decreasing it in others. Since we can't control the weather, a dam's performance is always going to be variable.

The fluctuations in a dam's output also means it can't be very responsive to changes in demand. It will require other renewable sources and storage to help even out its day-to-day

---

4   USEIA, "U.S. Hydropower Output," August 15, 2011.

and seasonal changes. There is also the issue that dams perform other functions, like flood control, that overrides changes in operation to meet electricity demand. The overall role of inland hydropower falls into the same category as solar and wind. It is nondispatchable power that feeds the grid as part of a mixed system.

Perhaps the greatest hurdle to overcome when looking to expand inland hydropower is the limitations of geography. Even with all the rivers in the United States, there are only so many suitable places for building hydroelectric stations, and the low-hanging fruit has largely been picked clean during the last century. Thanks to programs like the New Deal's Tennessee Valley Authority, we have a lot of dams across the country already, giving us 7 percent of our yearly electricity needs.[5] Their output has been pretty constant since about 1975, which was the end of the heyday for building new capacity.

Expanding our hydropower system would mean going into more marginal areas, which may not be the best use of resources. The potential environmental impacts would also complicate the situation. Changing a river by building a dam alters flood plains, agriculture, wildlife habitat, and migration. In fact, California doesn't count hydropower as renewable for this very reason. Additionally, more marginal locations need new technology development to effectively make use of the lower power density. That is not in line with our requirement to only use the technology currently available.

We don't necessarily have to build more dams to get more power since there is still room to make better use of the ones

---

5   USDOE, "The National Hydropower Map," June 2018.

we already have. There are hundreds of smaller dams spread around the country that aren't setup for electricity generation or connected to the power grid. They were built for other purposes and were never electrified. One easy option would be to upgrade these already existing resources, removing the need to invest in nearly as much infrastructure. By some estimates, we could get maybe another 112,000 TJ of energy from these dams, enough for three million homes.[6] We could also recapitalize some of the older fleet with better generators and turbines to yield another 47,000 TJ per year.

These investments, unfortunately, won't make the biggest dent in our fossil fuel demand. Combined, they add up to less than 1 percent of our yearly energy needs. Yet, doing so is an efficient use of resources that can be accomplished quickly, so it will be part of the strategy. An expansion of inland hydropower through new construction, however, will not be a priority.

SALT WATER
Rivers aren't our only water resources. Over 97 percent of water is in the oceans, and one need only visit a beach and watch the waves to imagine the wealth of potential energy there. By one estimate, the amount of power off of our shores could be enough to satisfy at least 15 percent of our grid.[7] Given that massive potential, it's worth evaluating the different technologies that can harness it.

---

6   USDOE, "Hydropower Vision," July 26, 2016, 57.

7   USDOE, "Tapping into Wave," January 27, 2012.

TIDAL BARRAGES

As with dams, the ultimate source of tidal energy is gravity. Only it's the moon's gravity pulling water up rather than the Earth pulling it down. Water is drawn onshore during high tide and recedes at low tide. This is different from a wave, as the water level rises and stays constant for a set period of time. If you control where water flows, you can have it spin rotors—essentially smaller, slower turbines—when the tides move in and out. The concept is almost medieval in origin, and coastal mills have operated on this principle for centuries. We would need a larger scale than that. Instead of an unencumbered approach to the beach, an entire shoreline area would be walled in, with a gap every so often with a rotor, not unlike a wide-area dam. This entire structure is called a barrage.

The energy provided by a barrage suffers from several of the same limitations as dams. It is fundamentally a nondispatchable power source because the time of day and duration it can generate power is outside of our control. The tides only come at fixed times, so the power output will never be continuous or responsive to our needs. It is at least predictable since the tides are well understood, and in that way, it would act like a baseload source. It would take greater planning to keep the grid in balance throughout the day, but that isn't insurmountable. There are several such facilities in operation, so we know it is feasible to operate, though they are few and far between.

There are really only two large-scale barrages currently in operation. The oldest, going back to 1966, is built across the Rance River in France, where it empties into the English

Channel.[8] The other is located in South Korea, although its barrage is constructed to form an artificial lagoon.[9] Though their forms are slightly different, each operates on the same principles and are a working part of their countries' infrastructure.

These two examples help illuminate the potential of this power generation approach. Both produce about 2,000 TJ of energy per year, enough for about 50,000 homes each. However, the resource requirements to get that energy are very different. The French station is only 750 meters long (about half a mile), while the South Korean is over twelve kilometers in length (about seven and a half miles). Even if those are boundary cases, we're talking about many miles of earth, rock, and steel that need to be committed if we want to build more. That should give us pause when we need to move our resources as quickly and efficiently as possible.

Beyond the resource cost, barrages have several other hurdles to overcome before building them makes sense. The choice of location has to coexist with other human uses. Building a barrage over a river blocks ship travel, just like a dam, so building in a high-traffic area probably won't be viable. Wildlife is also affected by construction and operation. In France, they've seen the depopulation of certain fish species due to the barrage. Even if a location is viable now, we'll also need to find options that would be able to survive the sea level rise coming with climate change in the coming decades.

All these things will have to be weighed when planning to build a barrage, making it difficult to discern just what fraction of our power grid they could constitute. Fundamentally,

8   Power Technology, "Tidal Giants," updated July 14, 2020.

9   Patel, "Sihwa Lake," December 1, 2015.

we need to start by conducting a comprehensive survey of the US coastline before answering that question. The strategy will prioritize doing such a survey to guide future decisions. There are likely some amenable areas that are low-hanging fruit for building, and we can do so once they're identified. Until then, the strategy will treat them like new dams: not a high priority.

OTHER OCEAN POWER GENERATORS

We could avoid the large-scale building requirements of a barrage by installing sub-surface turbines to capture the energy of tides instead. These would work much the same as their wind-powered cousins. Moving water hits underwater blades to turn a turbine. However, they're still in the research and development stage, so we can comfortably discard this approach.

Another way to get energy from the ocean's motion would be to rely on waves instead of tides. While they seem to be constantly crashing onto the seashore, waves are variable and thus a nondispatchable source, but they do have a surprisingly high power density.[10] Capturing wave energy is slightly different since you're capturing the water's up and down motion instead of its movement toward and away from shore. The generator actually looks more like a flashlight you shake to recharge, only on a much larger scale.

The most commonly presented way for harnessing waves puts the generators out from the shore on the ocean's surface. They take the form of floating pontoons or buoys anchored to the seafloor and connect to the shore by undersea cables. While there are myriad examples of test cases attempting to

---

10 Bonifacio, "Wave Energy," October 24, 2010.

prove this technical approach, none have really scaled up to a full grid-scale implementation.

Beyond the requirement for using existing technology, other factors don't recommend this approach. For one thing, it would require a huge number of units spread over a large area of the sea to make it worthwhile. Each piece of floating equipment would be a navigational hazard, making the entire area essentially closed to other uses. We must also anticipate what the result of a hurricane would be—likely more debris and trash filling the ocean. Maintenance would be obnoxious under the best of times as you try to repair all the connections and cabling on a moving platform, so the overall longevity of the infrastructure is another cause for concern. These factors together do not make a compelling case for widespread adoption.

One wave-based approach does have a better track record. A test facility in Scotland was built on a cliff overlooking the ocean instead of floating out at sea.[11] It was small and only worked for a couple of years, but it was connected to the grid. As a hardened structure that's physically placed on the coast, it can better survive inclement weather and is easier to maintain. The major issue is the limited options of where you can put this type of installation. The construction of one in Scotland took place on a rocky bit of coast with a sharp decline into the water. Just like with the barrages, we'd be limited by the geography available to us when scaling up the deployment. It's difficult to get an accurate picture of how much of this resource we could harness based on the available data. Thus, we shall include searching for amenable locations as part of our earlier survey for barrage locations.

---

11   Seenan, "Islay Pioneers," September 13, 2000.

***

Taken together, our options for water seem to be less immediately actionable than solar and wind. We know the potential is there. It's just not conclusive how much of it we can successfully tap into. We have dams that will keep putting out a lot of power in aggregate. We will connect the nonelectrified dams already in existence and make some efficiency upgrades, but that'll be about it for onshore hydropower. The first step for the oceans will be to complete our survey to find suitable locations for barrages and wave generators. With that information in hand, we'll be able to identify the low-hanging fruit to start rapidly exploiting those resources. Given the large coastal population of the United States, those easy builds will be a great way to supplement our expanding offshore wind power.

SACRIFICE: AN ECOSYSTEM
It would not be out of line to say we've put a fair bit of stress on our oceans. Between plastic, acidification, the collapse of reefs and fisheries, and deafened whales, it is remarkable they're still full of life. The transition to a new energy system must be at its core about preserving the environment wherever possible. The barrage discussion briefly mentioned that those structures can cause problems for local fish populations, which implies their widespread adoption would cause damage on a significant scale. Part of our location survey has to include some assessment of the ecological impact.

This perspective may seem at odds with our discussion of the desert tortoise. After all, we must take action to avert the disaster of climate change, even if it is nonideal. The conclusion is there exists an overall moral imperative to take action that would threaten one species in the face of global-scale extinctions. However, that was only one mostly isolated creature in the desert, and applying the same logic to an entire interconnected oceanic ecosystem requires some additional consideration. To help evaluate this situation, the damage caused to the ocean by climate change has to serve as the baseline of comparison for any new renewable energy installations.

The oceans soak up a lot of the carbon we throw into the atmosphere. Not in the way one would typically think of, through increased plant growth, but by basic chemistry. When carbon dioxide is dissolved by water, it forms carbonic acid.[12] More dissolved carbon in the ocean makes the water more acidic, and its acidity has increased by 26 percent since the industrial revolution. That rise has myriad negative consequences for creatures like corrals, which rely on a specific acid-base environment to form their shells. The bleaching of the Great Barrier Reef is a stark example of changing ocean chemistry, and it will only get worse without our transition away from fossil fuels.

More heat is also having a notable impact on the oceans. Water temperature is increasing just the same as land temperature, with similar effects. Notably, warmer water drives sea creatures further north.[13] These changes are not necessarily apocalyptic. After all, there have been times when previous climates included tropical poles. The issue is the rapid pace of the changes won't afford sea creatures enough time

---

12 The reaction is $CO_2 + H_2O \rightarrow H_2CO_3$. pH is a measure of acidity on a logarithmic scale, and a small change in pH represents a comparatively large change in acidity. See Appendix for calculation details. USEPA, "Understanding the Science," accessed August 6, 2020.

13 NOAA, "New Study," May 17, 2018.

to evolve and adapt to the new conditions. Climate change is happening now over decades instead of millions of years. The consequence of rapid change in the past has been mass extinctions, and there is no reason why this situation would be any different.

Disrupting habitat by building infrastructure will exacerbate some of the problems facing our ecosystems. Taking away breeding grounds for various fish species near the shore to build barrages will put them under even greater pressures and complicate their survival. A change like that can spread up the food chain, devastating species that rely on the threatened creatures for food. Life will be necessary for ultimately reversing climate change, so some actions to rebuild the grid might actually be counterproductive to our overall goals.

Problems like ocean acidification and warming will be with us for a long time. The ocean has massive inertia due to its size, such that adverse effects from climate change will persist after the transition. Therein lies the conundrum when trying to save the biosphere—both the cost of action and inaction may be great. We can move forward without regard for the impact and potentially cause irreversible damage, or we can be more measured and allow destructive forces to get even worse. It is a narrow path we must tread if we wish to preserve as much of the world as possible.

We'll need to know not only the potential of each location for generating energy and the resources required for construction, but the impacts on various parts of the ecosystem as well. Combined, such information will allow us to make optimal decisions. Sometimes the energy benefits of building in an area will overwhelm any damage to the local ecosystem. Other situations will be more ambiguous. We just need to be prepared to make imperfect decisions and trade-offs to keep us moving toward the overall goal. We can also make some sacrifices ourselves to help push the balance in favor of building infrastructure. We can choose to offset the ecological harm of energy generation by pulling back in other areas. If a barrage is threatening a certain fish species, we could cut back on fishing to relieve pressure on the overall population. Our lifestyle would change somewhat, but we should be as open to depriving ourselves as we are to burdening ecosystems. The point is we have to start making decisions in the framework of their overall impact on climate change, even if it means some mild inconvenience.

CHAPTER 6

THE EARTH

My favorite of the thirteen Yule Lads would probably be *Skyrgámur*, a.k.a. Skyr-Gobbler, since I also enjoy starting the day with some high-protein yogurt. Oh, you've never heard of the Yule Lads? Well, they're one of the curious cultural concoctions of the great island nation of Iceland. Icelanders aren't only known for their Christmas pranksters. There's also the prevalent belief in elves and a dating app that checks records to make sure y'all aren't too closely related.[1] Fun! On another unique note, Iceland is a country that gets almost a quarter of its electricity from geothermal power plants.

Geothermal power draws energy from the heat within the earth. That heat is used to create steam and turn a turbine and generator to make electricity. The second bit isn't so interesting since that's the basic operating mode for most power plants. While coal and gas are fundamentally limited, the Earth's energy is basically inexhaustible, at least for several billion years. A combination of primordial heat from when the planet formed and radioactive decay keep the core

---

1 Jacobs, "Why So Many Icelanders," October 29, 2013; Conradt, "This App Keeps," March 2, 2016.

a balmy ten thousand degrees. For reference, that's as hot as the surface of the sun. Some of that heat makes its way to the surface and out into space, to the tune of 1,400 exajoules every year. In other words, thirteen times what the United States consumes.[2]

Unlike solar, wind, or water, geothermal electricity production is constant. Not being affected by surface conditions like the sunset, weather, or the tides means it is our first and only option for dispatchable renewable power. For this reason alone, geothermal deserves serious consideration by our strategy. If it passes muster, investing in this energy source will take the pressure off of us to build overcapacity in other sources and decrease the amount of energy storage we have to bring online. Geothermal will help our entire effort move more efficiently and decommission fossil fuels more rapidly, provided it's readily available.

The ability of a country to exploit geothermal energy entirely depends on the underlying geology. Iceland has uniquely abundant geothermal potential, as evidenced by the numerous hot springs dotting the country. The entire island is basically located over volcanoes and fault lines, a situation that brings the Earth's internal energy to the surface in its most concentrated and useful form. Most countries are not so fortunate. A select few have managed decent geothermal infrastructure so far, though not to the same scale and certainly not anywhere near their full potential.[3]

The United States is actually the world leader in installed geothermal capacity. You just can't tell because it's such a small part of our overall energy mix. California alone

2   Johnston, "Radioactive Decay," July 19, 2011.

3   NS Energy Staff Writer, "Profiling the Top," January 8, 2020.

has more capacity than any other country, but even that chart-topping infrastructure can only meet 6 percent of the state's overall electricity needs.[4] We'd need much more than that to make a substantial difference, so our first priority is to determine our potential geothermal capacity.

Unfortunately, we are somewhat limited in the geographical extent of buildable geothermal power. The United States' priority regions include the Mountain West and Pacific coast, as shown on the accompanying map.[5] The majority of the country is simply nonviable (region C), and the Midwest and Eastern Seaboard will not be able to benefit at all. Only a few select areas within region A will even be able to host a substantial amount of infrastructure, but that will still be useful for our goals.

Geothermal Potential of the Contental United States

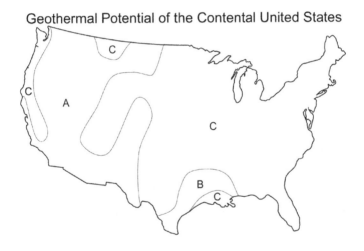

4   California Energy Commission, "California Geothermal," accessed February 14, 2021.

5   Regions prioritized based on the data presented in: USDOE, "GeoVision," 2019. Map created using public domain image: Codomo, "File:PNGedU-Soutline.png," May 20, 2006.

The most viable clusters of geothermal activity can help diversify the Western United States' grid. The furthest Northwest locations are adjacent to large population centers along the coast that would directly use the power. Since the areas west of the Cascades are marginal for everything except offshore wind, geothermal will help mitigate the need to build transmission infrastructure that brings power from further afield. The same will be true for the Plains east of Yellowstone and around Colorado, whose best alternative is wind as well. High-value resources in southern California would directly support the large populations and industrial base out there, combining with ample solar and offshore wind to create a renewable energy juggernaut.

More marginal geothermal regions can still add to our energy transition, even if they aren't directly adding more electricity to the grid. Instead, we could use the Earth's heat directly to meet a variety of our needs, and Iceland shows how this is done on a large scale. Their plentiful geothermal resources have allowed them to replace the majority of traditional furnaces with heat brought in from underground.[6] Doing so decreases the amount of fossil fuels burned in homes and businesses for space heating without adding additional burdens to the grid through electrification.

The only other option for decarbonizing heat sources is to use electricity derived from renewable sources. Doing so will slow our transition by requiring more renewable generators to be installed to replace both fossil fuel power plants and fossil fuel-burning appliances. Geothermal heat bypasses this problem and allows our renewable installations to focus

---

6   Orkustofnun National Energy Authority, "Direct Use," accessed July 31, 2020.

on the former source of emissions. It is also more efficient to use geothermal heat because it doesn't require multiple energy conversion steps. We lose about 60–70 percent of the available energy when converting heat to electricity and then back to heat. Prioritizing those investments would thus help increase the overall velocity of our transition.

Cities like Boise have used this approach for over a hundred years.[7] In their system, hot water is pumped from underground and distributed throughout nearby buildings. This kind of district heating allows many sources of emissions to decarbonize all at once. Manufacturers in some industries can also benefit from the same technology. It would be a variation on the industrial use of solar thermal discussed previously. Energy intensive but relatively low-temperature, applications like drying during cement manufacturing would be able to benefit immediately.[8] It won't work everywhere or for everything, but it will in enough places to make the investment worthwhile.

Just because a certain area is theoretically amenable to geothermal doesn't necessarily mean we can build there. Iceland is able to rely so much on geothermal because the energy is naturally brought right to the surface. However, in many promising locations, the heat we want is trapped below miles of rock. Building a plant will often require deep wells and extensive piping to bring the heat where we need it. Construction can thus be resource intensive and time-consuming to accomplish. US facilities are currently clustered in the most favorable locations, so expanding geothermal at scale

---

7   City of Boise, "Geothermal," accessed August 6, 2020.

8   Orkustofnun National Energy Authority, "Industrial Users," accessed July 31, 2020.

will run into this problem. That is one reason why geothermal has not been an investment target for several decades.

A substantial fraction of the current US geothermal capacity came online during a very specific point in time. It was not built to preemptively combat climate change but to respond to the oil crises of the 1970s.[9] The first crisis began in 1973 when multiple nations stopped oil exports to countries that supported Israel in the Yom Kippur War. The second crisis followed additional unrest in the Middle East following the Iranian Revolution and Iran-Iraq War. Back in the United States, these events caused gas lines, where people had to wait their turn for a couple of gallons of rationed gasoline. There were even ration stamps, something we typically associate with wartime shortages. The overall effect on the country was recession since the postwar economy depended on access to cheap energy sources.

The deprivation created by the oil crises led to several changes that almost seem anachronistic. There was a renewed focus on reducing energy demand, increasing efficiency, conserving resources, and developing new energy sources, all critical aspects of combating climate change. On a small scale, President Carter famously installed a solar water-heating system on the White House roof.[10] Developing larger, grid-scale resources like geothermal were also suddenly on the table, leading to a temporary construction boom. Unfortunately, fossil fuels returned to being the cheapest energy source once the crises were over, reversing what little progress made.

The geothermal facilities built in response to the energy crises made use of our prime real-estate, curtailing our

9   USEIA, "Nearly Half," November 20, 2019.

10   Biello, "Where did the Carter," August 6, 2010.

options for easy expansion. New construction will require more resources and time, leading to higher costs. Private investors have traditionally shied away from geothermal development for this reason. Even in states aggressively trying to decarbonize, other renewable options present fewer short-term barriers and more rapid returns.

Perceived financial constraints guide current estimates of geothermal energy's potential. The US Department of Energy calculates that we could get upward of two exajoules per year from new geothermal sources, between 1–2 percent of our overall needs, based on a range of cost estimate scenarios. Cost being the operative word since there is nothing else preventing us from exploiting those resources. We have the know-how to find and reach the pockets of heat deep within the earth, and we have the drilling tools to get our equipment down there. The oil and gas exploration industry does pretty much the same thing every day for fossil fuels. Fundamentally, we could gain much more energy than those two exajoules per year if we choose to do so.

Geothermal energy is simply too useful to be limited by cost models. It is our only option for a fully dispatchable renewable power source without storage. Being dispatchable means we can use geothermal power to directly shut down fossil fuel power sources without building additional storage. That attribute must give geothermal power precedence, and we will be prioritizing it over all other renewable options.

Once we set aside the financial constraints, our major limitation is time. It usually takes the better part of a decade before a new geothermal plant can go from conception to completion. That only emphasizes how important it is we start work immediately. We'll need surveys completed and sites to be shovel-ready, with equipment manufacturers and builders standing by to start construction. Workers from the oil and gas industry can help us here with their expertise. We'll certainly need all-hands-on-deck to keep this linchpin of our strategy on course and on time.

SACRIFICE: A PARK

The sacrifices we've talked about so far have been relatively impersonal. Most of us will probably never see a desert tortoise in person, a rich person's ocean view is incredibly petty, and environmental assessments are relatively abstract. But what if you're asked to sacrifice something you've experienced, touched, and used to build memories? What if it were something so culturally relevant it is protected by law and almost sacred to millions of people? What if it were Yellowstone National Park that had to be sacrificed to stop climate change?

The heat rising through its geysers and hot springs are the source of Yellowstone's geothermal potential. Building in the park would, of course, displace what's already there. Depending on how much is developed and the quantity of heat extracted, we might even cause Old Faithful to stop performing on time.[11] It could be a truly world scale operation, and Yellowstone could power swaths of the country with clean, renewable energy.[12] But reaching such an end state would require tremendous dedication on our part to accomplish.

The first obstacle is it is illegal to develop at Yellowstone, and that law would be difficult to overturn.[13] Although some

---

11   National Park Service, "Hydrothermal Systems," August 6, 2019.

12   Hall, "Yellowstone Supervolcano," August 8, 2018.

13   Geothermal Steam Act of 1970.

business interests support opening lands for extractive industries, the broader response is to push back against such activities because people generally like protecting national parks. Keeping certain places off-limits and in a natural state helps protect wildlife, which has allowed populations of wolves and bison to rebound from near extinction. There's also the idea we need to preserve unique features of cultural importance and be stewards for future generations so they might enjoy them as well. Nostalgia for family trips and youthful memories is powerful like that.

The easiest part to argue against is the need to maintain a pristine environment. Have you visited Yellowstone lately? The whole park is a developed landscape of paved roads, parking lots, hotels, restaurants, boat landings, walking paths, and gift shops. There is nothing like seeing the majesty of nature's creatures digging in trash cans or people waiting in traffic to reach a scenic overlook. Yellowstone is about as wild and natural now as any other attraction. Building geothermal power plants there wouldn't be bulldozing virgin forest, merely rebuilding over already developed land. Yellowstone is not now nor will ever again be pristine nature, and our only choice is how best to continue using that resource.

Switching from a tourist-oriented development to energy infrastructure won't even impact the environment too much. Geothermal power's footprint above the ground isn't very substantial, a few buildings and power lines at most, and it certainly wouldn't exceed what's already been built in Yellowstone.[14] If the Chernobyl exclusion zone is any indication, wildlife might even do better with fewer tourists around. As long as you otherwise protect the majority of the area left

---

14   USDOE, "Geothermal Power Plants," accessed February 9, 2021.

alone, *people* are the only ones who will miss out on experiencing everything the park previously had to offer. That will be the primary sacrifice that we have to overcome, our memories and future expectations.

This would be a deal-breaker for a substantial number of people. The places that have shaped our memories and lives do carry meaning, so of course, we want to preserve them, and the instinct to oppose the development of protected spaces is perfectly natural. Except now, the landscape is at risk of igniting because climate change is turning the entire forest into kindling. Nature does not care about protecting our memories and experiences. Wildfires and extinctions will not stop just because we've decided an arbitrary parcel of land is protected. Yellowstone and every other park will change no matter what we do, and that change will be much more destructive if we do nothing instead of taking proactive action. Preserving the park for future generations as it is also won't matter if there are no future generations to enjoy it. We have to be willing to consider emotionally wrenching decisions like developing a national treasure because survival *must* come first.

CHAPTER 7

THE MOON

———

I was a big fan of trains as a small child. Something about such large pieces of equipment interested me for some reason, driving me to consume train-related media and dress as if I were an engineer. The crown jewel of my toys was the train set in the basement. It was relatively simple, just a basic loop and some cars, but they did move on their own thanks to a couple of electric motors. The system didn't run on wall power, instead relying on, for a kid, gigantic D cell batteries. Replacing those isn't cheap, so my dad opted to buy rechargeable ones. Unfortunately, this was the early 1990s, so they took forever to charge and didn't last very long. With the benefit of hindsight, I could attempt to claim that experience taught me some lesson about energy storage, but that would be a lie. I just wanted to play with trains.

Energy storage absolutely has to work for our strategy to have a chance of success. Since we certainly won't have near enough geothermal power to meet all of our needs, we'll have to rely on intermittent and nondispatchable renewable sources for the bulk of our transition. The pace we can install storage infrastructure to compensate for their unreliability will determine how quickly we can take fossil fuels offline.

Our strategy is actually much more feasible now than if we had tried to implement it thirty years ago when I was a kid thanks to the new technologies that are available. The rest of this chapter is dedicated to evaluating those options. Our primary metrics have to be speed and scalability because our choices here determine our overall odds of success for long-term recovery.

BATTERIES

No storage technology has improved so rapidly over the past several decades as rechargeable batteries. Batteries offer several helpful attributes for grid-scale storage. They hold electricity directly, meaning they can be rapidly charged using excess power on the grid, then immediately be discharged when we need to compensate for a shortfall. There is already a massive manufacturing base for them, which facilitates rapid deployment. Finally, batteries are proven as being able to function as grid-scale energy storage. Banks of high-capacity batteries have taken root on both coasts and the Midwest, where they're already taking the place of fossil fuel peaker plants.[1]

Our ability to continue building battery installations will depend on the types of rechargeable batteries we decide to use. There are multiple options for us to choose from, and the performance of each type will determine its potential for grid-scale storage. We also have to judge them by their material constraints, that is, just how many we can feasibly build in a short period of time. Evaluating each option by

---

[1] Neuhauser, "Where Batteries," May 21, 2019; Spector, "The Biggest Batteries," September 3, 2019; USEIA, "Battery Storage in the United States," July 15, 2020, 10.

these two criteria will help us narrow down our options and make the proper choices.

The most important performance characteristics for batteries are energy capacity and lifespan. The best batteries have a high capacity because they can provide more energy for a longer period of time. That means fewer batteries are required for the same task, and we can save on our total resource investments. Unfortunately, capacity isn't permanent. Your rechargeable battery's performance will degrade over time, holding less and less power every time you charge it. If you have an older smartphone, you've probably noticed it requires more frequent charging now than when you bought it. After a certain number of charge-discharge cycles, our grid storage batteries will need to be replaced with new ones. We want to pick those with long lifetimes to avoid replacing them for as long as possible.

There are four main types of rechargeable batteries we could choose from. Lead-acid batteries, like the one in your car, are the worst in terms of both capacity and lifetime, so we can safely discount them at this stage.[2] Lithium-ion batteries occupy the opposite end of the capacity scale but have only middling lifespans. Nickel-cadmium (NiCd) and nickel-metal hydride (NiMH) rechargeable batteries offer the highest overall lifespans, sometimes over double a lithium-ion, but have only middling energy capacity. This serves them well in critical aerospace and telecommunications applications, but it means a bank of these batteries would be substantially larger than a lithium-ion facility with the

---

2   Lead-acid batteries have a maximum capacity of approximately 180 kilojoules per kilogram (kJ/kg), compared to 290 kJ/kg for NiCd, 430 kJ/kg for NiMH, and 680 kJ/kg for lithium-ion. Epec, "Battery Cell Comparison," accessed August 6, 2020.

same power output. Whether or not that is feasible depends on the availability of raw materials used to build each type.

These three types of batteries rely on some uncommon metals that will help set limits for how many we can deploy. The total world output of lithium, for instance, is less than 100,000 tons per year.[3] If all mined lithium went toward producing the best lithium-ion batteries, we could build 2,400 terajoules (TJ) of new energy storage capacity every year. That capacity does not seem like much, considering our total energy needs are thousands of times greater. For comparison, 2,400 TJ is the total output of only 132 wind turbines. However, that amount of power entering the grid over the course of an hour would be equivalent to adding 56,000 of the largest wind turbines to the grid at a moment's notice. That's quite a reserve to have in our pocket.

Our other options are deployable to a similar extent. Nickel is available in much greater quantities than lithium, but cadmium is limited since it is only manufactured as a by-product of other ores.[4] NiMH batteries rely on other uncommon materials like rare-earth metals and cobalt, as do certain variants of lithium batteries that would compete with them. Fortunately, unlike fossil fuels, building batteries do not destroy their raw material inputs as they are used.

Once the rare metals we need are out of the ground, we can use them indefinitely through recycling. NiCd systems already see high rates of recycling, thanks to the need to keep toxic cadmium out of the environment.[5] This shows it would be possible to build a circular system continuously

---

3   USGS, "Lithium," January 2020.

4   USGS, "Nickel," January 2020; USGS, "Cadmium," January 2020.

5   ICdA, "Collection and Recycling," accessed May 5, 2020.

regenerating our battery supply by reusing material. Unfortunately, lithium batteries are currently difficult to recycle. The processes to do so efficiently are still being developed and implemented, which creates a complication given our requirement only to use available technology.[6]

A further issue for the scalability of lithium batteries is competition with other applications. Every modern electronic device—from the smartphone in your pocket to the laptop in your backpack—relies on the power density of lithium batteries to provide the longest possible time between charges. That high capacity is also why all electric vehicles have switched from using NiMH to lithium. All those other consumers will deplete the reserves we would otherwise need for grid storage. That isn't necessarily a bad thing for the strategy.

Transportation is a major emitter of carbon dioxide. Our discussion in chapter 1 reflected on how decarbonizing that sector will rely on electric vehicles powered by a renewable grid and lithium-ion batteries. Every pound of lithium dedicated to electric vehicles will still be working toward our overall goal of reversing climate change. And it will take a lot of lithium to fully decarbonize the auto market. The United States' transportation sector consumes about 30 exajoules of energy per year. Assuming that's evenly split over 365 days, we need an energy storage capacity on the order of 82,000 TJ dedicated for cars and trucks. With 2,400 TJ added every year, it would take thirty-four years at the current lithium mining rate to fully replace gasoline and diesel vehicles. We

---

6   Hogg, "Batteries Need," September 30, 2019; Bush, "Closing the Loop," January 21, 2019; Energy Storage World Forum, "Are Energy Storage Systems," accessed April 22, 2020.

will therefore leave lithium batteries for cars and trucks for the foreseeable future.

That leaves our other two options for grid storage. Between NiCd and NiMH, it would be wise to focus on NiCd, since NiMH requires greater quantities of uncommon materials. NiCd will fill a similar niche as cadmium telluride solar cells. We need to do something with all the toxic cadmium we've mined, so we might as well put it toward building recyclable batteries. The amount we have available won't be anywhere close to our overall energy storage needs, but it will help make a dent.

THERMAL STORAGE

The primary selling point for solar thermal power generation is it can natively provide input for daily energy storage. As we discussed in chapter 3, the method is relatively straightforward: molten salts are pumped into insulated tanks while other power sources feed the grid. When they're needed, those salts are used to generate steam to make electricity. Like batteries, the energy output of thermal storage can ramp up and down as needed. Essentially, we're trapping heat during the day and storing it until we need it to produce more electricity. While it makes sense to combine storage with solar thermal in the Southwest, it doesn't solve the problem for the rest of the country.

Thermal storage can still be a widely distributed option because you don't require sunlight to heat up the molten salts. Electricity from any power source can be redirected to heat them using the same principle as an electric furnace or stove. The salts would be able to soak up extra energy on the grid and hold it for later, providing the same benefit as a battery. We just need to install the capital to do it, and we already have a head start thanks to the fossil fuel plants blanketing the country.[7]

The fundamentals behind operating a fossil fuel plant and thermal storage plant aren't that different. You can conceptualize these facilities as containing two parts—a heat generator and a steam turbine cycle. The latter component will be the same regardless, while the heat source only has to change from natural gas or coal to molten salts. All we need to do is rebuild that half of the process, and we'll be good to go.

The primary benefit of this approach is it would be quicker and more efficient to retrofit those existing facilities than build something new. It would mean working on already developed land, retaining the workforce, and building capacity across the country to capture energy from all of our power sources.[8] It also speeds the transition since creating more thermal storage would inherently decommission fossil fuels. Plus, we wouldn't have to invest in massive, new transmission infrastructure. That part of the grid wouldn't have to look or operate too differently than it does now.

Like batteries, the amount of electricity you can put on the grid using thermal storage will depend on how much material you have to work with. Eventually, the salts will go cold, and you won't be able to generate any more power. Thermal storage would need to be able to provide energy over the course of several hours if it is to become a workable part of our strategy. To determine how feasible that is, we first need to figure out the scales required and any material constraints.

7   Deign, "Germany Looks," March 18, 2019.

8   For a map of every fossil fuel power plant in the United States, see: USEIA, "U.S. Energy Mapping System," accessed September 14, 2020.

The first step for designing a theoretical thermal storage plant is to set its total energy capacity. We'll keep it simple and require that it outputs one gigawatt of power over eight hours, on par with the capacity of a large fossil fuel facility. In total, that will require about 260,000 tons of salt and a 174,000 cubic meter tank to store it.[9] That is quite a lot of material. It would be the same volume as about sixty-eight Olympic swimming pools. We already produce tanks near that size for crude oil.[10] These are the large white cylinders you might see at refineries or transportation depots, which usually have several acres dedicated to hosting them. We have many of those spread across the country, so the resources needed to build such tanks are certainly available. The land required for tanks is also relatively small, considering solar farms regularly occupy several thousand acres. Land and infrastructure wouldn't be an overall bottleneck for deployment.

The weight of salts in that tank is a large amount and well within our ability to manufacture. The United States produces fourteen million tons of ammonia every year.[11] One ton of ammonia can manufacture about five tons of nitrate salts, so our theoretical plant would only consume 0.4 percent of our total production capacity. Salts also don't go away once they're used but are constantly cycled through the system for twenty to thirty years. Disposing of the salts is relatively easy as well. It's essentially fertilizer that can be applied to crops after its decades-long lifespan is over. There is no material

9   See appendix for calculation details.

10   All Oil Tank, "Crude Oil Storage Tanks," accessed August 26, 2020.

11   Ammonia production estimate from: USGS, "Nitrogen (Fixed)–Ammonia," January 2020.

barrier for scaling molten salts to whatever quantity we could feasibly need.

Thermal storage will provide the first major pillar of our energy storage infrastructure. We'll proliferate both solar thermal and standalone thermal storage facilities as much as possible. These plants will help even out hour-to-hour and day-to-day grid fluctuations. Unfortunately, heat is not storable forever. The molten salts will slowly bleed heat to their surroundings, even in the best-insulated tanks. That means we need some backups in place to help further stabilize the grid in case of disruptions.

PUMPED HYDROPOWER

Mountain snow can act as a kind of energy storage. It is deposited in the winter, creating a bank of stored energy that is released when it melts and runs downhill in the spring. Snowmelt can be used by a hydroelectric station to generate electricity as it travels downriver to the sea. The problem is the timescale doesn't quite align with our goal of building a reactive energy storage system across the country, which will instantaneously even out demand. We can bypass nature to build more reliable energy storage by choosing when and where we pump water to higher elevations instead.

In a pumped storage system, water is moved uphill to artificially create the conditions necessary for hydropower. When there is excess energy on the grid, water is pumped to a reservoir at a high elevation from a lower reservoir.[12] The top reservoir is designed with one exit we control, keeping the water in place like an artificial lake. When the grid needs

---

12 For a visualization, see: USDOE, "Pumped-Storage Hydropower," accessed August 27, 2020.

more energy, the water is then allowed to flow back down to the lower reservoir and run a generator on the way. Pumped storage is thus dispatchable since you can tap into it whenever you need to, with the added benefit of not having to worry about energy loss over time. The only downside is it isn't a very dense means of storing energy, providing less than 2 percent of the energy storage capacity as batteries or molten salts on a pound-for-pound basis.[13]

The low energy density becomes less of a deal-breaker once you start measuring volumes in acre-feet.[14] The largest US pumped storage reservoir in Marion County, Tennessee, holds about 405 million tons of water at a 500-meter elevation. The energy storage capacity of the system has been rated to be about 131 TJ in total, equivalent to four and a half thermal plants we designed earlier. That amount of storage capacity is not insubstantial for our purposes.

The pumped hydropower approach to energy storage is one of the few with a long history of contributing to the grid. The first were built in the United States back in the 1960s, with the bulk coming online the following decade.[15] Thanks to that lineage, these facilities scattered across the country represent the vast majority of currently installed energy storage infrastructure. Unfortunately, the total US pumped storage capacity has not drastically increased in about thirty years. Overcoming inertia and expanding our inventory will depend on dealing with a couple bottlenecks.

---

13   See appendix for calculation details.

14   An acre-foot is a unit of volume equivalent to 43,560 cubic feet or 1.2 million liters.

15   USEIA, "Most Pumped Storage," October 31, 2019.

Unlike batteries or molten salts, the main limitation for pumped storage isn't based on materials. The fundamental barrier is finding land amenable for a dual reservoir system. Using amenable natural geography for our purposes is the only efficient method available. The alternative is we build a massive system of water towers for the same purpose; however, we would need 190 tanks of the size we calculated for our molten salts plant, each lifted a quarter mile off of the ground, to match the capacity of the reservoir in Tennessee. Building them would not be congruous with a rapid grid transition.

Overcoming this bottleneck will require a similar survey as we discussed in chapter 5, as the data doesn't seem to exist yet.[16] We'll need to identify the sites with the greatest capacity potential, access to water, proximity to grid infrastructure, and ability to run during winter. The water we pump will do no good if the top reservoir freezes solid, after all. With that information in hand, we'd be able to start building and bringing the most promising sites online. We'll want to start as soon as possible. Pumped hydropower facilities take years to construct, provided we overcome the bureaucratic hurdles.[17] Before a project can even begin, the builder needs to complete multiple environmental assessments and obtain permits and approvals from multiple state and federal agencies. This entire process takes at least four to five years, even without opposition.

Even if we start building today, pumped storage likely won't meet all of our needs. Without the completed survey

---

16   Some reports lay some high-level groundwork but don't have the granularity for the analysis we need. For example: Hunt et al. "Global Resource Potential," February 2020.

17   Spector, "Montana Developer," August 13, 2019.

of potential locations, we won't be able to accurately gauge how much of our requirements it can fulfill. Until that information becomes available, we have to proceed, assuming pumped storage won't be able to fully complement thermal storage alone. Otherwise, we might be losing time when we could be building alternative capacity.

COMPRESSED AIR

Another way to use pumping to increase energy storage capacity is the use of compressed air. The *compressed* part of the technology refers to how air is pumped to very high pressures as it is captured and stored underground. When we need electricity, some of it is released back into the atmosphere while passing over a turbine to generate electricity.[18] Air in this instance takes the place of water, but we are still operating under the same principles as hydropower. Energy is added to a working fluid, stored, then released when needed.

A back-of-the-envelope calculation shows compressed air about a hundred-fold more energy dense than pumped hydropower.[19] Yet, while there are several dozen examples of pumped water storage in the United States, there are only two compressed air operations globally—one in Germany and one in Alabama.[20] Both have been operating for several decades, so the issue isn't technical. The main problem is, again, one of finding appropriate locations.

While we could, in theory, build this form of energy storage anywhere, there are several constraints. We need airtight containers that will hold the air at high pressure

---

18   Wang et al. "Overview," May 2017.

19   See appendix for calculation details.

20   Seltzer, "Why Salt," August 4, 2017.

until we need it. Large metal tanks could get the job done, but pressure vessels that can withstand those conditions for long periods of time require a lot of space and a lot of resources to build. Underground caverns provide a more efficient and speedier alternative. They can easily be made airtight by sealing up the entrance, and they can provide vast volumes to work with. The best locations are over abandoned salt mines, like the two facilities currently in operation. Their geology makes them both airtight and impervious to damage by oxygen.

Unfortunately, our potential sites are limited. We can only build this storage once a salt mine is depleted, and only a couple of regions even have salt deposits that can be mined in the first place. No other geologic formations have been rigorously tested for use as compressed air storage. There have been some evaluations of other options, but nothing meeting our requirement to only use proven technology.[21] These constraints mean compressed air storage won't be widespread, but we will develop it where we can.

MULTI-LAYERED ENERGY STORAGE

We've covered a good number of options in this chapter, so let's take a moment to review what this means for the strategy. Just like with our power generation, the new grid's energy storage will have to be diverse. Our end state is clear enough, but additional prioritization needs to happen in the short-term to facilitate a speedy transition. We'll be using a layered, defense in depth approach to ensure all of our needs are met.

Our hour-by-hour workhorse will be thermal storage. Not only will it go hand-in-hand with concentrated solar power,

---

21 PNNL, "Compressed Air Energy Storage," August 2019.

but it will also efficiently reuse converted fossil fuel plants to cut down on capital expenditures. A small amount of NiCd batteries will supplement that capacity, but all of our lithium reserves will go toward decarbonizing the transportation sector.

While the fossil-to-thermal transition is underway, we can plan for our second line of storage to operate on a day-to-day timescale. The locations for both pumped hydropower and compressed air will take time to identify and develop, so we'll need to complete that survey as quickly as possible. However, until we have the survey results, we won't know just how much of each we can build, requiring constant reevaluation as the strategy is implemented.

SACRIFICE: AN APP FOR THAT

Depending on how familiar you are with batteries, you may have noticed an omission in the discussion of electric vehicles. We could, in theory, use their batteries as intermittent grid storage. The thinking goes you're only driving your car for a fraction of the day, so when you're parked, we could plug it into the grid both to deliver energy from the battery at peak times and soak up energy when the demand is lower.[22] While your car is at work during the day, it would charge using plentiful solar power, and then, in the evening, your car would be able to return some energy to the grid while you're at home. It wouldn't take so much energy away to leave you stranded, but enough to help level out the grid over the course of the day.

Similar approaches could help reduce grid strain with appliances as well. For example, you could set your washing

---

22 For example: Emilio, "Smart Grid for Electric Vehicles," September 5, 2019.

machine or dishwasher only to run when renewable electricity is more abundant.[23] The interconnected system where power-consuming devices talk to utilities over the Internet to control some of their functionality is called the *smart grid.* Such a system would help operators balance nondispatchable power sources by flexibly controlling demand instead of building more storage. The idea in and of itself does not violate our need to use existing technology. It comes down to connecting devices together over the Internet and completing the software engineering to make sure everything communicates. But therein lies the problem: there is no way such a system would be secure enough not to threaten the grid and everything attached to it.

A smart grid would function through the Internet of Things (IoT), the collection of smart devices connected to the Internet besides computers, phones, and tablets. A doorbell with a camera you can access through an app is part of the IoT, as is a light fixture you control through your phone. Unfortunately, this system is tremendously unsecure. Malicious persons have already hijacked Internet-connected devices for some of the largest coordinated cyberattacks in recent years. One attack in 2016 used hundreds of thousands of IoT devices to bring down the Internet for swaths of the East Coast, and we can expect such events to become more commonplace in the future.[24]

Connecting smart grid devices to the Internet would only provide more infrastructure that can be attacked or be used for attacks. The power grid itself is already the target of

---

23 For additional examples: USDOE, "What is the Smart Grid?" accessed August 23, 2020.

24 Fruhlinger, "The Mirai Botnet Explained," March 9, 2018; Asokan, "Massive Botnet Attack," July 26, 2019.

malicious foreign actors trying to damage the United States, and a smart grid would only give them more vulnerabilities to exploit.[25] The results could be catastrophic. A recent attack on the water system in Florida almost led to a mass poisoning of the public, which was only thwarted by a vigilant operator.[26]

The situation would only become worse over time. Legacy products, electronics no longer produced or supported, will be attached to the smart grid for decades. Plenty of IoT devices are already obsolete and no longer supported.[27] A car might not have a replacement for a decade or more, so what happens if the manufacturer stops supporting security updates for older models? While it may be nice to run your washing machine during nonpeak hours, the tech companies that provide the hardware and software to keep it going may just evaporate before the end of the appliance's mechanical lifetime.

Smart device companies also don't want to support their products long-term anyway. They make money when a device is sold, giving them a natural incentive to encourage obsolescence that forces consumers to buy more products. That mindset is neither conducive to arresting rampant consumption, another problem exacerbating climate change, or building robust infrastructure. If Microsoft can only provide security updates to globally used software for about ten years, your washing machine's firmware would seem to have little chance of remaining secure.

---

25 Sobczak, "Report Reveals," September 6, 2019.

26 Pegues, "Feds Tracking," February 9, 2021.

27 For example, consider the first generation of smart watches: Paul, "IoT Has," June 11, 2018.

Even a decade-long lifespan would be the best-case scenario, where indifference slowly degrades your system security instead of outright malfeasance. Let's say you get the product from a manufacturer in a country with a less than stellar track record around privacy and security. You can never be 100 percent sure the device is clean of malicious code waiting to be activated. We already know there's the risk of being spied on because we've found out smart speakers record our conversations as a built-in feature.[28] With devices that control mechanical objects, there's the risk of someone using a backdoor to operate it without your control. Having access to so many power-consuming devices would present an opportunity to drastically disrupt the grid or cause widespread mayhem. Think about what would happen if every smart stove received instructions to heat all of its elements at maximum intensity simultaneously. A hostile nation could use that as leverage to great effect.

A smart grid would be great in a more perfect world by balancing demand to help us transition faster. It would also be more convenient for us, with all the benefits that come from being able to control our appliances remotely. Unfortunately, the risks are simply too high, and the strategy cannot have it be a part of our solution. We will have to sacrifice some of our desires for ease and convenience, along with the assumption adding more connectivity to our lives is always a good thing. If the past few years have taught us anything, it's the Internet is a double-edged sword, and we should be careful to avoid cutting ourselves.

---

28 For example: Molla, "Your Smart Devices," September 20, 2019; Komando, "You're Not Paranoid," December 19, 2019.

CHAPTER 8

THE WINTER

—

Some of my earliest childhood memories involve the parties a family friend would throw to celebrate the end of the school year. He lived out in the country on a property with some forest. In anticipation of the event, he'd gather a pile of wood for building a bonfire. Not a small pile either, a massive one several yards across. The heat was so intense you couldn't get within ten feet of the thing. These events were a yearly highlight for me, to the point where as soon as we pulled in, I would be asking about when the fire was going to start.

Fire is so ubiquitous, it's easy to forget what exactly is happening when something burns. In essence, fire is just a chemical reaction that produces heat and light as a byproduct. A lot of energy can be released by combustible material, which is why fossil fuels are so useful. They're ready-made stores of energy we can tap into whenever we need them. In that respect, it's hard to compete with fossil fuels in terms of their energy storage capabilities.

We need another layer to the energy storage part of our strategy to account for seasonal variations. Renewable energy is, on the whole, less plentiful in winter. Days are shorter and sunlight is less direct, limiting our ability to collect solar power. Hydropower output similarly declines as water freezes. We won't be able to divert as much energy into storage during those months, which risks an undersupplied grid at night. If we want to avoid fossil fuels staying around to make up the difference, we'll have to deal with this issue.

Some of the seasonal needs could probably be met by pumped hydropower and compressed air. Once you pump the water to high elevation or air to high pressure, it isn't going anywhere. However, we have to assume the number of potential building sites will be nowhere near adequate to meet this need. Our only remaining options that are both renewable and satisfy our requirement to use existing technology are combustible substances. That is, things we can burn.

This approach to energy storage mimics the operation of a fossil fuel plant. The mechanics would be virtually identical; only we'd be burning renewable materials. Instead of coal or natural gas, we could burn wood or liquid fuels derived from plant matter. We'd harvest these fuel sources in the summer when renewable electricity is abundant and stockpile them. Whether piling wood or keeping liquid fuels in tanks, they'd be stable until we need them. There are multiple approaches for gathering burnable, renewable materials, each with its own strengths and limitations.

WOOD

Humans have historically derived their energy from burning wood, and we still do so today to generate electricity. Consider Great Britain, where 4,000 tons of wood pellets imported from the United States are burned to generate electricity every year.[1] The justification for burning wood is it is carbon neutral. The trees take carbon dioxide out of the atmosphere when they grow, and it is returned to the atmosphere when they are burned. Burning wood creates a complete cycle where no net carbon is released, hence *carbon neutral*. Whether or not that approach is scalable is something we need to determine.

We can start by figuring out exactly how much energy we can get per unit of forest. At the lowest level, we can get over 16 megajoules (MJ) of energy from burning one kilogram (kg) of wood.[2] For context, wood is, pound-for-pound, about twenty-three times more energy dense than the best lithium batteries. That still doesn't guarantee it will be the solution to all of our problems since there are fundamental limitations on the amount of wood we can burn every year.

The bottleneck for harvesting wood is the amount of land we dedicate to growing trees. They will have to be fast growing and monocultured to be the most space-efficient, even though that would create its own ecological problems.[3] Under those conditions, we can expect to produce about 15 terajoules of energy for every square kilometer (TJ/km²) of forest we dedicate to energy production.[4] That amount of energy isn't very substantial for the amount of land it requires. For scale, it's less than *one* wind turbine's output. Meeting just 1 percent of our yearly energy needs would require a

1   Beeler and Morrison, "The UK's Move," July 20, 2018.

2   See appendix for calculation details. NIST, "NIST Chemistry WebBook," accessed August 28, 2020; Jessup and Prosen, "Heats of Combustion," April 1950.

3   Dart, "The Dirty Little Secret," June 30, 2018; Howe, "Don't Believe the Hype," April 17, 2018.

4   See appendix for calculation details.

forest approaching the size of South Carolina. A similar area of solar panels would provide 22 percent of all our energy needs. In that context, scaling wood production to make a dent in our energy needs just isn't feasible.

ETHANOL

Ethanol, or grain alcohol, is another carbon neutral biofuel we derive from plant matter. It's one we're already producing in massive quantities, just not for energy storage. The primary driver right now is its use as a gasoline additive. The ethanol in your gas tank increases the fuel's octane rating and prevents knocking, both attributes that improve the function of the engine. We won't need ethanol for that function once we finish transitioning to electric cars and would be able to retool the existing infrastructure to produce it for seasonal energy storage instead.

Making this fuel starts on a farm. A cereal grain, predominantly corn in the United States, is grown as food for microbes that ferment starch into ethanol. This is the same process used to make adult beverages, only on a much larger scale. Almost 200 factories dot the Midwest and pump out a million barrels of ethanol per day.[5] For our purposes, that part of the supply chain would remain intact. We'd just divert the ethanol into holding tanks until it's needed and burned over the winter.

Ethanol even has a greater energy storage potential than wood. With an overall energy density of about 27 MJ/kg, we would need 40 percent less ethanol to provide the same amount of heat.[6] Like wood, we will be limited by how much

---

5   USEIA, "U.S. Ethanol Production," June 28, 2017.

6   See appendix for calculation details.

land we can dedicate to growing crops that are fermented into ethanol. We can get a sense of scale based on the quantity we're already producing. The United States consumes about 54.5 billion liters of ethanol every year through the gas pump, a volume requiring 141,000 km² of farmland to produce. Unfortunately, that means we get less than 2 TJ of energy per square kilometer of corn, substantially less energy than wood.[7] It's only about 10 percent of a single wind turbine's output and less than 1 percent as land efficient as solar panels. The same conclusion we made for wood has to apply here: ethanol cannot be part of our strategy. All that land would be better put to use generating other forms of renewable energy or sequestering carbon from the atmosphere.

BIOFUELS
Ethanol's lack of utility does not necessarily mean other fuels derived from biological sources can't find a niche in our new energy system. Consider aviation fuel. The United States consumes about seventy billion liters of jet fuel per year, a higher-value commodity that can't be replaced by batteries.[8] The energy density of jet fuel is fifty times greater than the best lithium batteries, meaning long-distance flights carrying the same cargo and people would be impossible without liquid fuels.[9] We can't get around that fact, so our choices are to either continue fossil fuel production or find a carbon neutral option to make jet fuel.

---

7   See appendix for calculation details.

8   USEIA, "As U.S. Airlines Carry," June 6, 2017.

9   Gofman, "Energy Density," accessed September 14, 2020; Clean Energy Institute, "Lithium-Ion Battery," accessed September 14, 2020.

A major fraction of jet fuel can be derived from fats. You can get those fats from cooking oil, industrial byproducts, or by farming them directly. Algae, for example, absorbs carbon dioxide from the atmosphere during photosynthesis, producing fats, among other things.[10] Once the crop is harvested, the fatty molecules are separated and used to synthesize jet fuel components. Since carbon is being drawn from the atmosphere to make the fuel and returned after it is used, it is a closed loop and carbon neutral source. The technology is generally proven, and only the current higher cost is preventing more widespread adoption.[11]

The limitation of a biofuel is the resources used to create it. Sun and carbon from the atmosphere are free, but land is not. Just like ethanol, developing land for growing biofuels will take away the area that could otherwise be used for carbon sequestration. Algae can reportedly produce up to 5,000 gallons of fuel per acre per year, which means we would need at least 15,000 km^2 of algae ponds to meet our current aviation demand.[12] That's only about 11 percent of what we already dedicate to growing corn for ethanol. The need for these liquid fuels will be with us until some new technology comes along, so biofuels will have to be part of our strategy in some fashion. A limited amount of land remaining dedicated for fuels is a reasonable trade-off since it means we can make a sector carbon neutral that can't otherwise be decarbonized.

While making aviation carbon neutral is useful, we still haven't solved our overall seasonal energy storage issue. All

---

10   Reddy and O'Neil, "Jet Fuel from Algae," January 28, 2015.

11   Le Feuvre, "Are Aviation Biofuels," March 18, 2019.

12   See appendix for calculation details. All About Algae, "FAQ," accessed August 29, 2020; ABO, "Algae and Land," April 30, 2020.

of the plant-based fuels we've discussed simply require too much land to make the quantities of combustible chemicals we need. Solar, wind, and other renewables are just so much more efficient at gathering energy from a given area. Our next step is then to look at ways of directly converting their electricity into energy storage by producing artificial fuels.

SYNTHETIC FUELS

Biological sources aren't the only means of producing combustible fuels we can use for energy storage. There is a suite of chemical reactions that we can use on an industrial scale for manufacturing hydrocarbons. Gasoline and diesel are both examples of hydrocarbon fuels we currently use. Essentially, we can make those same chemicals, just without having to mine and burn more fossil fuels.[13] The energy density of hydrocarbons is almost double ethanol's, meaning we'd need to stockpile the least amount of them compared to any fuel we've discussed so far.[14]

We can make a range of liquid hydrocarbons using the Fischer-Tropsch process.[15] It's the same route used to produce synthetic motor oils. Some countries, like South Africa, have entire industries based on this system already, although they are using fossil fuels as the source of their inputs. Those raw materials boil down to hydrogen and carbon monoxide, and the largest source of both gasses right now is natural gas. Keeping fossil fuels in the ground is our primary goal, so that

---

13   De Luna et al. "What Would it Take," April 2019.

14   See appendix for calculation details.

15   The Fischer-Tropsch process takes a mixture of carbon monoxide (CO) and hydrogen (H_2) gasses (collectively syn gas) and produces liquid alkanes over a catalyst: $nCO + (2n +1)H_2 \rightarrow C_nH_{2n+2} + nH_2O$

isn't an option. We need to make the process carbon neutral, and that means sourcing our inputs from renewable sources.

The first material constraint is the availability of hydrogen. The only renewable source of hydrogen that satisfies our need to use existing technology is splitting water with electricity. I've done this experiment at home, where you put some live wires in a bowl of water to break it down into oxygen and hydrogen gas.[16] It's certainly possible to do that on a massive scale, we just need to build the equipment. Theoretically, we could use hydrogen itself as a renewable fuel. However, it is difficult and dangerous to store, requiring specialized materials and new infrastructure we'd have to build from scratch. Renewable hydrocarbons present an altogether safer alternative.

A renewable source of concentrated carbon monoxide is straightforward to acquire. We could tap into the effluent of a carbon dioxide emitting industry, like cement manufacturing, or simply burn our trash and brush.[17] In either case, the carbon dioxide would be captured and purified. Converting it to carbon monoxide happens through a reaction with hydrogen, which we'll already have on hand, producing water as a byproduct. The carbon monoxide and more hydrogen are then fed into a reactor, and liquid fuels come out the other side.

A major limiting factor for hydrocarbons as a storage medium is the energy required. Splitting water requires a lot of energy, as does capturing, purifying, and reacting carbon dioxide. Since making fuels is essentially the reverse of

16   For more information, see: USDOE, "Hydrogen production," accessed August 30, 2020.

17   Timperley, "Q&A," September 13, 2018; Rodgers, "Climate Change," December 17, 2018.

combustion, we'll ultimately need to dedicate more energy to making them than we will get from them when they're burned. But that is a commonality with any form of energy storage. It won't be 100 percent efficient, and we'll need to install more renewable power sources to feed into our seasonal storage than their nominal output would otherwise suggest.

Our approach will be to build substantially more renewable generation than we need at the peak of the year. In the summer, when there's an abundance of sun, wind, and hydroelectric power, excess energy would feed chemical plants producing liquid fuels. The year's crop of hydrocarbons would then be stored for the winter and burned as needed, making it the energy equivalent of agriculture. The overall material efficiency makes more sense this way since wind and solar are so much better at capturing energy than farming our fuels. It would be a substantial investment, but one we have to make to fully decouple ourselves from fossil fuels.

TRASH GAS

The waste we routinely discard can be a boon to our search for seasonably storable fuels beyond being a carbon source for liquid hydrocarbons. Plenty of microbes eat our organic trash in oxygen-free environments and produce methane as a byproduct, the primary constituent of natural gas. We can capture the resulting trash gas by simply covering our dumps and pumping the methane into a storage vessel. From there, it can be burned as part of any natural gas power plant we keep around for this purpose.

Harnessing renewable methane helps us in a couple of ways. Firstly, methane is actually a more potent greenhouse gas than carbon dioxide, trapping more heat per molecule and leading to a more accelerated climate change.[18] Burning it to make carbon dioxide provides a net climate benefit as a result. Secondly, much of our energy infrastructure is already setup for natural gas. By using biogenic methane, we can decrease fossil fuel use without building new power plants or retrofitting existing ones. Even though liquid fuels are easier to store, we will still have all the existing natural gas infrastructure available, so we might as well use it for something productive, saving us time and resources.

We wouldn't be able to meet all of our storage needs with trash gas. Recent estimates indicate we could get 1 to 6 exajoules of energy per year if we fully exploited our waste streams.[19] That would account for, at most, about 5 percent of our yearly energy requirements. Certainly not enough power for all of our needs, but it would help make a difference by mitigating some seasonal shortfalls.

***

Combustible fuels will be our final line of energy storage, allowing our new grid to function year-round. Their energy density and ease of long-term stockpiling will make them indispensable for the foreseeable future. Building seasonal storage must take equal billing with geothermal as our primary target for resource investment moving forward, as it will take time to build that capacity. Our first step will be to better harness trash gas since the infrastructure is already there for using it. Next, we'll need to invest in liquid fuel production. Biofuels will combine with synthetic hydrocarbons

---

18   Princeton University, "A More Potent," March 27, 2014.

19   IEA, "Outlook for Biogas and Biomethane," March 2020, 6–7.

to meet specific needs, like jet fuel, then be applied to grid-scale storage.

The precise amount of fuel we need every year will depend on how the grid evolves throughout the transition and our evolving energy needs. A scenario where geothermal capacity is greater, for instance, will require lower amounts of long-term energy storage than one with less geothermal capacity. For now, we can safely press forward on each approach without worrying about making inefficient investments. If it turns out we need less, the production of bio and synthetic fuels can simply be dialed back. We'll just need to continually evaluate the situation as we make progress to keep everything in balance.

SACRIFICE: COAL OR CODE

The transition to a different energy mix will invariably impact the people working in the fossil fuel industry. Major shifts in the economy always lead to such effects, but we can choose to make it less difficult with the proper planning. The rise of the automobile industry can provide some historic parallels. It wasn't only the horses that disappeared into the ether once cars came on the scene, but the industries built around horses as well. No horses mean no more horse-drawn carriages, and most of those manufacturers went out of business. The company H. A. Moyer was an exception, who saw the writing on the wall and switched to making cars and auto parts. Embracing the new paradigm allowed them to adapt to the new order and keep people employed.

This is important because one of the surest points of resistance to the energy transition will be working people who have a stake in the status quo. The millions of people who directly and indirectly owe their livelihoods to fossil fuels will, as a group, work to preserve their jobs through the democratic process. We saw this in the 2016 election, where appeals to coal miners proved popular, despite the century-long decline in employment that is fundamentally irreversible due to the economics of coal compared to natural gas and the increased automation of mining technology.[20] The cultural memory of high wages for mining in an otherwise economically depressed area is a very powerful force to go against.

A division also emerged in deliberations around the proposed Green New Deal. Some groups within organized labor expressed their misgivings over not being directly consulted on the introduced framework. Even though the document itself is broadly prolabor, those who represent workers in the hereafter doomed industries have an obligation to represent those interests.[21] The point is, while the transition is necessary and inevitable, without consideration for and buy-in from these constituencies it will be stymied.

One approach for helping displaced workers is to help them retrain for a different career. If your job is no longer relevant to the economy, you need to make your labor more marketable by developing a new skillset. We can collectively ease that process by devoting resources to help folks as they acquire education and move back into the workforce. However, while it is likely true that "anybody who can throw

---

20   Federal Reserve Bank of St. Louis, "Full-time," accessed September 14, 2020; Federal Reserve Bank of St. Louis, "All Employees," accessed September 14, 2020.

21   Irfan, "The Green New Deal," June 19, 2019.

coal into a furnace can learn how to program," a focus on retraining ignores several important points.[22]

The first is psychological. Imagine you have just been told the skills and career you've built for years will suddenly have to change. And, in the interim, you won't be able to provide the same quality of life for yourself or your family. That probably wouldn't make you feel too good about your future, and it probably wouldn't encourage you to support the transition that is putting you out of a job. Instead, it would probably make you angry, anxious, and maybe even depressed. A lack of opportunity and hope leads to the deaths of despair that have become endemic across the country, especially in places where good-paying jobs have faded away.[23] Instead of being encouraged to retrain, there's a good chance you'll either hold out in the vain hope things will return to the previous status quo or just leave the workforce entirely.

Another critical consideration is the overall socioeconomic situation. Fossil fuel jobs don't necessarily have local replacements, so a displaced person would likely have to find work elsewhere that provides the same kind of salary, often far away. This happened in Janesville, Wisconsin, when the GM plant went under. People had to take lower paying jobs, travel long distances for work, or simply give up.[24] Since fossil fuel extraction and refining are tied to specific places, we can assume the same thing would happen as a result of our strategy. Finding a new job is made even more difficult if it would involve leaving an established home and family

---

22   Quote attributed to Joe Biden from: Kelley, "Biden Tells," December 31, 2019.

23   For example: Gander, "'Deaths of Despair,'" November 26, 2019.

24   Goldstein, *Janesville*.

behind, regardless of economic opportunity. The model of economics that assumes people will move based on the market just doesn't hold up in the face of the available data.[25]

The assumption new jobs will even pay comparatively well is not necessarily true. Most people would probably be taking a pay cut, since most professions haven't experienced real wage increases since the 1970s. The pain will be magnified if you're going from a unionized industry to one that isn't. So, not only do you have to overcome the difficulties of retraining, finding a new job, and moving, you'll probably take a hit to your standard of living as well. The motivation behind holdouts who resist change makes sense in this light. Why would they support a clearly dying and harmful industry instead of moving on? Because holding onto hope, however false, is less traumatic than the alternative.

Industrial workers aren't the only ones who will see their livelihoods threatened by this strategy. If we end the use of biofuels like ethanol, there will be a considerably lower demand for corn and agricultural products. Farmers in states like Iowa may be forced to quit or substantially change their operations. It's the same situation for alternative meat products, which has scared ranchers enough to cause a dozen states to enact laws protecting animal protein in the market.[26] There is no reason why getting rid of biofuels would be any different given the support farmers have at the state and federal level. While returning that farmland to forest and other unused status is absolutely essential to reversing climate change, these interests will undoubtedly push back against anything they perceive as a threat to their existing livelihood.

---

25 Cooke, "Americans Have Stopped," December 7, 2019.

26 Selyukh, "What Gets to Be," July 23, 2019.

This is not meant as a defense of the position to avoid taking action on climate change, but an acknowledgment of a reality that the strategy will have to deal with. The people whose material conditions depend on burning fossil fuels aren't going away, and they won't give up those jobs just because of the larger externalities at play. We have to assume these folks will use their political power to support the status quo, leaving us with two options: ignore them and rely on superior numbers to push through the necessary changes unilaterally or provide them an acceptable alternative.

There are opportunities to adapt our strategy to support the goal of helping displaced workers. One of the selling points of retrofitting fossil fuel plants into thermal storage is it would largely keep the local workforce intact. The rationale is they already work on half of the new power plant equipment, the steam turbine cycle, so they'll be able to apply their knowledge and skill to the new system. It also lessens the burden of retraining since they won't be learning something that's fundamentally different. Most importantly, they won't have to risk a pay cut. Other groups that have a direct transition pathway include oil and gas exploration workers, who could contribute to exploiting geothermal resources. The strategy benefits from their expertise, and we don't have to invest as much in developing a new geothermal workforce.

Examples such as these are ideal cases, and not everything is so transferable. It is unlikely we would be able to fully replace the jobs lost in coal and fracking. There isn't enough directly translatable work out there that would benefit the strategy, so we can't guarantee fully equivalent transitions. However, we can make it less painful by choosing how we go about retraining.

There are two main guidelines we should follow when engaging with the fossil fuel workforce. First, subsidize people cashing out early if they're close to retirement.[27] That way, they can finish with dignity and not dilute the labor market for a replacement industry. Second, we should retrain people in fields as close as possible to what they were doing before. It'll be easier, quicker, and more acceptable for those being retrained. Energy production will be just one part of adapting to climate change, and there will be ways for people to use their existing skills. None of this means miners aren't smart enough to code, just that we can't wall off the path to prosperity based on a narrow view of what kind of jobs are worthwhile.

Retraining needs to be focused on getting people out the door with the skills they need as fast as possible. We already have the infrastructure in place to aid this goal: technical schools providing trade-specific instruction. Not everyone needs a doctorate or bachelor's to contribute to the success of this strategy. The best insights of a scientist or designs of an engineer are only so much ink on paper unless there is someone who can turn it into reality. We need to sacrifice any elitist attitudes preventing us from recognizing the value and dignity of everyone's labor for our transition, and that means prioritizing some resources for the people who will build and maintain our new grid.

A final note is we need to encourage unionization in the clean energy sector. Unions provide higher than average pay and better conditions for workers, which helps incentivize people to work in this sector. It will also help by changing

27 That applies to agriculture as well, considering the average farmer is in their late fifties. USDA, "2017 Census of Agriculture Highlights," April 2019.

the priorities of those organizations. Once unions' fortunes are tied to the expansion of renewables instead of fossil fuels, lobbying on behalf of their members will require supporting the strategy.

It will also be necessary to involve unions when crafting specific policies, both to make equitable decisions and ensure they're not on the other side of the negotiating table.

PART TWO

DRAWDOWN

CHAPTER 9

THE SEA

I tried to learn the guitar when I was younger, having been inspired by all the metal music I was listening to at the time. While I dreamed of shredding massive solos, the skills acquired from a decade of saxophone did not exactly translate. I learned a couple of easy riffs but mostly floundered with anything moderately complex. Too many strings and frets and chords, and I'm just not that coordinated. I knew I was in real trouble when my teacher assigned me Cliffs of Dover by Eric Johnson. Great song, especially the live versions, but I could never play it properly with my stubby fingers.

The namesake for that song is similarly impressive, and it's an interesting example of carbon sequestration. The white part of the White Cliffs of Dover is chalk or calcium carbonate. This chalk was deposited over millennia as the shells of microscopic marine creatures (plankton) collected on the seafloor. Plankton make their carbonate shells by drawing carbon dioxide out of the atmosphere, similar to what plants do with photosynthesis. However, the shells don't decay, so every ton of chalk holds 440 kilograms of carbon dioxide on lockdown and out of the carbon cycle.

The sea creatures that made those cliffs still exist, sucking carbon out of the atmosphere. They're not alone either. The ocean encompasses two-thirds of our planet, and the myriad sea creatures therein have the potential to sequester massive amounts of carbon. That makes the sea a good place to start for our second priority—returning the climate back to normal. Changing the ocean carbon cycle means helping the environment consume more carbon dioxide from the atmosphere.[1] The most efficient tactic will be to make the ocean more productive, that is, brimming with carbon-sequestering life.

OCEAN FERTILIZATION

More ocean life means more carbon deposits, and not just as chalk. When a large animal like a whale dies, it floats down and is consumed by the denizens of the seafloor. Because the ocean is quite deep, carbon is essentially trapped down there. Unfortunately, it takes a long time and a lot of food to grow a whale or any other large sea creature. They depend on consuming massive amounts of plankton and tiny animals over the course of their lifetime. The ocean ultimately relies on algae and phytoplankton to support every other animal. These creatures feed fish, crabs, and krill, who are in turn eaten by whales and sharks. If we expand the bottom of the food chain, the benefits will trickle up into larger populations of everything else, so that's where we'll start.

Phytoplankton get their energy from the sun through photosynthesis, and they have the same basic requirements as terrestrial plants. They need carbon dioxide from the

---

1   For a primer on the ocean carbon cycle, see: NOAA, "Carbon Cycle," February 2019.

atmosphere and space on the surface to spread out and capture light, both plentiful resources. Plankton also need nutri-
ents like nitrogen and iron.[2] We spread fertilizer on fields to
increase the harvest, and the same approach could work in
the oceans. Essentially, we would disperse chemicals across
the ocean to provide whatever local deficiencies are limiting
plankton growth.

Nitrogen would be one place to start for fertilizing the
oceans. It's a critical nutrient required for making proteins,
and it's usually available in limited quantities. Microbes have
to pull it out of the air, a process called fixing, which takes a
lot of energy. Our industrial base already makes enormous
quantities of nitrogen fertilizer every year. Since part of our
strategy is to retire farmland from ethanol, we'd even have
excess manufacturing capacity when the time comes to fertilize the oceans.

Another option would be to add iron. Plankton use iron
in low quantities for critical processes, including fixing nitrogen. By some estimates, iron in the oceans is so effective at
increasing carbon dioxide absorption that a period of relative
abundance led to at least one ice age.[3] However, it has to be
the right form of iron, else all the rust falling off boats would
have solved the problem for us already. We'd need to add a
bioavailable form, like iron chloride ($FeCl_2$), but that is well
within our power to produce on a massive scale.

The application of either iron or nitrogen fertilizer is
relatively straightforward. First, you gather several tons of
fertilizer onto a boat. You then sail over the area you want
to fertilize, dispersing the chemicals as you go. That's it. The

---

2   Li, Legendre, and Jiao, "Phytoplankton Response," February 2015.

3   Underwood, "The Complicated Role," January 3, 2020.

simplicity is summed up by John Martin, the scientist who came up with the idea of seeding the ocean with iron. He said, "give me a half a tanker of iron and I'll give you the next ice age."[4] Still, it remains to be seen whether or not this is a viable approach that will work as intended.

Dumping fertilizer in the ocean to test this hypothesis is generally frowned upon. Whether or not you count it as pollution is a legal gray area and mostly up to the interpretation of the country in which it occurs. The practice is mostly not aligned with existing international protocols.[5] There is also substantial opposition from environmental interests concerned about unintentional ecosystem damage. Runoff from farmland brings a lot of fertilizer into oceans already, which leads to gigantic algae blooms. Such plankton proliferation creates huge oxygen-depleted dead zones that are uninhabitable for fish.[6] By purposefully fertilizing the oceans, we could increase the number of these destructive events.

The precautionary principle has to kick in at this point. We need to evaluate the potential risks of fertilization versus its utility. Going in blind and taking action without the data to back it up does not make sense. It's why we have our guiding policy necessitating existing technology. If we can find a happy medium that avoids environmental harm while still providing a carbon-sequestering benefit, that would be a path forward for the strategy. Unfortunately, the data that would guide our choices is somewhat sparse.

---

4   Dopyera, "The Iron Hypothesis," October 1996.

5   Convention on Biological Diversity, "Climate-Related Geoengineering," accessed September 14, 2020.

6   For an introduction on dead zones, see: Bruckner, "The Gulf of Mexico Dead Zone," accessed September 2, 2020; NOAA, "NOAA Forecasts," June 12, 2019.

A man named Russ George performed one of the only large-scale ocean fertilizing experiments in 2012. He and his crew spread 120 tons of iron across a patch of the Pacific north of Vancouver.[7] The goal was to recreate a boom in the salmon population that followed a natural iron seeding event in 2008 when an Alaskan volcano erupted and spread material across the ocean. Despite opposition from the government and scientific community, the fertilizing crew reported more plankton, which was quickly followed by more fish, whales, and cephalopods of all kinds.[8] The salmon run of 2013 alone hit a record high of 200 million fish. While anecdotes about increased fish harvests seemingly validate the approach, it is unclear whether there was any lasting impact on the climate.

There are some substantial technical limitations that prescribe a more reserved assessment. The first issue is quantifying the results. We need to know how much carbon sequestration we're going to achieve. Unfortunately, the amount of carbon dioxide absorbed during better controlled experiments has been decidedly lower than anticipated.[9] There is also a question of longevity. Most of the carbon dioxide will return to the atmosphere as plankton die and decay. Only about 10 percent actually becomes part of the larger oceanic carbon cycle. Most of that will also eventually make its way back into the atmosphere. With such minuscule amounts of carbon being permanently sequestered in

7   Falconer, "Can Anyone Stop," updated January 16, 2018.

8   Abrams, "Does Russ George," updated November 4, 2013.

9   Schiermeier, "Ocean Fertilization"; Keim, "Ocean Fertilization," January 29, 2009; Lampitt et al. "Ocean Fertilization," August 2008.

undersea geology, we would need a massive and sustained fertilization operation to make any long-lasting progress.

Those facts together do not recommend this method. We can't invest in an impermanent solution. Other parts of our strategy would make better use of any resources we would dedicate to ocean fertilization. The added risks of toxic algae blooms are certainly not justified. We'll have to use a different approach for the oceans instead.

ECOSYSTEM RESTORATION

An alternative to artificially increasing ocean productivity is to restore ecosystems to their prehuman state. We wouldn't necessarily have to be actively involved and could simply let nature rewild some of the developed lands and return them to a natural state. That would allow a greater range for carbon-absorbing vegetation to thrive, sequestering carbon on our behalf. There are several oceanic biomes we could focus on, each naturally capable of pulling substantial amounts of carbon dioxide out of the atmosphere for long periods of time.

MANGROVES AND MARSHES

The interfaces between the ocean and land can store large quantities of carbon dioxide if they're just left alone.[10] The types of plants that grow in these regions create soil conditions that trap carbon. They do this thanks to the water cover, which prevents organic debris from decomposing.[11] Layers upon layers build up over time, removing substantial quantities of carbon dioxide from the atmosphere and overall

---

10   Stecker, "Restoring Mangroves," July 31, 2012.

11   Runwal, "Tracking Carbon," September 27, 2019.

carbon cycle. Human development has disrupted many of these areas, so returning them to nature could play a large role in our strategy.

The restoration of two main ecosystems is possible in these areas. The first includes the mangrove forests that proliferate closer to the tropics, mostly Florida and some parts of the gulf coast.[12] Mangroves are funky-looking trees with complicated root systems that hold onto soil carbon while also providing safe breeding grounds for a myriad fish species. Mangrove forests require high temperature and humidity, giving way to the second biome, salt marshes, as you move further north. Salt marshes are more typically recognizable wetlands for the United States because they are swampy areas dominated by grasses. The grasses also hold on to the soils and prevent carbon from returning to the atmosphere.

Human activities have severely curtailed both ecosystems. Development has destroyed about half of global mangrove forests, denying us hundreds of millions of tons of total carbon sequestration potential.[13] Salt marsh development is also costing us tens of thousands of tons of potential sequestration per square kilometer.[14] Thus, rewilding these areas would make a substantial dent in the billions of tons of carbon we have to eventually capture.

The first step is to stop destroying the mangroves and marshes we have left. That hasn't always been a high priority since they've typically been viewed as wastelands unfit for human habitation. Activities ranging from aquaculture and farming to building beachfront real estate utilize cleared and

---

12 Romañach et al. "Conservation and Restoration," March 2018.

13 Worthington and Spalding, "Mangrove Restoration Potential," 2018, 3.

14 Macreadie et al. "Carbon Sequestration," March 2017.

drained wetlands. Stopping new development is relatively straightforward since we can strengthen our existing protections for wetlands to better protect mangroves and marshes. The difficult task would be reclaiming the territory we've already lost. Restoration would mean removing existing buildings and infrastructure. That will not be such a popular proposition. People like their beachfront property, and it's hard to imagine there's much appetite for rewilding in valuable real estate markets like Miami. The irony is, in a lot of areas, nature will reclaim those areas regardless.

Climate change is going to play havoc with our coastlines. Rising sea levels and increased storm surge from more powerful and frequent hurricanes will force people to abandon those areas and move elsewhere. Thankfully, our goals for carbon sequestration can help mitigate these eventualities as well. Mangroves and marshes help dampen the power of a storm surge and protect areas further inland. Since the outcome will be the same either way, we might as well do some good by rewilding before disaster strikes.

The primary caveat becomes how to make the transition as easy as possible for the current inhabitants. Evacuating an area for the benefit of public safety has been done before, only at smaller scales. Places like Love Canal, New York, and Centralia, Pennsylvania—let alone Chernobyl—saw abandonment once living there was deemed a health hazard. There is no reason why preventatively getting people out of the way of hurricanes and sea level rise should be much different.

The most straightforward way we can accomplish migration is through buyouts. Most people simply can't leave behind their single biggest asset, a house, and expect to be financially secure. We will have to pay people in affected areas so they can move on and restart somewhere else. It would cost a decent chunk of change up front, but it would pay dividends over time. More people protected from storms and rising seas also means fewer flood insurance payouts for rebuilding, which would only become increasingly burdensome. We'll have to do it eventually, so we might as well do it now in an orderly manner instead of when people are forced to be refugees by climate change in the future.

MEADOWS

A less socially disruptive form of ecological restoration for the oceans would involve fostering underwater meadows of seagrass. Like mangroves and marshes, these plants trap carbon in the seabed thanks to the low oxygen environment they create, slowing decay.[15] They're ranked just as high in terms of total carbon sequestration potential as well.[16] Since seagrass meadows are underwater, we wouldn't have to worry about moving buildings and people, simply changing some practices that put them at risk.

Meadows have a potential range encompassing most of our Eastern and Western Seaboards. Unfortunately, they are in similar decline as mangroves and marshes. Instead of being cleared for development, they are being choked by our pollution—farm runoff, specifically. Fertilizer entering the ocean leads to algae blooms that block sunlight from reaching the seagrasses, essentially staving them.

Fixing seagrass meadows will require reducing our fertilizer use. That doesn't have to be a controversial proposition, even though it targets a politically important constituency like farmers. The problem with runoff is it's fundamentally

---

15   Homer, "Underwater Meadows," November 1, 2018.

16   UN Environment Programme, "Seagrass," accessed September 14, 2020.

inefficient and wasteful of our resources: every bit of fertilizer entering the ocean isn't going toward growing food. Reducing our usage is, therefore, more efficient for the farmer doing the application since less of their expenses are literally going down the drain. We would need to change our regulatory structure to accomplish that goal. It is certainly doable within the already massive scope of the strategy.

***

Our goals vis-à-vis the ocean will be to help restore the climate by encouraging the recovery of ecosystems that are highly active at sequestering carbon. It means redefining our development goals along coasts and being willing to implement more stringent pollution controls for agriculture. Very little capital investment is required compared to rebuilding the grid, just a matter of mitigating the costs of externalities and reprioritizing our policies. Nature can do the rest.

SACRIFICE: GLOBALIZATION
The oceans have always provided benefits to civilization far beyond being carbon sinks. They've been the highways for commerce and migration throughout our entire history. Even in ancient Rome, you could find cinnamon at the market grown thousands of miles away in India and Southeast Asia. Trade connected the continents, as it continues to do so today at an incredible scale.

Sea shipping is a pervasive and engrained part of our global economy. Many products you buy today are composed of materials that crossed the ocean multiple times during manufacturing and sale. Electronics provide an extreme example, where components can be designed in America, etched onto wafers in Europe, which are sent to Vietnam to be cut into chips, which are sent to Malaysia for assembly, which are sent to China for integration into a laptop, which is shipped back to the United States, where you use it to shop online for products with similarly tortuous supply chains. Moving all of these goods across the globe takes energy—a lot of energy.

The shipping industry accounts for about 3 percent of global carbon emissions, and there are few ways of getting around that.[17] Batteries may be nice for short journeys, or you could cover the deck in solar panels, but a transoceanic voyage needs a lot of power all the time. That can only be supplied by the high energy density of liquid fuels. Increasing our synthetic fuel infrastructure to meet both our seasonal energy storage and shipping demand will take time. One way around this problem would be to invest more heavily in our domestic manufacturing capabilities, reducing the scale of overseas shipping and reversing existing economic trends.

Globalizing commerce has been the operating paradigm for the past half-century. It follows orthodox economic thinking that each country, region, or factory needs to become increasingly specialized in producing goods to maximize efficiency. The downside is the United States has moved substantial portions of its industrial base overseas, to the tune of millions of jobs and tens of thousands of factories.[18] Losing that industrial base doesn't only hurt the people who lose jobs and increase emissions from shipping, but it risks us not having the manufacturing capacity to fully implement the strategy at the pace we want without foreign suppliers.

---

17 Selin and Cowing, "Cargo Ships," December 18, 2018.

18 Scott, "We Can Reshore," August 10, 2020.

Overseas manufacturers produce a substantial amount of our installed renewable capacity. For instance, about four in five solar cells installed in the United States are currently imported, despite the technology being pioneered in this country.[19] Our supply chains present several risks beyond the emissions required to bring those materials here. What happens if there's a supply disruption once we start deploying renewable energy infrastructure in earnest? Perhaps there's a problem in a factory overseas, a natural disaster shuts down the supply chain for several months, or maybe a foreign manufacturer decides they just don't like us. If for whatever reason, we're not able to get the equipment we need from the globalized economy, our strategy grinds to a halt.

Mitigating that risk would involve bringing critical manufacturing back to the United States. We have all the major raw materials and a large population to operate the factories. Everything you need to be a self-sufficient economy is right here. Onshoring would also help spread the economic benefits of the transition to a greater number of people through the jobs it would create. Manufacturing provides good-paying work, so bringing factories home can have an immediate impact on the material well-being of many people. There will also be greater political will for enacting the strategy once it is clear that doing so will bring these jobs.

The primary downside to investing in domestic manufacturing is it will increase prices. We were able to offshore so much of our capacity because cheaper labor overseas enables lower costs for consumers at home. Overseas workers aren't paid nearly as much as Americans, and other countries often don't have the same health and safety requirements, making

---

19 Cummins, "The Price of Solar Panels," June 8, 2018.

it difficult for domestic labor to compete. Reversing that paradigm will also eat into the profits of those who have moved their capital overseas. They would certainly oppose moving manufacturing back to the United States, and their influence would make implementing our strategy more difficult overall.

The situation is further complicated because costs will likely increase in either approach, and the benefits of onshoring may not be as widespread as we might hope. Global shipping is enabled by cheap fossil fuels. Switching to more expensive synthetic fuels will naturally increase prices for any goods moved overseas. If manufacturing does return to the United States, it is also likely many of those production lines will be highly automated and not provide as large of a boon to employment as anticipated. It will also be expensive to move that manufacturing capital back to the United States, and it will take years before we're able to manufacture at the scale we need. Thus, we arrive at the catch-twenty-two situation of globalization. No matter what we do to change the existing system to combat climate change, there will be downsides making the transition painful.

It is also important to recognize trade is not inherently a good or bad thing. It is a tool for accomplishing our goals, and trade can be incredibly powerful for enabling a diverse and advanced economy. It will also be necessary to ensure those countries that can't support an indigenous industrial base can have access to the equipment they need to build a renewable grid. The choice comes down to how we as a society choose to use that tool and what sacrifices we are willing to make. We could compromise and only onshore manufacturing most critical for the strategy or increase trade more with our nearest neighbors using electrified land transportation. Until the existing consensus changes, however, we must engage with the existing international system to start making progress on our strategy. Regardless of how that evolves, we will certainly have to tolerate higher prices and sacrifice some of our buying power.

CHAPTER 10

THE LAND

My time in the Boy Scouts was formative if less than pleasant. I have the unfortunate distinction of being an Eagle Scout who hates being outdoors. In a program centered around camping, that creates some issues. From outhouses filled with spiders to canoes filled with spiders, I have had my fill of outside, even if I do recognize the importance of *nature*. The only downside is most of the skills and experiences I built don't have a lot of everyday relevance, except maybe spending a week in a tent at the height of August in Iowa. That would give anyone perspective on and create an imperative for mitigating climate change.

One of the worst experiences I had involved a long sleepless summer night up at camp, as sweaty an affair as any. The local terrain was mostly swamp. One night that was our destination, and we were made to pitch makeshift shelters. The thing about Wisconsin summers is there are always mosquitos, and mosquitos like to breed in stagnant, swampy water. Trying to sleep in the open becomes an unending nightmare of buzzing noises and itching. Add onto that the wild card of some adolescent hitting people with sticks in the middle of the night while screaming *tattoo*, and you've got an event for the scrapbook.

My personal preferences notwithstanding, these wild areas will be critical for our strategy. Just as with the oceans, the most efficient method of sequestering carbon on land is going to be to let nature recover. We need vegetation on a massive scale to soak up all the carbon we've emitted, so it makes sense to work on both land and sea at the same time. Also, like the oceans, there are multiple ecosystems we can rebuild to store terrestrial carbon.

USEFUL BIOMES

There are many different kinds of outside. The United States is so vast that almost every biome is present in some way. We've got everything from tropical swamps in the South, forests along both coasts, and the Great Plains between them. Each of these environments can play a significant role in drawing carbon out of the atmosphere and keeping it sequestered permanently. Each square kilometer of wildland is potentially thousands of tons of additional carbon storage. There is still some prioritizing we can do, and each type of biome will have different attributes that will gate how much they can contribute to our strategy.

SWAMPS AND BOGS

While I certainly can't recommend camping in them, the wetlands themselves aren't to blame for my discomfort. They were just doing what they're supposed to. Their misalignment with human preferences has led to a general decline in the range of wetlands across the country. This is unfortunate because wetlands are incredibly valuable for our strategy.

Inland wetlands hold onto carbon in the same way as the cousins on the coast. Take peat bogs, for instance, which store almost a quarter of all soil carbon despite encompassing only 3 percent of land area. Their soil is held in place by extensive root systems covered in water, which prevents the rapid decay of organic matter. The mosses that grow in peat bogs also create a mildly acidic environment that further impedes decomposition. It's why you will occasionally find perfectly preserved mummies when you dig into them. I never found anything that cool while out camping, but it does speak the longevity of carbon stored in wetlands. When they're protected and restored, bogs and swamps have the potential for taking in vast quantities of atmospheric carbon and keeping it sealed away indefinitely, making them indispensable for the strategy.[1]

The ability to store carbon has, unfortunately, been one of the reasons for their decline. Peat bogs have historically been mined for fuel, much like coal. The solidified plant matter is cut out like bricks, dried, and burned. If you're a Scotch fan, you've probably enjoyed the flavor peat smoke gives to barley. Most bogs were simply viewed as wastelands that were drained and developed for agriculture and other purposes. This seems to be a common trap society has fallen into, giving up subtle, long-term benefits from environmental services in favor of short-term gains.

The good news is it should be relatively straightforward to repair that damage. The goal for rewilding is to return ecosystems to what they naturally would be had we not interfered in the first place. For wetlands, one need only repair the

---

1   Wang and Dodla, "Wetland Soil," July 29, 2013; Gewin, "How Peat," February 2020.

disrupted underlying hydrology, and the land should start to recover naturally. That process usually involves employing some heavy equipment to fill in the drainage systems made to dry the land. Once that's done, nature can largely take care of the rest.

Estonia serves as a good example of how this can be successfully accomplished.[2] A lot of their wetland area, which covers a quarter of the country, was drained during the second half of the twentieth century by the Soviet Government. Left alone, the remaining organic matter in the dry bogs would decompose and contribute to carbon dioxide emissions. Thankfully, repairing the underlying hydrology has rebuilt many of these ecosystems in only a matter of years. These experiences overseas show this could be a quick and easy method for the United States to start sequestering carbon.

Rebuilding wetlands will require some changes in our behavior beyond land use. Peat mosses are routinely harvested for use in the gardening industry, and some areas still burn peat for fuel, further depleting the resource. We can simply ban such practices, as well as more stringently control the development of existing wetlands.[3] Otherwise, we just leave them alone to do their thing. There are plenty of wetland areas spread across the United States, and that's where we would start to rebuild them.[4] The only barrier would be how much of the now-developed land we can get our hands on.

---

2   Niiler, "Tiny Country," August 4, 2017; Barthelmes et al. "Peatlands," 2015, 8.

3   For additional information, see: Votteler and Muir, "Wetland Protection Legislation," January 29, 2002.

4   Soper and Osbon, "The Occurrence," 1922, 80–82.

Swamps, bogs, and wetlands of all types will take center stage for our reclamation of terrestrial carbon sequestration. They have an outsized impact compared to their size, and their somewhat limited range means we wouldn't have to acquire as much land to rewild as other options. However, that doesn't mean they can get us all of the way there. Some of the drained wetlands aren't going to be coming back. We're certainly not going to uproot an entire city just to rebuild them. We also can't build new wetlands without massive earth-moving projects. Thus, we'll have to look to other ecosystems to help supplement our carbon storage capacity.

FORESTS

One of the reasons peat bogs were drained in Scotland was to clear space for tree plantations. It didn't work that well because if the soil conditions were good for trees, they wouldn't have been bogs to begin with. That doesn't mean reforestation is not a solid path forward for reversing climate change in other areas. On the whole, planting more trees is a very effective method of rapidly drawing down atmospheric carbon.[5] The potential scale is absolutely enormous. With all the timber that's been felled over the past couple of centuries, we have the opportunity to replant *billions* of trees.

Those trees sequester carbon in a couple of different ways. The first is obvious. They need carbon to grow and build themselves. An acre of trees will absorb around five tons of carbon per year.[6] Just as important is their ability to build and stabilize soils. In the colder regions, where snow cover slows decomposition, soils continually accumulate

---

5   Fargione et al. "Natural Climate Solutions," November 2018.

6   CMRSDP, "A Landowner's Guide," October 2009, 8.

and sequester carbon. Cutting down trees to make room for development or agriculture removed both the carbon stored in the trees and soil.

Rebuilding forests is already an ongoing activity, such as Pakistan's Ten Billion Trees campaign.[7] The additional carbon storage comes with another human-centric benefit: jobs. Planting that many trees require tens of thousands of people, creating additional opportunities for people displaced from fossil fuel industries. Those people likely wouldn't have to move either, considering almost every part of the United States can host more trees.

The only downside to restocking our forests is it isn't something we can just do and forget about. Fires are an endemic feature of these ecosystems we will have to deal with. Over time, accumulated brush and plant matter will build up until, with an advantageous spark, they ignite into a widespread conflagration. The only way to have wildfires under some modicum of control is to do proper forest maintenance and controlled burns. The current rise in California's fires is partially linked to the government banning the controlled burns Native Americans used to perform.[8] It may seem counterintuitive, since we want to keep from burning and putting more carbon into the atmosphere. However, the only alternative is increasingly out of control events that are much less favorable for our goals.

A small investment in additional forest management does not take away from the conclusion that increased tree cover will absolutely help our strategy. The potential scale is so

---

7   Khan, "As a 'Green Stimulus,'" April 28, 2020.

8   Sommer, "To Manage Wildfire," August 24, 2020.

immense we cannot ignore reforestation's potential.[9] It will have to be an ongoing part of the strategy, encompassing as much amenable land as we can get our hands on.

GRASSLAND

It's important to remember the vast middle of the country never evolved to accommodate forests. The Great Plains between the Rocky Mountains and the Mississippi River require their own attention, as they will be the third terrestrial target of the strategy. Despite the lack of large vegetation like trees, the soils beneath the prairie are remarkably useful for sequestration. The native grasses evolved extensive root systems allowing them to survive periodic fires and retain carbon.[10] Problems arise when you replace natural grasslands to make way for crops that don't provide the same benefit. Curtail their range enough, and you'll wind up with a dust bowl after a bad drought, just like what happened in the 1930s.

We'll almost be starting from square one with rebuilding grasslands. The majority of these areas no longer exist in a wild state, being long since developed for agriculture. In Texas, for example, over 90 percent of native prairies are gone, and the remainder occupy small, disconnected islands.[11] Since the rate of carbon sequestration is fairly low, only around a ton per acre per year, we'd need to rewild a whole lot of this area to start making a substantial dent in our atmospheric carbon.[12]

9   Maslin and Lewis, "Yes, We Can Reforest," May 7, 2019.

10 UC Davis, "Grasslands More Reliable," July 9, 2018.

11 Ahmed, "How Texas Prairies," September 6, 2019.

12 TgO, "Tallgrass Prairie," accessed September 4, 2020.

Fortunately, repairing these areas are relatively straight-forward. Like marshland, we have to do a bit of work to clear space for the proper vegetation, mainly removing scrub brush so the grasses can take root. Unlike forests, we won't have to do much beyond that. The true cost of returning these areas to nature will be in competition with the other uses we have for the land.

FINDING LAND

Wetlands, forests, and grasslands have all been diminished to make room for human activity, so replenishing them will mean we have to make some trade-offs. The limiting factor in each biome we seek to restore is the amount of land we'll be able to work with. That acreage will determine how quickly we can take carbon out of the atmosphere and how soon we can return the climate to normal. However, every acre we reclaim means diminishing our potential for growing food and other activities. Reclaiming land for carbon sequestration involves striking a balance between our climate goals and the benefits we receive from development.

We also have to consider the social aspect of our activities. Land is a commodity owned by individuals, and those individuals will have to be convinced to part with their land for the greater good of this project. That is the tricky bit. People have a lot of emotions tied to land, especially if it's a homestead their family has inhabited for generations. Trying to tell someone what to do with their land will be a difficult prospect, especially if it's land they could otherwise use to support themselves.

Agriculture will be the most significant competition. We certainly don't want people to go hungry as we're fighting climate change. There are a couple of areas where we can start to make a dent, starting with ethanol. We currently dedicate about 141,000 square kilometers to growing the corn used to make ethanol, and all of that will become superfluous once we decarbonize the automobile sector. The other main set of farmlands we can reclaim are areas already marginal or at risk due to climate change. Arid lands in the West and Southwest that require a lot of water, fertilizer, and effort to cultivate would be efficient targets. They already take more resources than may be warranted, and their viability will only decrease as the climate continues to change. We may as well be proactive and deal with them now and focus on maintaining more productive lands for agriculture.

The major question is how to go about accessing the farmland that needs to be rewilded. The most straightforward option would be to financially compensate the current owners. We could buy the land outright, but that is the costliest option in both money and public goodwill. The strategy may not look too appealing to many constituencies if the government appears to be strong-arming people out of their land. Farming is a pillar of the classic American tableau, after all. Direct purchases only make sense if they're done to rescue people from land that would become worthless. If a farm is going to become nonviable from climate change anyway, we can buy the land from the owner to help them build a new life elsewhere. You can better make the argument we'd be freeing people from a rapidly depreciating asset, much like performing buyouts along the soon-to-be-inundated coastline to get people out of harm's way.

A better option for the majority of land would be to subsidize the choice of returning it to a more natural state. We already pay farmers not to plant crops certain years, and we pay significant amounts to incentivize the massive production of corn.[13] It makes sense to pay people to plant trees and native plants, then continue paying them to keep it that way.[14] People would have the motivation to engage while ensuring they'd be able to earn a living and keep land in the family. There are already federal programs through the US Department of Agriculture that incentivize removing environmentally critical lands from cultivation. We would only need to broaden the scope of what is included and subsidized for climate purposes.[15]

We still have to consider the broader economic effects rewilding will cause. Farms aren't the only businesses relying on agriculture for their livelihood and removing that base will impact the small towns relying on farms for their livelihood. This would come at a time when these places are already dealing with problems like hospital closures, declining economic opportunities, and brain drain.[16] Hopefully, creating new jobs for completing the rewilding and subsequent land management will alleviate some of the pressure caused by the transition. Making sure we can support everyone in society has to be a part of this process, and our carbon sequestration activities are no different.

Finally, there is also the possibility of changing farming practices to better sequester carbon, even during cultivation. These activities mainly fall under the banner of preserving soil health, which is the common denominator for all of our best carbon sequestration options. Current tillage practices

---

13   Frank, "Why Does the Govt.," August 4, 2009; Urry, "Our Crazy," April 20, 2015.

14   There are some limited precedents in our tax code that do this already. Hoover, "Financial and Tax Aspects," 2004.

15   USDA, "Conservation Programs," accessed December 29, 2020.

16   Siegler, "Small-Town Hospitals," April 9, 2020.

encourage carbon depletion from the soil and a reliance on artificial fertilizers. We could instead adopt modern conservation practices like no-till planting or the use of cover crops to hold soils together. We'd still be able to produce an abundance of food, but in a way that doesn't work against our overall climate goals.

Keeping or returning land to an undeveloped state will require some changes beyond agricultural practices. My mother always used to complain about this guy named Urban Sprawl, who was constantly taking over farmland and building new housing developments outside of town. Therein lies an example of us suffering from an abundance of resources. Our country's plentiful space has allowed us to occupy a lot of room for building houses, strip malls, gas stations, and whatnot. It's even codified in many zoning laws that preclude high-density housing in many areas.[17] We need to change that situation, as the continued expansion of low-density development wastes a lot of land we could otherwise use as a carbon sink.

The same reason we don't want to dedicate a lot of land to solar panel installations by themselves should apply to most other forms of buildings. We need to be incentivizing higher-density development and redevelopment that keeps everything in much closer proximity, freeing up land for carbon sequestration. However, we also want to balance higher densities by including vegetation within a city, since plants are needed to dampen the heat island effect. This phenomenon causes cities to be much hotter than surrounding areas because the concrete used in roads and buildings traps heat. Investing in urban parks, tree-lined roads, and rooftop

---

17   Schuetz, "To Improve," January 7, 2020.

gardens where solar panels don't make sense helps counter this effect while providing a modicum of carbon sequestration. Urban planning will need to make better use of these spaces, and communities will need to divert more resources into making it happen.

SACRIFICE: STEAK AND BRISKET

A potential criticism of retiring farmland, even the part used for ethanol, is we would be unnecessarily endangering our food supply. One could argue we'll need as much agricultural production as possible in anticipation of looming food insecurity issues caused by climate change. That isn't unreasonable. The same changes that will make marginal land in the United States nonviable will affect other countries just as much, but they may not have the same overall abundance as us. It's likely many people will become uprooted from their subsistence agrarian roots and become climate refugees, all of whom will need to be fed. There is one way of both feeding everyone and sequestering carbon, but it will require a sacrifice on our part.

Our current agricultural system is not very efficient, and not just through all the food that gets thrown out every day. In terms of calories produced, most of what we grow never even makes it to our plate. Most states dedicate the majority of their farmland, collectively more than three and a half times the size of Texas, to produce food for the animals we eat.[18] Since the conversion of plant to animal calories is less than 15 percent efficient, we're only getting a fraction of the benefit for all the inputs we dedicate to making meat. Beef is

---

18 Cassidy et al. "Redefining Agricultural Yields," August 2013; USDA, "Farms and Land," April 2019; Foley, "A Five-Step Plan," May 2014.

by far the worst, giving us one pound of meat for every thirty pounds of grain we feed the cow. All those acres dedicated to growing corn and soybeans for feedlots are land we could be rewilding for sequestration.

Beyond preventing recovery, raising, and processing animals also actively contributes to climate change. About seven billion tons of carbon dioxide are emitted by this sector every year.[19] It's a bit of a running joke to say environmentalists are worried about cow farts, but that too is literally a problem. Methane is a much more potent greenhouse gas than carbon dioxide, and livestock collectively releases a lot of methane.[20] Add to that all the emissions from manufacturing fertilizers, harvesting equipment, transportation, and animal agriculture sectors become the second largest contributor to our overall emissions.[21]

Meat production isn't great for our objectives, but that doesn't mean it's an easy problem to rectify. The first issue we must overcome is how meat consumption is engrained in our culture. One of our central mythologies is centered around cowboys who drove cattle to market, after all. It explains why there are often visceral reactions to the idea of consuming less meat.[22] This is not something we will be able to overcome, at least not in any reasonable timeframe, which means we won't be able to snap our fingers and just make meat disappear to free up additional land for us to use as carbon stores.

It should be noted I'm not making a moral argument against meat here, only the utility of its present production

---

19   UNFAO, "Key Facts and Findings," accessed September 14, 2020.

20   To be precise, cow belches are the predominant problem.

21   UNFAO, "The State of Food Security," 2020, 100–103.

22   Bromwich and Yar, "The Fake Meat War," July 25, 2019.

levels in the face of the climate crisis. I certainly still eat it, even though the climate would be better off if I didn't. A certain population of people will be vegetarian or vegan, but we can't count on seeing massive growth within either group in the short-term. The only alternative is to proliferate food products that can satisfy our craving for meat while having less of a climate impact.

There are several ways to go about producing protein using fewer resources. One is to wait and see if the lab-grown meat industry can take off. This removes all but the muscle tissue from the equation, which is cultured in a laboratory. Theoretically, you can avoid some of the inefficiencies since you're only providing the calories needed to grow and sustain the cultured tissue instead of the entire animal. While press releases do show progress on this approach, it still hasn't crossed the technological threshold enough to say it meets our requirement to use existing technology.

The less high-tech option would be to decrease the number of animals we farm. Instead of concentrated feeding operations, we could require all animal meat to come from more pastoral growing methods like sustainable grazing. The result would be some meat on the market, but much less than is currently available. That would be tricky, as even just decreasing the amount of meat available will cause significant disruptions. It would no longer be possible for meat to be included in every meal, which is still going to be unacceptable to some people. There will also be a class dimension, since the rich will continue consuming as much as they want, while everyone else is pushed out of the market by higher prices. That doesn't seem fair.

The only way around that problem would be a rationing program like my grandparents dealt with during World War

II. Each person would be given an annual allotment of lower emission animal protein. It would transform meat into more of a special occasion product, not something to be consumed in vast quantities at low quality. One would certainly better appreciate a quality ribeye steak if it is a less common occurrence. Many people wouldn't like that either, but it would be the only way to ensure an equitable situation. However, that still wouldn't meet the need for day-to-day protein sources.

Myriad products are made from cheap meat that will need to be replaced as part of a culinary transition. Consider the chicken nuggets you buy in bulk for your kids. These are quick, microwaveable, and mass-produced forms of protein that are too convenient to abandon entirely. Those will be our primary targets for replacement: all the things you can find in the freezer section. Fortunately, we have some pretty spot-on replacements for these meats. Products like the Impossible or Beyond burgers use textured vegetable proteins to sufficiently replicate the taste and texture of animal meat. They'll never be able to replicate the properties of a filet mignon, but that isn't required to make a considerable impact. They're best at replicating the mass consumed, relatively low value products like ground beef and sausages, and they provide enough taste and texture similarities to justify the switch.

Switching to meat alternatives on a large scale is going to ruffle feathers for altogether different reasons. One argument is these are not healthy foods, despite what their plant-based origins may imply, or they're too processed or based on genetically modified organisms (GMOs).[23] Such arguments don't hold up to scrutiny. Plant meats are simply a vehicle

---

23 For example: Kendall, "The Impossible Burger," September 8, 2019; Barrett, "How the Impossible Burger," February 13, 2020.

for protein and fat that one should approach with the same dietary considerations as animal meat. *Processed* is such a vaguely useless term that it covers everything from chopping a carrot to making sprayable cheese. Finally, GMOs have never been adequately shown to have adverse health effects.[24]

There's also a strange classist angle against plant proteins. Some commentators and critics were fine with them until they moved out of the luxury restaurants and became available to the general public, and they suddenly became a problem.[25] Food has always had a performative consumption angle to it, but such a privileged consideration doesn't make sense in the face of climate change. We should be subsidizing the production of plant-based protein, not decrying it.

The benefits of switching to alternative meats for our strategy drown out the manufactured distractions. The land area that could be made available for rewilding is one thing. It is absolutely massive given the scale of present meat consumption. What we do with the remaining cultivated land is almost equally important. Instead of growing corn, we could rely on peas and soybeans, legumes that are naturally nitrogen fixers. That means we don't have to manufacture and distribute nearly as much fertilizer as before, which frees up a ton of energy and hydrogen for other strategic purposes. It also means less runoff, so less of those unintended algae blooms that hurt our seagrass sequestration. Overall, less meat consumption makes everything easier for our transition. We just need to have the collective will to resist that juicy steak.

---

24 The state of GMO research is well summarized in: NASEM, *Genetically Engineered Crops*.

25 Trembath, "Food Activists," August 12, 2019.

CHAPTER 11

THE STONE

———

The term *fossil fuel* is a bit of a misnomer. It creates the idea dinosaur juice is being pumped into your gas tank, but none of the coal, oil, or gas we extract comes from that time period. Oil comes from algae and other sea creatures that became trapped under the seafloor, gradually transforming due to heat and pressure on a geologic timescale. Coal is a little more interesting because it has an entire age named after it—the Carboniferous, which ended about 300 million years ago. Vast swampy forests, not unlike the wetlands of today, allowed the accumulation of organic matter that eventually became coal over millions of years.

The geological epoch that gave us coal exhibits the power of sequestering carbon. All of those trees growing but not decomposing had the dual effects of drastically increasing oxygen and decreasing carbon dioxide levels. The first allowed the evolution of massive arthropods, like giant centipedes, but that's not part of the strategy. The more useful effect was the drawdown of carbon dioxide that punctuated the end of the carboniferous with intense cooling and the massive growth of glaciers across the planet.[1] Nature had essentially done what we're aiming to do in this part of the strategy, albeit a bit farther than we should go.

We most likely can't rely on these same natural processes to correct our current predicament. We've thus far built up our strategy for carbon sequestration by restoring nature as much as possible, but we can't assume it will be a 100 percent solution. The restoration areas were in their own equilibrium before human civilization arrived, meaning all the emitted carbon dioxide from burning fossil fuels likely can't be incorporated into the previous steady state carbon cycle. There are also ecological limits to how much carbon dioxide nature can absorb on short timescales.

More direct carbon capture is likely required for a complete reversal of climate change. Fossil fuels effectively trapped billions of tons of carbon underground for millions of years. Thus, it is logical that taking carbon out of the atmosphere and reburying it might be an effective way around our present difficulties. We would essentially complete the loop, returning all the coal, gas, and oil that's been burned back into the Earth where it can no longer do our climate any harm. Since we won't be consuming those fuels anymore, we'd be able to dial back conditions to what they were before, permanently ending the crisis.

DIRECT AIR CAPTURE

Capturing carbon dioxide from the atmosphere by industrial means is easier said than done. The primary issue is the incredibly low concentration of carbon dioxide we're dealing with, despite the vast quantities we've emitted. Only

---

1   Feulner, "Formation of Most," October 2017.

0.04 percent of our atmosphere is carbon dioxide. That's the equivalent of half a sugar cube dissolved in a gallon of water. We would need to process incredibly large quantities of air before an appreciable amount of sequestration is achieved. That presents several difficulties for our strategy, regardless of the technology we use.

One option for removing carbon dioxide is to basically freeze it out of the air. It has a higher melting point than oxygen and nitrogen, so if you cool air below -57°C it will freeze out. Much like a dehumidifier collected water by chilling the air in your basement, this method pulls out the carbon dioxide and leaves behind dry ice. The downside is refrigeration requires a lot of energy and would require substantial additions to our grid investments.

Alternatively, we could choose from a number of different chemical capture techniques. In such a scheme, air is bubbled through a basic (opposite of acidic) material that reacts with carbon dioxide to trap it.[2] The concentrated mixture is then heated during a different stage to release a concentrated stream of carbon dioxide for capture by some other mechanism. The downside is, again, energy. Running air through the absorbing material takes energy. Heating it to release carbon dioxide takes energy, and energy is needed to convert that carbon dioxide into something else we can easily sequester.

Direct air capture is technically feasible but would require a substantial investment on our part to make it a reality. In addition to rebuilding the grid, we would have to invest in massive amounts of energy generating infrastructure, to the tune of hundreds of gigawatts of extra capacity, to make this

---

2   Johnson, "Capturing Carbon," February 25, 2019.

variety of carbon capture viable.[3] Plus, after we're done with this phase of the strategy, that new capacity would be useless. We could alleviate part of that cost if we abandoned air in favor of preexisting streams of concentrated carbon dioxide.

CARBON CAPTURE AND SEQUESTRATION

We can make carbon capture easier on ourselves by trapping emissions before they enter the atmosphere. Instead of pulling dilute carbon dioxide from the air, we would attach additional equipment to the tail end of industrial processes. Such a facility would switch from venting their waste into the atmosphere to routing their concentrated emissions to a carbon capture system. It would take some investment in capital and energy, but it would be an altogether more efficient alternative.

While a coal or natural gas plant produces a concentrated stream of carbon dioxide, we absolutely cannot use them as sources for carbon capture. Capturing and sequestering the emissions from fossil fuel sources will only delay the transition since it leaves the rest of the fossil fuel infrastructure intact.[4] It would allow us to become complacent with the status quo while doing nothing about the carbon that's already in the atmosphere. At best, it only delays the overall transition by consuming resources we could invest elsewhere. Fundamentally, we can only permanently solve our emissions problems by stopping fossil fuel consumption.

---

3   von Hippel, "Thermal Removal," May 2018.

4   This is likely why fossil fuel-friendly sources generally favor carbon capture from power plants, for example: Biniek et al. "Driving CO_2 Emissions," July 30, 2020; Bhambhani, "Everyone Wants," November 21, 2019; C2ES, "Carbon Capture," accessed September 6, 2020.

Another option is to use nature as a giant carbon collector for our carbon capture needs, beyond simply increasing the amount of vegetation. All the new trees, shrubs, and grasses can serve as energy-free sources of concentrated carbon. We need only harvest them, move the plant matter to an incinerator, burn it, and capture the resulting concentrated stream of carbon dioxide for sequestration. So long as the leftover minerals are recycled back into the ecosystem, we can use the same area of land to continuously pull carbon out of the atmosphere until the problem is solved.

Once we have our concentrated stream of carbon, whether it comes from plants or industry, we have to decide what to do with it. The vast majority of carbon we capture will have to be reburied in some way. Depending on if we transform the carbon dioxide into something else, there are multiple avenues for doing so.

STORING GAS

One method of sequestration is to pump carbon dioxide underground. One can think of it as the reverse of natural gas exploration. We find a site with the appropriate geology that can accept the gas, bore a well into the rock, pump in the gas, and seal the well once it's full. If everything holds, the gas will stay down there permanently, just as natural gas had been locked away before we started extracting it. While it seems straightforward, there are a couple of technical issues to consider before work can begin.

We would need to store the carbon dioxide under greater than atmospheric pressure to sequester any worthwhile quantity. Gasses are much more dilute than a solid or a liquid, meaning we have to compress them to maximize our underground space. Compressing gasses to higher pressures requires a lot of energy. The same reason compressed air energy storage is viable for the strategy is why gaseous carbon storage is painful. We must make an energy investment to solve the problem.

Even if that energy calculus is favorable, we must also consider whether this will be a permanent solution. There are several avenues for underground sequestration to cause us future issues. Carbon dioxide is a reactive chemical that will create acidic conditions where it is stored. With the help of a little water, carbon dioxide dissolves rock like limestone. We can plan for that when choosing a site, but the ground beneath us is a dynamic system. Tremors and movements, even those made when pumping the carbon underground, could create instabilities. If we choose an unstable or unsuitable location, there is a chance all the stored carbon will escape, providing no real benefit for our strategy.

There are pockets of carbon dioxide gas that have been stable underground for millions of years, implying that gaseous sequestration is fundamentally possible. It just remains to be seen if we can reliably engineer those conditions. There are ongoing tests and studies examining this approach, ongoing being the operative word.[5] With unproven technology that doesn't guarantee a permanent solution violating two guiding policies, we can't justify the investment required to make underground gas storage part of the strategy at this time.

Carbon dioxide's reactivity can, in some circumstances, be turned to our advantage. If it's done in a controlled way, mineralization is a process that can sequester carbon

---

5   For example, in the European Union: O'Callaghan, "Storing CO_2 Underground," November 27, 2018.

within certain kinds of rock without necessarily damaging the underlying geology.[6] The general procedure is to pump highly concentrated carbon dioxide, with some water, into a geological formation containing minerals that can form carbonates. Essentially, you do the reverse of cement manufacturing by exposing calcium oxide to carbon dioxide to form stable calcium carbonate.[7]

There are more than enough mineral reserves within the Earth to accommodate the carbon we've put into the atmosphere, provided we have the time. Mineralization is a slow process, as born out by several test cases that only show ton-scale absorption over the course of months.[8] That isn't the rapid pace we would hope for, but it's a place to start. The technology is feasible and the resulting storage permanent, so it makes sense to include mineralization as part of the strategy. We would use our available geological resources to save building infrastructure and energy as much as possible but knowing it will need to be supplemented by other approaches.

STORING SOLID CARBON

It would be so much easier to bury carbon if we could do it as a nonreactive solid. A cubic meter of anthracite coal contains about one and a half tons of carbon, which is 67 percent more than crude oil and over 3,000 percent more than carbon dioxide at compressed air storage pressures. We wouldn't have to worry about all the geological engineering required

---

6   USGS, "Making Minerals," March 8, 2019; Snæbjörnsdóttir et al. "Carbon Dioxide Storage," January 2020.

7   The reaction is: $CO_2 + CaO \rightarrow CaCO_3$.

8   Kelemen et al. "An Overview," November 2019.

to mineralize carbon dioxide with a solid alternative. We could simply bury it anywhere we wanted.

The problem is getting back to a solid form of carbon in a scalable way. It is chemically possible to turn our stream of concentrated carbon dioxide back into solid carbon, essentially synthesizing artificial coal. Scientists have already demonstrated a method of doing this in a way requiring relatively low-intensity conditions and that can run continuously.[9] Unfortunately, it isn't developed enough for our requirement to use existing technology. The process has been demonstrated in the laboratory, not at scale—and that is a substantial gulf to bridge.

There are always complications when transitioning science from the benchtop to an industrial operation. It's something I ran into during my years as a scientist. One of my early projects was to develop chemicals for making plastics from biological sources.[10] We were able to do it, proving the concept, but only for milligrams at a time.[11] Scaling up would have taken years of additional research and design. We would have had to build a small-scale model of the complete chemical factory to unambiguously prove it was feasible. The point is that making a process work requires as much or more time and resources as making the initial discovery, and project-ending problems can occur at any point.

This reality is unfortunate because directly synthesizing elemental carbon from the air would be very amenable for the strategy as a whole. Provided we had the energy, we could run it constantly until the problem is solved. This approach

9   Service, "New Way," February 26, 2019.

10   Schwartz et al. "Integration of," October 2013.

11   A milligram is one one-thousandth of a gram.

would be incredibly useful and worthy of future investigation, but until it's fully demonstrated, we can't assume it will be available to us.

ENERGY SOURCES

Dedicating energy for carbon capture and sequestration is complicated by the fact it will be a fundamentally impermanent activity. Once all the excess carbon dioxide is out of the atmosphere, our job is forever done, and we will no longer need all the equipment. It would be wasteful to invest in more renewable infrastructure only for it to go to waste once its purpose is fulfilled. Given these considerations, we should have a plan in place for getting the energy for separating, concentrating, and storing carbon as efficiently as possible.

There is a synergy here with a power source we haven't talked about much so far: nuclear. We dismissed expanding nuclear power in chapter 2 because nuclear fuel is fundamentally limited. Once we mine all the fuel, nuclear power is gone forever. However, that won't be so much of a problem if we're using it for a specific task with an expiration date. Instead of taking these power plants offline as more renewables are installed, we could instead direct their electricity solely to feeding carbon sequestration activities. The steady power output of a nuclear plant is ideal for an energy-intensive operation that needs to constantly run at a high capacity. After, we would be able to retire them without harming the grid's stability.

The only limitation is time. The nuclear fleet is aging and likely won't last far beyond the completion of our grid transition. We would have to build more reactors to meet our needs for carbon capture and sequestration. If we do it right, new nuclear capacity could help us deal with our ever-present nuclear waste problem at the same time if we employ breeder reactors. These units can burn-up that waste to make it less dangerous. They're just not yet fully developed yet. While our requirement to use existing technology puts a pause on such an approach, it's something to look out for in the coming years.

BUILDING WITH CARBON

Carbon doesn't have to be put below ground to take it out of the atmosphere for the long haul. Most buildings are designed for decades of use, so if we could use carbon storing materials for construction, we could make a dent in the problem. It would mean having to move our building techniques away from concrete and steel and back to wood. Every ton of wood used in a building is carbon kept out of the atmosphere, helping us reach our goals faster.

The best way to use more wood in buildings would be to use mass laminated timber construction. This differs from the light-frame construction of your typical house in the United States. Mass laminated means multiple layers of boards are glued together to create a solid piece that is as strong and fire-resistant as the cement and metal it replaces. They already do this in Europe for multi-level apartments and other commercial buildings, so there is no technical barrier for doing it here.[12] We'd only need to update the building codes to allow for it and invest in a little additional capital to retrofit sawmills for manufacturing.

There are some downsides to scaling up this material. A common critique is that it would encourage clearcutting since less mature trees can be inputs for mass laminated

---

12   Robbins, "As Mass Timber," April 9, 2019.

timber. Solving this issue would require additional forestry management and oversight, which we would want anyway. The other limitation is the relatively small amount of carbon this wood would store. There are only so many buildings, and all of them have a set lifespan.

The wood used in construction would eventually be disposed of when buildings are demolished. That means we wouldn't permanently remove that carbon from circulation, which puts us on the wrong side of our need for permanent solutions. At best, we would reach a new steady state where a set quantity of carbon is constantly cycled in and out of the atmosphere, making the overall carbon dioxide levels somewhat lower than present. It would also reduce the demand for cement, which can't be fully decarbonized by the nature of the material, helping keep more carbon dioxide from entering the atmosphere that needs to be sequestered. More wood construction wouldn't make the largest impact, but it could be some low-hanging fruit that helps.

SACRIFICE: DISPOSABLE CONSUMERISM

Continuing to emit carbon dioxide will only make our task of taking it out of the atmosphere harder. That's why we want to decarbonize the power grid first, but there are ways we can help accelerate the process without building more energy infrastructure. Most fossil fuel expenditures are used to feed the production and transportation of goods for us to consume. We can, therefore, reduce the amount of electric power we have to replace by simply consuming fewer things. That may be easier said than done in a society that depends on consumption for its economy to function.

It is a completely natural phenomenon for demand and growth to eventually plateau. Barring outside intervention, it happens with any product when you saturate the market. You can only overcome this law by selling replacements once the original item breaks or when the buyer wants to upgrade. These factors combine to give us the horribly inefficient system we have, where consumer products are designed to have short lifespans and built-in obsolescence.[13] Whether it's a smartphone that refuses to upgrade or fast fashion clothing that quickly falls apart, we are constantly incentivized to continue consuming new things when we shouldn't have to.[14]

A straightforward solution is to require manufacturers to only produce long-lasting goods. The longer a product goes before breaking, the fewer have to be made to meet demand, and energy is conserved. The corollary to changing to that mode of consumption is it requires more robust and expensive items. Done poorly, this could create a new burden on consumers, especially for poorer folks who can't accommodate the added up-front costs. Done properly, it will eventually pay dividends since consumers won't have to continually purchase things that fall apart.[15]

We can also reduce wasteful consumption by reviving a different approach to broken things. You used to be able to take items like a broken radio or television to a repair shop. My father actually started his teaching career with classes on how to repair electronics, keeping those items in circulation a little while longer. My dad ultimately switched to teaching computer networking when I was a kid, but not because he

---

13　While this article draws the opposite conclusion, it provides a history of the practice: Hadhazy, "Here's the Truth," June 12, 2016.

14　McFall-Johnsen, "The Fashion Industry," October 21, 2019.

15　Terry Pratchett summarizes this concept in the novel "Men at Arms," excerpt available here: Huffman, "Boots Theory," December 11, 2019.

was tired of electronics. He had to shift topics because modern devices were no longer worth it to repair.

The repair industry fell by the wayside once we started offshoring our manufacturing sector in exchange for cheaper imported goods. It doesn't make sense to pay someone to fix a microwave oven when you can buy a new one for fifty bucks. That is, assuming you could even have it repaired in the first place. A number of electronics manufacturers actively discourage users from repairing their products. Some go to extremes to prevent you from breaking their monopoly on the parts and labor required for something as simple as fixing a broken screen or replacing a battery.[16] This does not need to be how we do business. We should better protect a user's right to repair their devices and encourage designs that make repairing easier.

Every device will eventually reach its end of life. This is also an issue for our new energy infrastructure. Solar panels and wind turbine blades have a limited useful lifespan, after which they need to be disposed of. As a result, we need to build for recyclability as well. We can make choices during the design process, making renewable energy generators easier to disassemble and recover the raw materials contained within them.[17] If we mandate items be designed for recycling, we can make use of our existing resources almost indefinitely instead of having to mine and extract additional inputs.

Activities like encouraging durability, repairability, and recyclability will need to have some forcing function driving their adoption. We can safely assume the overconsumption problem won't be solved if left to the market. It's already

---

16 Goode, "Right-to Repair," November 27, 2019.

17 De Clercq, "Europe's First," June 25, 2018.

decided this is the optimum way to maximize profits. That's essentially the same problem with fossil fuels. A straightforward way of ameliorating this problem is to tax manufacturers more heavily on cheaply made and quickly disposable products based on how quickly they will wear out. It would raise their prices and disincentivize consumption while also increasing demand for the less-taxed, higher quality options. Going one step further and additionally subsidizing the better alternatives would guarantee lower overall consumption while maintaining the potential for a high standard of living.

There would be trade-offs in switching to a less consumptive economy, foremost among them being convenience. If you need a new article of clothing for a single event, for example, you don't want to have to dump a lot of money into it. Therein lies one of the problems we need to overcome, the performative consumption that drives a lot of our behavior. It isn't something we can legislate, but a set of rules we can collectively decide. We need to shift our thinking around objects from one of aesthetics to one of utility. A product may no longer be *in style*, but as long as it still performs the function you need, we should not be so eager to throw it out. We just need to be willing to sacrifice our impulsive decision-making a bit, preferably before the decision is made for us.

CHAPTER 12

THE SKY

There comes a time in any child's life when they learn the word *why*. You will know it happens because that word will incessantly fall from their lips. Not only will any one thing become the subject of why, but it will continue down a never-ending string of whys until you, the adult answering the question, struggle to further contemplate the fabric of reality. If you're a lucky child, like I was, there will be an adult in your life who humors your whys because they are both nice and actually knowledgeable about enough things to provide a satisfactory response.

Perhaps one of the more common whys follows the observation that the sky is blue, because there is no readily apparent reason for this fact of nature. It is only natural to ask why. Unfortunately for the young question asker, comprehending the full explanation requires an awareness that light is a wave and different colors of light behave differently. In short, light scatters off particles in the air, and blue light scatters more than red or green light, so the sky is blue.[1] Whether or not

---

[1] The precise phenomenon is Rayleigh Scattering. Peshin, "Why Is the Sky Blue?" updated April 10, 2019.

that satisfies the child will depend on them and the authority of your delivery.

The concept behind the sky's blue appearance, that light can be manipulated by the atmosphere, could help us in our quest to return the climate to a prewarming state. So far, in this part, we've discussed methods of removing carbon dioxide, but that is only half of the equation. The heat it traps ultimately comes from the sun. If we could alter that energy input, the carbon dioxide would have less heat to trap, and climate change would reverse. We do have options for doing that, namely by adding specific chemicals into the atmosphere to reflect sunlight back into space.

Our solar blocking scheme would rely on adding sulfur to the air in a controlled way. In short, some form of aircraft spreads a stream of sulfur chemicals, such as sulfuric acid or hydrogen sulfide, into the upper atmosphere over a wide area. Those chemicals then agglomerate onto dust, and those aggregates (called aerosols) scatter incoming light back into space.[2] This effect essentially creates a solar mirror around the world. We would need millions of tons to alter the balance enough to make a dent, but that mass would certainly be less than the billions of tons of carbon we would otherwise have to remove. Sulfur chemicals are also plentiful thanks, ironically, to the waste generated by the oil and gas industry.[3]

While this intervention sounds radical, there is precedence for it having the desired climate effect. The same thing happens every time a volcano erupts and expels massive

---

2   An introduction on aerosols can be found at: NASA, "Aerosols," November 2, 2010.

3   Depending on the type of oil being refined, there can be massive yellow piles of sulfur kept on-site. For Example: G., "File:AlbertaSulfurAtVancouverBC.jpg," July 10, 2005.

amounts of sulfur. A great example was the 1815 eruption of Mount Tambura in Indonesia, which led to the year without a summer. Enough light was blocked that there were periods of freezing temperatures in August as far south as Virginia.[4] We certainly don't want to go that far, and we wouldn't because we can control how much sulfur we release.

There is not much hard data on the human-made version of this climate-mitigation approach because no one's done the experiments necessary to test its viability. Our requirement to only use proven technology raises the first barrier, which is unlikely to change any time soon. The scientific and political establishment generally gets heartburn when we start talking about large-scale geoengineering projects. Just like there is opposition to ocean fertilization, the uncertainties inherent with altering the atmosphere in such a drastic way makes people cautious.

The experience we have with volcanoes tells us the effects will wear off, lowering the risk somewhat. On the timescale of a year, the aerosols we add will fall out of the atmosphere. In case we do accidentally add too much and create another year without a summer, the effect won't be permanent. That safety stop also means we would have to continually add sulfur to the atmosphere to maintain the necessary cooling effect. We would only create a loop of resorting to the easy fix that doesn't solve the underlying problem.[5] Our requirement for permanent solutions thus discourages this approach as well.

A successful deployment of aerosols also risks encouraging inaction on the broader goals of the strategy. People

---

4   Appalachian Magazine, "200 Years Ago," May 20, 2016.

5   Futurama satirizes the absurdity of such a situation in the season four episode "Crimes of the Hot."

might become complacent about the need to decarbonize the power grid and sequester carbon when the problem becomes less acute thanks to a solar mirror. Less dramatic evidence of climate change will likely disincentivize action as attention is drawn elsewhere. However, since temperatures aren't the only issue caused by excess carbon in the atmosphere, such as ocean acidification, it also won't help the overall health of our planet. Much like carbon capture from fossil fuel plants, we can't afford to invest resources in a solution that risks encouraging the status quo.

With three strikes against it, any kind of climate engineering that relies on blocking light won't be part of our strategy. That includes literal mirrors in space that some have proposed since the downsides are the same regardless.[6] Our guiding policies force us to rely on ecosystem restoration and carbon sequestration for our strategy's needs.

SACRIFICE: AIR TRAVEL

Saying the year 2020 was defined by the coronavirus is an understatement. It left millions dead, destroyed the livelihoods of millions more, sabotaged a generation's education, and created a morose and dour mood regarding the future. Very few silver linings punctuated the daily stream of pandemic news. One of the only encouraging events was the reduction in air pollution during the early phases of quarantine.[7] Thanks to fewer cars and trucks on the road, there were fewer particulates and emissions clogging the sky. While hard to see, thanks to everything else going on with the

---

6 Kaufman, "Could Space Mirrors," August 8, 2012; Calma, "As a Last Resort," August 26, 2019.

7 Khoo, "Coronavirus Lockdown," April 8, 2020; Milman, "US Greenhouse Gas," January 12, 2021.

virus, it paints a picture of what a decarbonized future may look like. It provides evidence that nature is, in fact, resilient, and we can turn back the clock on the damage we've done.

Changes in transportation were some of the easiest to see during the pandemic. In addition to fewer cars, the reduction in air travel has been like night and day.[8] Thousands of fewer flights helped reduce emissions from aircrafts. Since air travel represents 3 percent of our problem, that reduction can help quite a bit. We will be replacing fossil-derived fuel with renewable, synthetic varieties, but building that new capacity is a big lift that can only get easier if we decrease the overall demand.

Reducing air miles is already part of some people's personal climate adaptation plan. The approach has a modest number of followers thanks to pushes starting in Europe. There is a word in Swedish, *flygskam*, that literally means flight-shame, and it describes the feeling one has when confronted with the carbon footprint of flying.[9] That is a sacrifice of convenience for the common good that is to be lauded. More people sacrificing their plans for vacations and travel in order to help repair the climate is unambiguously good. The limitation is it relies on personal choices instead of systemic change, and it is therefore unreliable.

Our politics and priorities will have to change substantially if we want to seriously cut back on air travel. It would mean returning to the era of highly regulated and infrequent flying before the 1980s.[10] Just like with steak, flying would

---

8   Petchenik, "Then and Now," April 7, 2020.

9   Kennedy, "I Quit Flying," November 29, 2019; Irfan, "Air Travel," November 30, 2019.

10 For a history of this policy change, see the discussion in: Appelbaum, *The Economists' Hour*, chapter six.

become infrequent and more special occasions. We would no longer board a plane on a whim to take a last-minute getaway, nor would we be able to take a short flight between neighboring cities. The world would be a little smaller, but it would start to be cooler.

Such a suggestion would lead to push back from many quarters, and not without reason. I myself travel by plane at least twice a year for the holidays because it's the only efficient means to get to my parents' and in-laws' houses in a reasonable length of time. Without flights, I would certainly see my family much less frequently, and that's a pretty big emotional ask for most people. The only way to avoid that disruption is if we simultaneously promote non-emitting alternatives that can do the same job as flying.

A better transportation system would have to include options for long-distance travel that can operate using renewable electricity. The transition to electric cars will help decarbonize our day-to-day travels, but that's not as viable for long distances, at least not comfortably or timely. Multiple 2,000-mile car trips per year are certainly not appealing to me. The only real alternative would be passenger trains, which can get much closer to the speed of air travel while being wholly powered by electricity.

One of the reasons the no-fly pledge has taken off more in Europe than the United States is because they already have better trains than us. I remember taking the TGV in France (literal translation: very fast train) from the Mediterranean coast to Paris in only a couple of hours. That time was more comfortably spent than on an airplane, with more space to stretch my legs and less dehumanizing security conditions. My group and I could relax and enjoy the experience, instead of being crammed like sardines into a small metal tube. Such a trip would not have been possible in the United States. Our infrastructure is stuck a century behind. You can't make the excuse the United States is simply too large for trains. The breadth of the European continent matches our own. Nor can you say such works are outside our capabilities. Our country once relied on the railroad for all long-distance transit, and it still does for freight.[11] It only comes down to a mismatch of priorities not unlike the problems we have with the fossil fuel industry.

Public policy has historically favored driving cars and building infrastructure for them. The Federal Aid Highway Act of 1956, as one example, marked a quarter trillion dollars in today's money for building highways. We have also avoided paying for the externalities of car travel by pushing those costs onto the environment and population at large. As a result, the subsidization of car travel only starved the rails of passengers, creating the vicious cycle of decreased investment, leaving our system on life support ever since. There is no technical reason it should take eight hours to go from DC to Boston by rail right now, but that's what happens when you don't spend money on better infrastructure.

Our goal for decarbonizing air travel means we need to invest in a new high-speed rail system, but there are a couple of barriers before us. We'd basically have to start from scratch since none of our existing infrastructures can handle the speeds required to compete with aircraft. Power distribution infrastructure will also have to be expanded to provide the lines with electricity. Not only will those investments require a lot of material resources, but also political capital to make it through the eminent domain proceedings required

---

11   Lee, "Watch American Passenger Rail," March 11, 2015.

to build on peoples' land. That could pose an issue if there isn't substantial support to make this transition.

The primary barrier will be cultural, as there will be a desire to maintain the current air travel status quo. Even in their fastest incarnations, trains will inevitably be slower. The resulting convenience is not something many people will so easily sacrifice. Our consumption habits and priorities would have to change to accommodate a more leisurely pace. That shift isn't necessarily a bad thing. Societies that don't have a stressful, efficiency focused, workaholic culture tend to be happier, so it wouldn't have to be too great a sacrifice overall. We just have to be willing to slow down a little bit.

PART THREE

SOCIETY

CHAPTER 13

THE MARKET

———

I am a 90s kid. All the cartoons, toys, music, and cultural ephemera are inextricably part of my sense of self. That's not always for the best, considering how earwormy the pop music of the time can be. I will never be able to forget the Macarena, no matter how hard I try. What is easy to forget through all the neon and grunge is the 90s followed the decades of the Cold War, a conflict over whether capitalism or communism would reign supreme. The collapse of the Soviet Union decisively ended that economic debate. The market won. Since then, the prevailing order has been to rely on private enterprise to guide our society.

It is undeniable markets and businesses are powerful societal institutions. Financial hubs move trillions of dollars every year to mobilize the labor and raw materials required to bring a capital investment to fruition. These are things that will need to be accomplished for our strategy to work. Resources will not spontaneously configure themselves into solar panels and wind turbines just because we want them to. As a result, we have to consider how best to use the existing forces and institutions that dictate commerce and decision-making.

We also have to acknowledge the capitalist organizations have their own goals and priorities that do not necessarily align with the greater good sought by the strategy. They will always make decisions to maximize their financial return as the paramount priority. We cannot assume business interests will spontaneously take action on climate change just because it is necessary. If they would, we likely wouldn't be in our present predicament. We need to look to history when defining our approach to business, and there is an undeniable pattern showing what we can expect from the market if left to its own devices.

TRUSTWORTHINESS

I completed a large milestone while I was writing this book. My wife and I found, bought, and moved into a house after renting for over a decade. It makes sense financially and provides the stability needed to start putting down roots. Recognizing that fact is simple, but becoming a homeowner is easier said than done. There are so many things to consider. You've got to look at the roof, HVAC, finishings, appliances, school district, walkability, parking, commuting, ad infinitum. Another, less obvious, thing to look out for is when the house was built. If it predates 1978, there's a decent chance there is lead paint somewhere. You always need to make sure the lead is properly remediated or removed. Otherwise, you risk your family's health. Whether it's flaked off chips kids eat or dust in the ventilation system, exposure to lead paint leads to impaired mental ability and development.[1]

The funny thing is that we've always known it was dangerous. Ancient histories provide accounts of lead miner's

---

1   Drum, "Lead," January/February 2013.

poor health, and the leaded wine and lead pipes used by the Romans certainly did them no favors. It then may seem odd that one would choose to use lead in myriad products even within living memory, but that's what the market forces incentivized. The story of leaded gasoline provides a complete example of how relying on private business to affect positive change is a dangerous choice.

LEAD POISONING

Early automobiles regularly suffered from knocking, that is, misfiring within the engine. Knocking causes poor performance, so it was a primary target for innovation. Early research in both industry and the government had shown ethanol was an effective anti-knocking additive to gasoline and as a fuel in its own right.[2] It was better than gasoline since it could create a higher compression ratio and more powerful engines. The only downside was ethanol can be produced by anyone with access to grain and yeast, making it unpatentable.

The proposition of using ethanol for fuel was not amenable to existing business interests based on oil. The petrochemical industry would get cut out of a large market, and chemical companies were disinclined to invest in a supply chain they can't fully control. Enter tetraethyl lead, a horribly poisonous chemical that solves both problems for both interest groups. When added to gasoline, it serves as an anti-knocking agent, while its formulation was patentable and required dedicated manufacturing capacity. This resulted in the preservation of the existing system.

---

2   Kitman, "The Secret History of Lead," March 2, 2000.

The initial implementation was not without pushback. A string of poisonings and deaths at the production plants engendered increased scrutiny and warnings about the public health hazard of leaded gasoline. In response, the affected companies resorted to lying about the problem and covering up the evidence. Thomas Midgley Jr., the inventor, went so far as to rub the fluid on his skin and breath in the fumes in front of the press to show it was safe. What wasn't reported was the extended convalescence he required to recover from the resulting lead poisoning. To help avoid the stigma, the word lead was also never used, if at all possible. The chemical became known as "ethyl," and the subsidiary producing it was renamed the Ethyl Gasoline Corporation.

Another prong of the lead defense strategy relied on the government. General Motors turned to a government agency, The US Bureau of Mines, to conduct a study on the safety of leaded gasoline. Unfortunately, that agency was under regulatory capture at the time, meaning they were essentially working on behalf of the industries they were meant to regulate. As a result, the report concluded in the industry's favor. The conclusions about the safety of leaded gas were picked up by business-friendly press, helping to provide a counter narrative to state and local governments that were trying to regulate it.[3]

Certain government officials then became some of the most ardent supports of leaded gasoline, despite the earlier research into ethanol. The sitting Surgeon General, for example, promoted its use abroad, convincing the United Kingdom to adopt leaded gasoline despite the findings of their own scientists. The Federal Trade Commission banned

---

3   The New York Times, "No Peril to Public," November 1, 1924.

competitors from mentioning the health impacts of lead. The formation of a lobbying group, the Lead Industries Association, entrenched this interest in the policy making sphere. All these actions combined ensured the predominance of leaded gasoline for decades.

The continued accumulation of lead in the environment may have escaped notice were it not for scientific advancements in geology. A major goal of the field since its inception was to determine the age of the Earth. It took the discovery of radioactive decay before it became possible to make an accurate estimate of that figure. Measuring radioactivity allows geologists to compute the ratio of an element like uranium to its decay products, which reveals the age of a certain sample. Clair Patterson, one of the scientists dedicated to this task, ran into a problem with this technique. Lead is a decay product, and extra background lead makes measurements incredibly difficult. He had to create exhaustively clean conditions thanks to the thousand-fold increase in the environmental lead we had created by burning leaded gasoline.

Finding such quantities of lead in the environment is distressing, especially for the industrialists creating the problem. That kind of information getting out would certainly cause problems for their business model's future viability, and they feared a public backlash. As a result, they first tried to bribe Dr. Patterson into silence. After he refused, they went after his livelihood, causing Dr. Patterson to lose grants and pressured his university to fire him. Thankfully, he resisted those attempts to silence the truth as well, and the information gained public attention. Nothing says innocence like threatening the people testifying against you.

The days of lead were numbered once the federal government started acting in the public interest. Part of the response was ancillary. The new catalytic converters required by law to clean-up smog are poisoned by lead, making leaded gasoline nonviable anyway. The Environmental Protection Agency began the phase out of lead in the 1970s, which saw an immediate court challenge. The lead industry lost on appeal, and the phase out was able to begin. Further attempts to slow the death of lead relied on appeals to preserve jobs and the economy. However, public opinion was against them by that point, and not even the Reagan administration was able to roll back the regulations. Lead was fully outdated by the 1990s, and the environment has become cleaner for it.

The story of lead is a prototypical example of how businesses respond when it is revealed they manufacture a dangerous product. There was preexisting and subsequent knowledge confirming the danger of lead. Regardless, they covered-up that information, worked to prevent the government from taking action against the problem, and did their best to avoid any consequences for their actions. The lead industry did these things simply because selling tetraethyl lead was profitable. There are almost exact similarities between this story and how the fossil fuel industry has responded to climate change.

DENYING CLIMATE CHANGE

We've known chemicals like carbon dioxide trap heat within the atmosphere for a long time. There are scientific articles on the greenhouse effect as far back as the 1800s.[4] We also can't make the excuse it was an esoteric discovery since newspaper articles from the early 1900s are clear in attributing a warming climate to carbon dioxide released from burning

---

4   Arrhenius, "On the Influence," April 1896.

fossil fuels.[5] Just like the health impacts of lead, we knew this was going to be a problem. The people at the time were only mistaken in assuming it would take several hundred years longer to become an issue than it has in reality. The companies that produced fossil fuels certainly knew about the effects of carbon dioxide emissions as well. Their own internal assessments prove it well enough, which even anticipate the worst impacts of climate change.[6] That didn't stop them from obfuscating the problem.[7] They put up a smokescreen for decades, ranging from spreading misinformation about the state of the science to making threatening commercials about how everyone would lose their job without fossil fuels.[8] This is from the exact same playbook as the public relations used to sell lead to the public.

The greatest efforts were aimed to prevent any kind of coordinated public response. The same tactic of obfuscating the truth continues to be employed. Companies dump hundreds of millions of dollars to impact the outcome of initiatives that would limit fossil fuel exploration.[9] The industry also throws money at elected officials via campaign contributions, often to both sides. Democrats and Republicans are on

5   Rodney and Otamatea Times, "Coal Consumption Affecting Climate," August 14, 1912.

6   Watts et al. "Half a Century," October 9, 2019.

7   Hall, "Exxon Knew," October 26, 2015.

8   For a timeline of events for one company's (Exxon) contributions to this process, see: Greenpeace, "Exxon's Climate Denial History," accessed October 6, 2020.

9   Aronoff, "The Fossil Fuel Industry," November 7, 2018.

the receiving end of this money.[10] So much corporate money floating around only disincentivizes officials from fully grappling with the reality of the situation and taking action.

Gaining political power has paid dividends for the fossil fuel industries. International agreements like the Kyoto Protocol are never ratified. Industry affiliated persons are appointed to lead regulatory agencies.[11] Federal lands continue to be open for oil and gas extraction.[12] Instead of investing in renewable technologies, we achieved energy independence through fracking.[13] Both parties support pipelines carrying oil and gas.[14]

The fossil fuel industry also wants to prevent itself from ever being held responsible, despite a growing public demand for consequences manifested through lawsuits.[15] While these legal battles haven't had much success to date, fossil fuel companies are concerned enough to be pursuing legal immunity.[16] In exchange for accepting a carbon tax, they would never be held responsible for the damage they've done nor be forced to sacrifice their former and future profits for the sake of the public good.

---

10 To see how much money your elected officials have received from fossil fuel interests, browse: OpenSecrets.org, "Politicians & Elections," accessed December 23, 2020.

11 Roberts, "Meet the Fossil Fuel," June 14, 2017.

12 To show this is a bipartisan problem, consider how the Obama Administration only put-up minimal barriers to this activity: Colman, "Democrats Split," September 4, 2019.

13 Zou, "How Washington Unleashed," October 16, 2018.

14 Martin, "Why are Democratic Governors," November 22, 2019.

15 Marlon et al. "Majority of Americans," June 19, 2019. For example: Rust, "California Communities Suing," February 5, 2020.

16 Milman, "Microsoft Joins," May 2, 2019.

The pattern with business is always the same. Whether it's lead, climate change, tobacco, asbestos, persistent fluorinated chemicals, or any other hazard, the playbook is to obfuscate the truth, exercise political power, and escape liability.[17] This situation is both logical and predictable. When profit is the only motivating factor for action, people will take action to maximize profit. Maintaining the status quo is always more profitable because it allows you to extract more wealth from the investments you've already made, regardless of the impact on public health.

Extracting, refining, and distributing fossil fuels is a very capital-intensive activity. Companies need a lot of equipment and resources invested before they can begin operations. Once those investments are made, not uncommonly costing billions of dollars, the only way to maximize profitability is to run them as long as possible. This is why any new investment in fossil fuel production has the expected lifetime of decades. Every stoppage or delay cuts into your ability to make a profit. Hence, an owner of any part of the fossil fuel supply chain has an overriding incentive to keep their capital running.

That desire is completely antithetical to taking action on climate change. There will continue to be unanimous pushback from the sector against renewables because it is more profitable to work as a bloc to protect existing capital than invest in innovation or new modes of operation. Their natural impulse to protect their capital is the entire reason we need a drastic strategy in the first place. If they had not obfuscated the situation for decades, we could have had a much easier transition. If they had not exerted undue political control, the transition would not have been controversial.

---

17   For more examples, see: Michaels, *The Triumph of Doubt.*

If they had done the right thing, we wouldn't be facing oblivion. Renewables will not have the resources necessary to overcome the inertia and power of fossil fuel interests, at least not without help.

DIVESTMENT

Not every market actor is irrational about climate change. A growing number of people in finance recognize the danger and have become part of a movement to move their investments away from fossil fuel extraction and consumption.[18] The goal of divesting from fossil fuels is to starve those industries of the funding they need to find and exploit new resources. Finding and extracting oil and gas requires billions of dollars, making this an acute pressure point. Ideally, that divested money will also be used to support renewable projects.

The fossil fuel divestment movement has had notable success over the past decade. Enough groups have committed to altering their portfolios that over eleven trillion dollars in assets are now walled off.[19] For reference, the annual gross domestic product of the United States is about twenty trillion dollars. If that value continues to increase and enough money is made unavailable, fossil fuel companies will have no choice but to substantially alter their business model. People, working collectively through the market, will dictate the practices of these businesses by making it unprofitable to continue the status quo. Reaching that tipping point may be

---

18   For example, consider the activist non-profit: 350.org, "About 350," accessed August 23, 2020.

19   Tyler-Davies, "A New Fossil Free Milestone," September 8, 2019.

tricky, as the movement will first need to overcome several unavoidable hurdles.

The overriding problem is one of participation. Divestment will only work if enough people are on board such that any remaining holdouts are unable to support the fossil fuel industry. That won't be easy to achieve, as some institutions have already said they will not divest. Harvard University is a prominent example. Despite claims of taking climate change seriously, it has categorically refused to divest from fossil fuels, even in the face of lawsuits.[20] In the words of Harvard President Drew Faust:

> While I share their [students advocating divestment] belief in the importance of addressing climate change, I do not believe, nor do my colleagues on the Corporation, that university divestment from the fossil fuel industry is warranted or wise.[21]

Similarly, some pension funds are hesitant to alter course so long as fossil fuels provide good returns.[22] Divestment also is unlikely to appeal to countries with state owned or supported enterprises, which will undercut their own primary revenue streams. Norway's Sovereign Wealth Fund,

---

20 Mufson, "Harvard Says," July 7, 2019. The lawsuit filed by Harvard students to force the university to divest was dismissed: Delwiche and Klein, "Judge Dismisses," March 24, 2015.

21 Fuast, "Fossil Fuel Divestment Statement," October 3, 2013.

22 Keidan and Cohn, "British Pension Schemes," January 20, 2020. However, some pension funds do participate in divestment: Collinson and Ambrose, "UK's Biggest Pension Fund," July 29, 2020.

for example, is reticent to fully remove fossil fuels from its portfolio.[23]

An insufficient, partial divestment without these players would likely even be counterproductive. Divested shares in a fossil fuel company don't just disappear. They are sold to other buyers who still want to be involved with this industry. As divestment grows, these shares will concentrate in the hands of fewer people. More shares allow greater leverage over the companies by the remaining investors, who now have an increased incentive to continue status quo operations. Similarly, fewer available lenders mean those that remain will be able to extract more favorable terms, increasing their own profitability. Unless everyone is forced to divest, there will remain opportunities for profit by those who either don't accept or don't care about the reality of climate change.

Conversely, a glut of divestment could also devalue these companies and potentially make them less attractive to the market. Many people selling all at once will deflate prices and, with a lower market capitalization, it may make it harder to attract new investors and lenders. While that will help, it doesn't affect the resources already committed. Wiping out the stock value of a company on paper does nothing to the infrastructure that's built to extract and use fossil fuels. Real capital will continue to exist and emit carbon so long as it is profitable to do so.

The second premise of divestment is that those resources will move to renewable projects. However, funds are always looking to maximize their returns, which doesn't necessarily align with the transition we need. Other sectors of the economy could be more profitable and absorb the divested

23   BBC News, "Norway's," March 8, 2019.

resources instead of renewables. There is also no guarantee that any investments in renewables will be coordinated to provide the comprehensive transition we need. So long as profit is the overriding concern, the necessary transition cannot be guaranteed.

Divestment does not appear to be able to deliver what our strategy requires. There are too many uncertainties, and we can't rely on things unproven to work. The impetus for divestment is laudable. It allows people to take collective action using the system available to them. Unfortunately, when the system only rewards actions that increase individual profit, it will hamper collective action.

RETOOLING MARKETS

Private industry and the market will continue to exist in the future, meaning it would behoove us to find some way of putting them to use. This is the thinking behind tweaking the financial incentives to encourage decarbonization and investment in renewables. Such incentives would alter the financial calculus by making it more profitable to transition from fossil fuels. Essentially, we would mold the power of profit-seeking to our benefit.

One way we could accomplish that is by altering prices, specifically the price of emitted carbon. This framework would charge an emitter some amount for the carbon dioxide they release into the atmosphere. When the price of emission exceeds the cost of investing in decarbonization, we create an incentive for companies to transition and maximize their revenue. The policy lever is simple since we can either dial-up or dial-down the price of carbon to engender change at the pace we desire.

This approach is often favored by industry since it leaves the structure of the market intact.[24] Even though this is a market-oriented solution, it does have to come from the government, as there are no other forces in society that can create such a mandate. So much of the energy sector is either a natural monopoly or oligopoly that individual consumer choice is not strong enough. Only the collective action of consumers through the government is strong enough. There are two main mechanisms the government can use for creating this new system: cap-and-trade and direct carbon taxes.

CAP-AND-TRADE

The oldest of the market-oriented climate change solutions is the cap-and-trade framework. The idea is that you can set limits for how much carbon dioxide a given company can emit (cap). If they emit less than their quota, they can sell those emissions to another company (trade). That trading is done on an exchange, with companies buying and selling on an open market. Lowering the caps over time increases the value of unused quotas. Eventually, the profit gained from selling emissions credits will exceed the cost of decarbonizing operations, giving companies the incentive to transition organically. This framework has a logic to it and is market-oriented.

The best example we have of a complete program is the one that exists in the European Union (EU). They've had this policy in place since the 1990s. The statistics the EU quotes seem very promising, with continually decreasing

---

24 For example: World Resources Institute, "Leading U.S. Businesses," May 15, 2019; Yoder, "Republicans Are Backing," June 21, 2018.

carbon emissions year-over-year.[25] This system has reportedly worked thus far by targeting the emitters that are the cheapest to decarbonize.[26] One would expect that at first, but cuts will become increasingly painful for companies. There's no data proving those cuts would continue to work at the same rate in the future. Natural gas is supported in certain policy circles since its abundance has allowed the closure of coal-fired power plants, because the latter emit more carbon dioxide per unit of energy produced. You can achieve short-term profits by switching to gas under a cap-and-trade system, but you've done nothing to excise fossil fuels from your energy infrastructure. Some EU countries, like Germany, have certainly worked to implement renewables while taking coal offline. However, the consumption trend for natural gas combined with continued investment in gas infrastructure makes the long-term success of this approach dubious.[27]

There will also be enforcement concerns. Every carbon-emitting source will need to be monitored and accounted for. That is an issue because we'd be creating a system where emitters have a natural incentive to underreport to increase revenues or avoid new investments. Making sure they don't will require a massive expansion in government auditing capacity, subject to budgetary constraints that will likely

25   European Commission, "EU Emissions Trading System," accessed September 29, 2020.

26   Climate Policy Info Hub, "The EU Emissions Trading System," accessed September 29, 2020.

27   Meredith, "A Contentious," October 31, 2019; The Economist Intelligence Unit, "Europe Coal Use," February 14, 2020; Sönnichsen, "Natural Gas Consumption," June 23, 2020.

impede the mission.[28] The penalties for violations will also have to be sufficiently high to discourage bad behavior, much more so than the typical fines currently levied for similar violations.[29]

A cap-and-trade regime also introduces perverse incentives that, by their nature, would impede progress. Central to this framework is the market for trading emissions. There is no reason why that market, left to its own devices, wouldn't be just as susceptible to speculation, bubbles, and malfeasance as any other exchange. There would be new kinds of futures and derivatives requiring just as much oversight as other financial instruments. Even if that weren't the case, cap-and-trade creates a new class of specialized financiers whose profits depend on the new market. If everything goes to plan, the trading will eventually stop as we complete decarbonization. When the market goes away, so do the returns they create, and those who profit from them will have an incentive to oppose our ultimate goals.

There is also the issue that cap-and-trade markets are downstream of and reactive to larger economic forces. Something like a recession will set back the entire operation. Less economic activity naturally leads to fewer emissions. Fewer emissions will depress their market price, so there is less incentive for companies to decarbonize. These events happen every ten years, and the one in 2008 undermined progress

---

28 If the IRS is any indication: Kiel and Eisinger, "How the IRS Was Gutted," December 11, 2018.

29 Lund and Sarin, "Corporate Crime," March 18, 2020; Henning, "Guilty Pleas," May 20, 2015. For example, securities fines only approached $5 billion in 2020 across several hundred cases: Michaels, "Wall Street Fines," November 2, 2020.

in the EU.[30] We need a program capable of consistent and steady progress, which is not a feature that these markets can currently provide.

CARBON TAXES

A cousin to cap-and-trade that avoids some added complexity is a more direct tax on emitted carbon dioxide. Instead of worrying about ever-changing financial instruments, you simply assess a tax at the point of emission. Every year a natural gas power plant will receive a bill for how much it burns, a cement producer for how much it releases, and so forth. The result would be to internalize the externalities of climate change. The cost is then passed down the supply chain, motivating decreased or reduced consumption of high-emission items.

Consider cars. Much of a vehicle's carbon footprint comes from manufacturing, including making the steel and aluminum for its body and the electricity powering the assembly line. A manufacturer that foregoes decarbonization would have the added cost of the carbon tax, driving up prices for consumers. A manufacturer that can use lower-carbon suppliers would be able to offer a more competitive product. Or they could charge the same price and pocket the difference.

Using prices to change behavior is fine in some cases. Alcohol and cigarettes aren't essential, so you're not driving people to destitution by taxing them. It's different for things like food, electricity, and fuel. Your needs for each won't change based on the presence of a new tax. The inherent weakness of a carbon tax is that one way or another, the average person will be paying the price. It will affect the poorest

---

30   Grose, "Europe's Carbon Market Crisis," April 20, 2013.

most severely. If you can't afford as much food, you will go hungry; as much fuel, you can't get to work; as much electricity, you can't heat your home. Poor people can't change their lifestyle like the upper class, the highest per capita emitters, because they're already on the margins of viability.

One method of cushioning a carbon tax is to provide the money back to the general population at the end of the year in the form of a dividend. That would make it a net-neutral tax for the populace, incentivizing behavior without inflicting so much pain. A model for such an approach is the Alaskan oil dividend, where a portion of the state's oil revenues are distributed equally among the citizens.[31] However, this kind of scheme won't change the day-to-day reality. A check at the end of the year won't help someone who can't buy groceries today.

Another downside to a carbon tax is the added risk of offshoring manufacturing. Businesses have no compunctions about leaving the country because of labor costs, and there is no reason this situation would be any different. Losing manufacturing capacity this way means less political support from people who lose jobs and more emissions from shipping. Avoiding that situation means tariffs would have to be part of the equation, as has been proposed in Europe.[32] Implementing them would require a lot of work and political capital for an impermanent policy, which might be better spent elsewhere.

31   For more information on Alaska's system, see: AOGA, "Permanent Fund Dividend," accessed August 22, 2020; DeMarban, "This Year's," September 28, 2019.

32   Colman, "Europe Threatens," December 13, 2019.

MARKET WRAP-UP

Cap-and-trade and carbon taxes are the only two policy options for climate change solutions that largely leave the solution to the free market. There are myriad variations on each that will change how decarbonization is incentivized, but the overall templates will be the same. And neither will serve our overall goals efficiently.

The fundamental problem is we will have to build an impermanent bureaucracy and enforcement system. All of that time, labor, and resources used to tinker with the trajectory of markets and personal consumption takes away from what could otherwise be applied to a coherent strategy. If the goal is to fully decarbonize, all those jobs will also go away once the transition is complete. There would be no need for either system once climate change is mitigated. Rather than spend all that temporary effort on tangential progress, we would be better served by action that directly solves the problem.

The second major issue is it is a passive system we can't directly control. Prices may cause some general shift in energy usage, but we won't be able to cause change to happen in a coherent and coordinated way. Just as with divestment, many individual actors working at random will not necessarily lead to an efficient transition. Building infrastructure on a continental scale will require careful planning that many independent market players will be unable to work toward effectively.

The market is one of the most powerful forces in our modern society, yet it is ill-equipped to solving climate change. Left to their own devices, fossil fuel-aligned businesses would continue the status quo. Their entire history indicates they will use every tool at their disposal to block a renewable transition. Divestment may have some effect, but its success is uncertain because it relies on collective action in a system that incentivizes private gain. Both carbon taxes and cap-and-trade exemplify the risks of trying to use random actors to achieve an intricate and complex project. Thus, we cannot rely on any of the market-oriented mechanisms to achieve our goals.

The main impediment to the strategy will be the people and organizations who benefit from our current mode of operation. The options above are their preferred choices because they leave these organizations with the most flexibility and the most power. Attempting anything else will be met by increased resistance. We need to approach this strategy with the full knowledge that what it requires will not be well-received in all quarters because it will threaten the short-term profits of powerful groups.

The pursuit of private profits means there is an inescapable incentive not to fix problems if it would be financially disadvantageous. This does not necessarily align with the perspective that market actors behave in rational self-interest. After all, there is no greater threat to long-term profits than the collapse of civilization. The issue is not with any individual, despite what their moral center may dictate, but what the system they work in incentivizes. The system only rewards those who maximize profits. It is the only way to acquire more power, resources, and influence in this economic system. It means never admitting the status quo is causing harm and resisting unprofitable changes. The only conclusion is the market won't help us respond to climate change.

SACRIFICE: DEVOTION TO GROWTH

Our society depends on many different numbers and values to quantify our economy's status, with few as important as the gross domestic product (GDP). This figure adds together the totality of the country's economic activity, all the wages, sales, and trades when money changes hands. The desire to maximize GDP undergirds much of modern economics, where actions are judged by their ability to increase this value. We certainly hang on to its changes with bated breath. Its changes can determine political fortunes of elected officials, such as in 1992 when a momentary hit to GDP cost George H.W. Bush reelection.

The overriding principle has always been to make GDP bigger, so the economy is always growing, and, in theory, people are doing better. The commonly applied analogy is a rising tide lifts all boats, with increased productivity increasing everyone's standard of living. So long as the water continues rising, we'll all be better off in the long run, regardless of individual circumstances. A continually rising GDP has been the overall economic goal. However, there is only so much water in the ocean.

The economy fundamentally relies on energy. Energy lets you perform more labor, the fundamental origin of value in an economy, within the same amount of time. Every small advance in energy extraction, from simple tools to wind and water mills to electricity, is responsible for the greater access to resources and higher standards of living human civilizations have achieved. The energy-dense and plentiful fossil fuels beneath our feet derived our current level of material wealth. Yet, those resources are inherently limited. Only so much coal, oil, and gas exist and continuing to burn them will irrevocably deplete the supply. Even if climate change wasn't driving us to keep fossil fuels in the ground, we wouldn't be able to perpetually maintain and improve our standard of living in an economy based on fossil fuels.

The fundamental problem with tying your economic system to the concept of ever-increasing growth is it is destined to fail. Even renewable energy has its limits. As large as it is, the Earth can only accommodate so many solar panels before they completely cover the surface. Growth in one area is not independent of everything else because the effort of applying resources to make something means they cannot be applied elsewhere. Every acre of solar panels is land unusable for another critical purpose like agriculture.

On a single planet with finite resources, we must ultimately reach a balance between competing needs. Any natural system will reach an equilibrium steady state in the long-term. Ironically, the present emphasis on growth contributes to a vicious cycle that undermines itself. We're already seeing this in some quarters. The ability to increase profits has relied on stagnant wages and high debt over the past forty years. This arrangement depresses the material conditions of younger generations, lowering population growth, reducing their ability to consume, and shrinking the economy.[33] Thus, a system bent on maximum financial extraction will, eventually, burn itself out. The only alternative is to purposefully create a steady state economy designed to provide indefinite stability.

The only sustainable option is to decrease our consumption in aggregate and reverse our overall growth. A

33   Friedman, "Student Loan Debt," February 3, 2020; Gould, "State of Working America Wages," February 20, 2020; U.S. Census Bureau, "2019 U.S. Population Estimates," December 30, 2019; Nova, "Why Millennials May Shrug," updated March 11, 2020.

new model of running the economy would instead focus on meeting societal needs. It would free us to start making choices that work toward stability and combating climate change. The state of Kerala, India, for example, has spent the past half-century implementing policies designed to meet the needs of everyone within the polity.[34] The result has been positive development indicators in terms of education and healthcare. The only price was accepting a slightly slower pace of overall development.

The major barrier to creating a more responsible economic system is some people have a lot to lose by the switch. Making a shift to a more sustainable economy would require a significant number of people willing to sacrifice the need to accumulate more. As a global society, we would have to decide that living with a quality but constrained standard of living is preferable to burning out.

---

34 Javed, "Lessons from Kerala," May 18, 2020.

CHAPTER 14

THE LEGISLATURE

———

My grandparents were part of the generation that grew up during the Great Depression. Instead of the prosperity of the 1990s, they grew up in a time of deprivation and hardship, and the mindset created by that experience followed them throughout their entire lives. One of my grandmothers had the habit of washing and reusing Ziplock bags, something anyone my age would discard without a second thought. Such were the desperate conditions of the Depression that even trash was forever marked as something of potential value, even during the post-war boom following it.

There were two primary contributing factors to the end of the Great Depression. The New Deal programs put people to work and built guardrails within the system to prevent future collapses. It worked to a point, but the New Deal began to stagnate until the attack on Pearl Harbor. The country's mass mobilization for the Second World War brought jobs back to every part of the country, and education funding for returning veterans built a base for post-war stability.

None of that would have happened if responding to the Depression was left in the hands of the private sector. The only institution that was able to respond to the dual crises of economic collapse and war was the federal government. Nothing else can marshal the resources necessary to prosecute a global war or immediately improve the material conditions of the general population. The same is true for our response to climate change. The government must take the lead for the transition on the scale we require.

Climate change is a universal problem that will affect everyone. Therefore, everyone needs to be involved in solving it through our representative democracy. Democracy is the keyword here. The alternative of abdicating responsibility to a smaller group of elites, those with means to unilaterally impact the political process, means they will make decisions that primarily benefit themselves instead of the general population. One would not imagine that an oligarch with a private bunker will have the same priorities as John Q. Public.[1] Thus, the government must be responsive to the needs of the people throughout the transition.

We also can't be bogged down in a debate over jurisdictional issues. Not everyone has the same conception about what the government should do and the proper limits of its power. One can have a reasonable discussion on the topic, and, in most instances, there can be a proper debate about the ideal separation of powers. However, the view that the government should be small and only concern itself with ensuring property rights must be discarded. The transition requires being able to access the resources and labor of an entire nation. We will never accomplish our goals by relying on myriad independent parties. We need a strong, centralized government response capable of responding to a global

---

1   For example: Stamp, "Billionaire Bunkers," August 7, 2019.

threat. We, the people, need to empower the government to do what is required.

The United States has not had a very strong response to climate change so far. We never ratified the Kyoto Protocol, and we've waffled in our approach to the Paris Agreement, both of which would have curtailed emissions. More importantly, there has never been a sustained and comprehensive national effort toward solving the problem. Some individual states have set out on their own, but those actions do not have the reach to fundamentally alter our trajectory. [2] Our situation must change if we are to have any hope of success.

APPROPRIATIONS

We have so far avoided the question of money when defining our strategy. While we cannot be worried about pennies as the world burns, it is also true that mobilizing the raw materials and labor we need will require money. That is its entire purpose. Our country is wealthy enough in population and resources to build the infrastructure we need. Whether or not enough arbitrary coins and pieces of paper exist does not change the fact we have the physical ability to do those things. Money is a tool and, like any tool, can be rationally wielded.

A national problem requires national solutions, which means the bulk of the work must be done by the United States Congress. Most parts of this strategy need to be included in a budget bill in some way. The first grouping is obvious—paying to upgrade all of the infrastructure for our grid transition. We will need appropriations for buying equipment like wind turbines, solar cells, and salts for thermal storage. Money will

---

2   For state-level examples: Zukowski, "These Red and Blue States," November 1, 2018.

need to be paid to the people who install and maintain the new power generation equipment. We will also need to buy access to land for renewable generator installations.

It is hard to put a price tag on replacing our infrastructure, but we can be confident it will be trillions of dollars. Tens of trillions of dollars, to be more accurate, the same order of magnitude as the yearly output of the entire country.[3] Still, that's a better monetary situation than if we did nothing.[4] A study by economists at Citi models decarbonization as cheaper than continuing to incur material losses from the effects of a changing climate.[5] As a result, it makes sense to pay for it now, upfront, rather than continue paying for damage indefinitely.

There will no doubt be opposition to any appropriations for the strategy because it involves government expenditure. Many of the political fights over the past decades around funding are instructive. The perennial pearl-clutching about the debt ceiling led to government shutdowns and legislation like the Budget Control Act of 2011.[6] The latter makes it much more difficult to appropriate the money we need and makes it easier to stymie increases in spending. Talk of new spending is now always punctuated by demands to cut programs elsewhere, usually somewhere politically painful.[7] This doesn't leave much room for the government to tackle pressing issues, but that may have been the intended purpose.

---

3   Holtz-Eakin, "How Much Will," June 11, 2019.

4   Levitan, "The Green New Deal," May 3, 2019.

5   Channell et al. "Energy Darwinism II," August 2015, 23.

6   Budget Control Act of 2011; Carney, "Senate GOP," May 23, 2019.

7   Both parties are guilty of this myopic thinking, for example: Dayen, "Nancy Pelosi," January 2, 2019.

Fights over spending caps and debt ceilings have primarily been a purely political tactic meant to put pressure on the party wielding executive power.[8] It makes the president look bad if the government shuts down or can't meet its obligations. If it were actually about lacking money or controlling inflation, we'd never have spent trillions of dollars on other priorities, like endless wars, quantitative easing, and tax cuts for the wealthy.[9] *Fiscal responsibility* will be wielded as a cudgel against the strategy by people who will use it as an excuse to protect the status quo for fossil fuel interests.

The only solution is not to play this game in the first place. Once we're debating spending, we'll be stuck forever in negotiations and budget-balancing that will only delay action. The strategy, therefore, won't be relying on offsets or byzantine pay-as-you-go schemes. It will use the constitutional power of Congress to appropriate funds. The Constitution is clear: "The validity of the public debt of the United States, authorized by law… shall not be questioned."[10] Wielding power like this is unorthodox, but climate change is an unorthodox situation. Congress must be bold in its use of appropriations to fully deal with the crisis.

NATIONALIZE THE GRID

Rebuilding the power grid will be a colossal undertaking, regardless of funding. The myriad interests and divisions

---

8 Thus far, it has primarily been the Republican Party that has used this tactic.

9 Almukhtar and Nordland, "What did the U.S. Get," December 9, 2019; Insinna, "Inside America's," August 21, 2019; Horton, "The Legacy," October 23, 2017; Hayes, "Why Didn't Quantitative Easing," updated December 10, 2020.

10 U.S. Constitution, 14th Amendment Section 4.

complicate it within the existing systems. There are actually three primary power grids throughout the continental United States and Canada, which are broken up into nine different markets, with hundreds of different companies operating within them managed by sixty-six different authorities.[11] Trying to create rapid, systemic change in such an environment will be difficult unless we simplify and consolidate the existing bureaucracy.

While all these entities are under the oversight of the US Federal Energy Regulatory Commission to ensure smooth operation, their investments are not so coordinated. This disunity is why states are able to set emissions goals and determine what kind of infrastructure utilities can build. In Texas, it allowed them to completely decouple most of their grid from other states, with some notable recent downsides.[12] To make things more efficient and coherent, it would better serve us if the federal government could determine the composition of all power-generating infrastructure. The simplest, cleanest, and most effective way to accomplish that is by nationalizing the US power grid.

Nationalization is the process by which the government takes control of an industry and operates it on behalf of the country. For the power grid, all those hundreds of individual companies and utilities would come under the umbrella of a single organization. That new institution would then have the authority to operate the grid in the public interest. In this case, that means both decarbonizing and providing energy as cheaply as possible.

---

11   USEIA, "U.S. Electric System," July 20, 2016; USEPA, "U.S. Electricity," accessed September 16, 2020.

12   Price, "'An Electrical Island,'" February 17, 2021.

We have strong evidence that creating truly public utilities will save people money in addition to meeting other priorities. Consider the Internet. Municipalities across the United States have created their own Internet service providers that perform the same functions as commercial players. These services are almost universally cheaper, sometimes by up to 50 percent, and offer higher average speeds than private companies.[13] As a result, each consumer benefits from Internet access being run in the public interest.[14] There is no reason why nationalized electricity generation would be different.

The reason a nationalized industry is capable of offering lower prices is that it doesn't have a profit motive. All else being equal, a government-run entity will perform the same function as a private business for less money because it doesn't need extra revenue to generate profit. Any attempt by a private business to be cheaper than the government has to come at the expense of service quality or wages and benefits. Private Internet service providers, for example, sometimes increase their profits by providing slower speeds at higher costs. Normally, such behavior would be tempered by market competition, but that is impossible for services that are natural monopolies.

A natural monopoly occurs when competition is logistically infeasible. It doesn't make sense to have multiple sets of competing roadways. Attempting to navigate such a system would be pointlessly inefficient. The only logical situation is one where the government takes responsibility for building

---

13 Brodkin, "City-Owned Internet Services," January 15, 2018.

14 Many states ban municipal Internet service due to lobbying by the industry. Chamberlain, "Municipal Broadband," May 13, 2020.

and maintaining roads for everyone's benefit. Electricity is a natural monopoly because it makes just as little sense to have duplicative power lines as it does roads.

Electricity prices are only presently constrained because of strict regulations on what utilities can charge. Nationalizing the power grid would only be going one step further by cutting out these middlemen. Instead of having to satisfy a small group of shareholders, power producers would only be responsive to the needs and concerns of the public. It would also allow us to make investments that wouldn't be profitable but are nonetheless required for our strategy. Expansion and recapitalization of the system would also be subject to public pressure through elected officials. If it is not run to satisfaction, those put in charge will risk losing their jobs, which is impossible when the private sector controls electricity.

Taking over a sector of the economy whole cloth certainly seems a radical proposition in a political environment that has advocated just the opposite for decades. That wasn't always the case. There is a precedent of the government taking over key industries when required. Certain manufacturers became nationalized during the world wars, and climate change is certainly no less a crisis.[15] Publicly owned electrical cooperatives also already present throughout the United States, whose existence proves the viability of this approach.[16] Legally, nationalizing the entire grid is covered by the commerce clause, as the grid transmits electricity across state lines.

---

15   Hanna, "A History of Nationalization," November 4, 2019.

16   For example, those represented by the American Public Power Association: APPA, "Public Power," accessed October 18, 2020.

Congress would provide the legal framework of a nationalized grid, but it wouldn't be the entity to manage it. The delegation of that power would go to an appropriate body within the executive branch. Ideally, to one of the existing departments that already executes money on this scale, so we don't have to spend time setting up a new agency. To update regulations governing grid upgrades, Congress will also need to update existing laws. Agencies involved in permitting, for example, would benefit from changing procedures so construction projects can move quickly. It will then be up to the president to use those authorities effectively.

SUBSIDIZING BEHAVIOR

Concepts like profit and revenue start to break down entirely for the second part of our strategy. Private enterprises cannot make money from drawing down atmospheric carbon unless they are paid to do so. Requirements for sequestration will also have no more impact than is required by law, as capturing carbon dioxide will always cut into revenues. Similarly, almost every example of massive ecosystem restoration has been done by a government.[17] If we're talking about rewilding areas the size of entire states, only the government can move the resources required.

We've discussed in chapter 9 how the government outright buying land for rewilding is not going to be very efficient. Instead, we can incentivize the myriad farmers and landowners to make the transition for us. Agriculture subsidies are already a substantial part of the federal budget, with some of the largest shares going toward crops that feed

---

17   For example: Khan, "As a 'Green Stimulus,'" April 28, 2020.

livestock and produce ethanol.[18] Since we want to decrease animal production anyway, we could shift those incentives to other crops, such as the legumes used to create alternative meats. Doing so would lower the overall cost of plant protein, make it price competitive, and encourage less meat consumption. With a simple redirection of funds, we would naturally change the incentives for land-use to be more in our favor.

There are powerful political forces that will have to be overcome to change agriculture policy in the United States. Thanks to the nature of the Senate, those who benefit from the current system have outsized power compared to their population. Consider Senator Chuck Grassley of Iowa, who, in his own words, stated, "I believe so strongly in ethanol as part of an all-of-the-above energy strategy."[19] Support for a renewable fuel seems incongruous for an otherwise conservative politician, but it makes sense given the state he represents. Much of his constituency are corn farmers. The ethanol subsidies bring money back to them, so supporting ethanol makes sense politically. Our strategy needs a way to tip the scales through similar means.

We will have to subsidize the farmers who currently grow corn for ethanol by paying them to rewild their land instead. Whether through direct payments, tax breaks, or some other financial instrument, they will have to be made whole for their lost income. Those payments would be best accompanied by a jobs program that employs people to do

---

18 USA Facts, "Federal Farm Subsidies," January 20, 2020. Ethanol indirectly subsidizes corn production through the market created by the Renewable Fuel Standard: Energy Policy Act of 2005.

19 Eller, "Grassley Pushes," November 20, 2019; Grassley, "Ethanol," May 11, 2018.

the rewilding and manage the forest. The resulting new sector will then have a vested interest in maintaining the new status quo.

A similar approach will be necessary in the fossil fuel-producing states that stand to lose from the transition. States like West Virginia, North Dakota, and Pennsylvania all have substantial populations employed in extractive industries that will go away during the transition. Just like ethanol, these activities are bolstered by government subsidies and tax credits.[20] We'll have to use the same approach, move those subsidies to something more productive while keeping people employed.

Coal is especially amendable to keeping people working. Mining that solid form of carbon is immensely destructive to the overall environment, leaving yawning gashes across the landscape and pollution flowing downstream.[21] There is plenty of work to do reclaiming the land and making it both better for human health and a carbon sink. We need only incentivize people's labor to make it happen.

Other sectors could help provide a safe harbor for displaced fossil fuel workers as well. We can create a boon for construction industries by subsidizing energy-efficient building upgrades. There are pilot programs that detail how this could work. The Property Assessed Clean Energy (PACE) programs are state-level financial mechanisms that remove

---

20 For more information on subsidies, see: EESI, "Fact Sheet: Fossil Fuel Subsidies," July 29, 2019.

21 Mountaintop removal is especially destructive: Appalachian Voices, "Mountaintop Removal 101," accessed September 16, 2020; Schiffman, "A Troubling Look," November 21, 2017.

the initial cost barriers to making energy-efficient upgrades.[22] The property owner subsequently pays back the money through a temporary property tax increase. Expanding this type of program countrywide would put people to work and help reduce the scope of the grid transition.

A decentralized approach for upgrading buildings and choosing land to rewild is required given the limited impact of any one specific action. One person installing solar panels with a capacity of kilowatts does not need the kind of centralized oversight that building an offshore wind farm with a capacity of gigawatts does. It does not make sense to expend government resources overseeing each minuscule part of the wider transition. A framework that allows individuals to act independently within a set of defined parameters would be more efficient for generating a collectively large response than micromanaging each small decision. Beyond that initial work, the government would let the program run itself and exercise a corrective course of action if there are emergent flaws.

Generating a change through subsidies will require money, no different than direct appropriations. To change the targets of farm subsidies, Congress would rewrite the relevant sections of the next farm bill. To move subsidies away from fossil fuels, Congress would rewrite that part of the tax code. Subsidies for upgrades will need an initial sum of money to start making loans. All of these things are fully within our power to do.

---

22 USDOE, "Property Assessed," accessed September 16, 2020; Pritchard, "How PACE Loans Work," updated October 1, 2020.

END THE FILIBUSTER

Enacting the laws we need will be made difficult by the structure of the Senate. The current rules require we need at least sixty senators on our side to bring most bills to a vote. Without that number, the opposition can grind proceedings to a screeching halt through unending "debate." Individual senators have the right to stand and speak on any topic they want, whether it's the motion at hand or names from the phone book. So long as someone is capable of standing and talking, and has forty people that agree with them, the Senate cannot move forward. This is called filibustering.[23]

Even the threat of a filibuster is all it takes to completely block legislation, and that has only become more commonplace in the past few decades.[24] A filibuster used to be relatively rare, but it has become the go-to method for the minority party to wield outsized power. Blocking legislation always makes sense if you control the Senate and not the White House. It makes the incumbent president look weak and increases your party's chances of winning the next election.

The filibuster will no doubt become an issue against our strategy because it targets entrenched interests. Too many senators have constituencies who rely on fossil fuels for this not to be a problem. The last time one party had a filibuster-proof majority was in 2008, and even that wasn't enough to pass an unfettered agenda. All it took was one senator—Joe Lieberman—to remove the public option originally part of

---

23 United States Senate, "Filibuster and Cloture," accessed September 18, 2020.

24 Tausanovitch and Berger, "The Impact," December 5, 2019.

the Affordable Care Act.[25] Even with sixty senators from a nominally climate-responsive party, all it takes is one senator disagreeing, and it's over.

The only way Congress currently gets around the filibuster is through the budget reconciliation process. Basically, this procedure keeps budgets from being held up by eliminating the filibuster for that one type of legislation.[26] However, not every change we need to make can be made part of a reconciliation bill and it can only be used sparingly. We will certainly need to be more active than that.

We must be prepared for the eventuality that sixty senators won't be onboard with the strategy, which means the filibuster must go. Thankfully, it is only an internal Senate rule. No legal change or constitutional amendment is required to end it. A simple parliamentary trick is all that is required. The Senate majority leader (the head of the party in the Senate supporting the strategy) raises a point of order that goes against the current Senate rules. The presiding officer (constitutionally the vice president, but it can be any senator so delegated) then denies the motion. This allows the majority leader to appeal that ruling and, with a fifty-one-vote majority, can overturn the rule.[27] In a Senate with a fifty-fifty partisan split, the vice president would need to cast the deciding vote. In a few minutes, we can end the filibuster forever.

This tactic has been used two times in the past. In 2013, the Democrat-controlled Senate eliminated the filibuster for Supreme Court and executive branch appointments. Harry

25 McGreal, "Why Joe Lieberman," December 16, 2009.

26 Davis, "The Rule," October 15, 2017; Klein, "Bernie Sanders's Plan," April 11, 2019; Matthews, "Budget Reconciliation," November 23, 2016.

27 Reynolds, "What Is the Senate Filibuster," September 9, 2020.

Reid invoked this so-called nuclear option to stop Republicans from stonewalling confirmations.[28] The Republicans did the same thing for lower court appointments in 2017. We'd just be following these precedents to completely eliminate an anachronistic practice.

The largest opposition to removing the filibuster would come from the senators themselves, even if they are otherwise amenable to our goals. There is always the risk you will find yourself in the minority one day, and the filibuster gives you a lot of power to prevent changes you don't want to see. That is a risk we will have to take. If keeping the filibuster means nothing will happen, we have no choice but to take action that at least gives us the potential to do something. To safeguard our strategy, we will just need to maintain enough public support to always control at least one of the chambers of Congress or the presidency. That is a tall order but necessary for making substantial progress.

SACRIFICE: NORMALCY

There is a desire for a general return to normal among swaths of the electorate. In this instance, normal is used to mean a repudiation of the politics we've experienced over the past few years. It means the banishment of divisive rhetoric and a return of sense or reasonableness to the public discourse. The hope is to trade the stress of a disagreeable and unpredictable news cycle for the boringness of traditional government. That is understandable, given how fragile and polarized relations have become in recent years.[29] However, such a regression

---

28 Kane, "Reid, Democrats Trigger," November 21, 2013.

29 For example, fewer people have friends with differing political views: Dunn, "Few Trump or Biden," September 18, 2020.

will not work in our favor. The same veneer of institutional respectability that allows people to ignore politics also permits behaviors to flourish that have entrenched inaction on climate change.

Disengaging from the political process would only permit those who benefit from the status quo to reassert themselves. They would be able to use their positions and power to fold themselves back into the decision-making process to threaten further progress. If no one is paying attention, fossil fuel lobbyists, for example, would go back to influencing politics. That means there will be less pressure on our elected representatives to pursue systemic change. A return to normal benefits no one because normal is what created the problem in the first place.

The pivot away from decisive action will begin almost immediately after a seemingly large victory has been achieved. Seemingly is the correct adverb. Consider some of the recent responses to Confederate statues.[30] The creation of these monuments was to preserve the racist status quo of the Jim Crow era.[31] Yet, a piece of stone is only the first superficial manifestation of racial inequality. Removing these statues can't fix the underlying issue, but it is visible enough to claim work is happening. Without taking the next more difficult steps, simply putting overt symbols out of sight and out of mind cannot correct systemic problems.

The climate equivalent of tearing down a statue is greenwashing. Using rhetoric and token action to feign concern about the climate problem. Oil companies provide a

---

30 For example: Ebrahimji, Moshtaghian, and Johnson, "Confederate Statues," updated July 1, 2020.

31 Best, "Confederate Statues," July 8, 2020.

prototypical example. They may run ad campaigns pledging to go carbon neutral or be part of the solution, but those promises are completely at odds with their present business models.[32] We would be wise to take their word with a grain of salt the size of an oil tanker. If we allow ourselves to tune out, it will be harder to mentally guard ourselves against this kind of activity, and we will more often take the well-produced images shown to us at face value. It also makes it harder to detect ruses when they are extolled by the elected officials we would otherwise support and trust.

There is a synergy here because obfuscating processes is often politically advantageous. Spinning a comforting excuse is sometimes more expedient than reiterating a difficult truth, especially when it lets you avoid making tough choices. If you're representing a region dependent on natural gas jobs, it's easier to protect your position by saying fracking can be part of a clean energy system rather than acknowledging the truth that fossil fuels need to stay in the ground. That creates a feedback loop where public and private incentives reinforce each other to discourage action.

Monitoring these happenings is critical to avoid complacency, but that is harder to do under normal conditions. The structure of the media as a whole will likely aid the fossil fuel-aligned interests in their pursuit of a return to normal, regardless of any one person's intent. The news cycle has evolved over the past three decades so that everything must be simple and rapidly changing, which does not allow the thoughtful consideration of complex issues. Given the interconnectedness of climate change and the time frame required

---

32   Crowley, "All Eyes," February 12, 2020; Chevron, "The Energy Transition," accessed September 24, 2020; Roberts, "On Climate Change," September 25, 2020.

to stop it, it will be easy for relevant stories to become lost in the shuffle as our attention is pulled elsewhere.

Serious examinations of policy would likely also threaten media company's interests in other sectors of the economy. For example, outside of climate change, you would be less likely to see a critical examination of US Internet service on broadcasters owned by or affiliated with Internet service providers. As long as a media company's parent or fellow subsidiaries benefit from fossil fuels, we're unlikely to see truly critical reporting around climate change and its solutions. Even if they don't have those ties, broadcasters will also be hesitant to risk alienating fossil fuel companies buying advertising space.[33]

Our most important challenge is to stay vigilant and engaged, lest we become complacent when someone gets on stage to declare "mission accomplished." We must sacrifice our free time to pay attention and take action to prevent the old normal from creeping back. Our goal needs to achieve permanent and successful change, not the silencing of confrontation and unpleasant truths. Normal must die for us to live. If we hope to maintain the countervailing forces against climate change and the previous status quo, we must be willing to be uncomfortable and unsatisfied for an extended period of time, perhaps for the rest of our lives. That mindset will be tiring, both mentally and physically. It may even lead to despair and a desire to quit with every setback. But it must be done because there is no viable alternative.

---

33 The Guardian provides a counter-example, forgoing fossil fuel advertising to maintain reporting standards on climate change: Waterson, "Guardian to Ban," January 29, 2020.

CHAPTER 15

THE EXECUTIVE

———

I once received a letter from the President of the United States of America. President Clinton, in fact. I was about five or six and had written on my concerns regarding drugs. It was probably after some school event or presentation, as were common during the 90s. In return, I received a pretty standard format letter with a wallet-sized photo of the president; both are probably still tucked away in a box somewhere within my parents' basement. Whoever actually wrote that letter congratulated me on taking an interest in civic problems, but I somehow doubt my early forays into public policy had much of an impact.

It would have been truly bizarre if Mr. Clinton had been the one to read and respond to my letter. A modern president has so many responsibilities it is inconceivable they would have the time even to consider doing so. The stress of the job is known to prematurely age whoever holds the office from the enormity of the workload. At least, much like a warlock, that sacrifice of vitality comes with the promise of great power.

The Office of the President has accrued immense authority over the years, and presidential power will play a critical role in our strategy. Superficially, no legislation that passes Congress with a bare majority has a chance of becoming law if the president doesn't support it, thanks to their constitutional veto power. While powerful, the ability to scuttle legislation only scratches the surface. Presidents set the policies of the executive branch through executive order and proclamation, they guide how resources are distributed, and they have the ability to reach and influence the public through the bully pulpit. All of these attributes will need to be used to their full extent if we are to fully confront climate change.

APPOINTMENTS

Congress may create the law, but the president is the one responsible for enforcing it. They can't do it alone. The millions of federal officials supported by untold numbers of contractors are the ones who will ultimately be responsible for translating policy into action. The vast majority of these people are career civil servants who fulfill their duties regardless of changing administrations and political priorities, except for those at the top of the hierarchy.

The upper echelons of the federal bureaucracy are composed of political appointees that serve at the discretion of the president. They are responsible for ensuring the administration's priorities are reflected in the output of their agencies. Many bodies will have a direct impact on our strategy, and we will want appointees simpatico to the strategy onboard. One of our priorities must be to staff these positions with those ready to implement the transition with the appropriate focus and gusto.

We can't afford to have high-ranking appointees who are either ambivalent or outright antagonistic to our goals. Given the scope of the powers delegated to the various executive authorities, they must be trustworthy. That means no lobbyists from fossil fuel interests, no donors, no one who is philosophically against using government power, and no one who lacks the courage to lawfully wield power for the public benefit.

Finding such people isn't going to be the hard part. They exist, only they are often shut out of the process. Having the president select them is the first barrier. Oftentimes, appointments go to people who aren't necessarily selected for their managerial skills and public service virtues. Ambassador postings are especially egregious examples. President Obama rewarded dozens of major campaign donors with cushy positions in places like Western Europe.[1] The practice continued under President Trump, proving this is a bipartisan issue.[2] Such practices will have to stop for our transition to work, meaning we have to hold presidents accountable.

The Constitution requires the Senate to provide consent on high-level political appointments within the federal government. Thus, we have a way to help ensure the right people are appointed, and we don't even need a majority of the Senate to do so. Let's assume the same party controls the Senate and the White House. All we need is a core group from the Senate majority, perhaps less than ten senators, to deny confirmations to people who either aren't qualified or don't support taking action on climate change. Doing so forces the administration to acquiesce to our demands, regardless of their particular climate change politics.

---

1 Levinthal and Zubak-Skees, "Barack Obama's Ambassador Legacy," January 4, 2017.

2 Kelemen, "Under Trump," August 18, 2020.

We will need senators willing to take a risk by going against their own party leadership for this tactic to work. Reaching that point will require elevating the right people to office and continued support to provide them the political cover they need. It's how Republican Senator Ted Cruz was able to wield power in the Senate and help cause a government shutdown, despite alienating some of his colleagues. Republican Senator Lindsey Graham, for example, once joked in response to such events: "If you killed Ted Cruz on the floor of the Senate, and the trial was in the Senate, nobody would convict you."[3] We need people who are willing to stand for the right thing, regardless of the fallout.

THE JUDICIARY

Passing laws and confirming the right administration officials doesn't necessarily mean progress will follow. Another group of unelected persons has the potential to block action—the Judiciary. Federal courts have the authority to strike down legislation as unconstitutional.[4] As a result, all of the new laws, programs, and regulations we implement will be at risk once fossil fuel interests immediately file suit against them. We know this will happen because industry often does so when agencies like the EPA issue a new rule. All it takes is a small set of judges siding with carbon emitters to leave our project dead in the water.

Only considering the court as a tool to achieve political outcomes likely seems anathema to many Americans.[5]

---

3 Treyz, "Lindsey Graham Jokes," February 26, 2016.

4 Marbury v. Madison.

5 There are plenty of editorials against doing so, for example: Shapiro, "The Case Against," June 24, 2019.

We are taught the judicial branch is only concerned with applying the law as it is written without partisanship. Judges must be fair and apolitical. Otherwise, the system of checks and balances within the government can't function properly. However, we have never achieved that ideal. Racial segregation, in one instance, was declared legal by the courts when the political mood supported such a decision. Yet, that decision was overturned by a later court with different views.[6] If the courts are truly unbiased arbiters, such fundamentally diverging opinions on the law's interpretation would not be possible.

Court's ruling in such a way has always existed. Case law is littered with examples of the judiciary ruling against otherwise popular or necessary laws. They can do this because the Constitution is not a proscriptive document that covers all possible situations. Choosing an interpretation of the Constitution is up to each jurist, and each judge will bring their own philosophies with them as they decide cases. People in power generally understand this dynamic. It's the reason Senator Mitch McConnell was so eager to fill judicial posts during President Trump's administration.[7] Those 200-odd appointees will be able to set the law for decades to come.

Even with an overwhelming Congress, a deep bench within the judiciary would no doubt stand in the way of the strategy if they oppose it philosophically. Experiences during the New Deal are instructive. The government created numerous programs that alleviated the Great Depression and were popular with the general public. Despite their popularity, many of these programs were struck down by a

---

6 Plessy v. Ferguson; Brown v. Board of Education.

7 Caldwell and Kapur, "McConnell Reaches Milestone," June 24, 2020.

reactionary Supreme Court.[8] They eliminated broadly useful entities, like the Agriculture Adjustment Administration that farmers relied on to survive, and laws like New York State's minimum wage.

Roosevelt's proposal for countering this threat to his policies was to pack the court. Essentially, this tactic increases the number of seats on the Supreme Court, allowing the president to fill them with more sympathetic appointees. We can do this whenever we want because the Constitution doesn't specify how many justices there may be. Unfortunately for Mr. Roosevelt, he couldn't get enough of Congress onboard to make the change, but at least the threat seemed to be enough to make the court less eager to interfere with newly enacted legislation.

The only real alternative to packing the court is to wait for current justices to retire or die in office. Deaths are too random to rely on. We can't force retirements because the Constitution does not allow us to, and passing an amendment requires an order of magnitude more support than just passing legislation. Justices also have a habit of retiring when they are more likely to be replaced with a like-minded person. Unless we can guarantee complete control of the presidency for decades, that isn't a viable approach. The only remaining option, with a simple Congressional majority and sympathetic president, is to pack the court.

The approach would be simple. Congress would pass a bill increasing the number of justices that would allow the necessary majority. Then, the president nominates people to fill those vacancies, and the Senate approves them.

---

8   Leuchtenburg, "When Franklin Roosevelt Clashed," May 2005.

There are risks to opening this box. If the power dynamics shift, opponents could simply pack the court again, beginning a never-ending expansion of the court. The integrity of the institution would diminish until the judicial branch loses its entire meaning, and we face a constitutional crisis requiring an amendment to resolve. However, when the alternative is no substantial climate action for a generation, it is something to judiciously consider. Perhaps, like in the 1930s, merely the threat of that happening will be enough to obviate the need for it.

REORIENT FOREIGN RELATIONS

One area where the president has a good deal of unilateral authority is foreign policy. The Constitution delegates the majority of that responsibility to the executive branch. Ratifying treaties ultimately depends on the consent of the Senate, but the actual negotiation of those treaties is firmly in the hands of the president.[9] They can set the scope and boundaries of diplomatic talks and arrangements, defining the realm of what is possible. Ensuring those parameters benefit the strategy is critical because any future engagement with the rest of the world will have to make climate change central to the process.

We will need to engage with the world in solving this problem. Even though the United States is the largest economy on Earth, fully decarbonizing our nation's power grid is not going to halt climate change on its own. Eighty-five percent of emissions come from elsewhere.[10] Every country needs to take action, which was the spirit of the Paris

---

9   U.S. Constitution, Article II section 2.

10   UCS, "Each Country's Share," updated August 12, 2020.

Agreement. While laudable, that accord was ultimately voluntary. We instead need to create strong, enforceable systems that complement our domestic policies on climate change.

TRADE

Controlling access to the domestic market is one of the few pressure points we have to create movement on climate change in other sovereign countries. Essentially, we would make it more difficult for other nations to sell their goods in the United States if they don't decarbonize by applying tariffs or other trade controls. Make the tariffs high enough, and you can basically shut out a country from our market. If carbon emissions are the primary consideration for tariff value, we can economically incentivize countries to decarbonize by making it cheaper to transition their power grids rather than lose revenue from exports.

Climate change can also become part of future trade agreements. These treaties are made between nations to facilitate the flow of goods and services. While their main purpose is often to remove trade barriers, other priorities are often included. The recently ratified United States–Mexico–Canada Agreement (USMCA), for example, included updates to NAFTA's labor standards.[11] If climate change were made central to such treaties, we would have some strong options for reducing carbon emissions on a global scale.

This approach has a good chance of being effective. France threatening to veto an EU-Brazil trade agreement helped push the Brazilian government to take action on the recent

---

11   The full text of the agreement can be found here: OUSTR, "Agreement between," accessed September 20, 2020.

Amazon fires.[12] Implementing carbon tariffs is also likely to happen, whether we initiate them or not.[13] There is energy in the EU for doing so to help protect their own industry from moving offshore as emissions are continually curtailed.[14] We could partner with like-minded allies to create a more universal, climate-focused trade regime. Whether or not this is compatible with existing trade agreements is a matter of debate, but that may not be so relevant. As the economic bloc that desires carbon tariffs grows, the rest of the world will feel more pressure to decarbonize, potentially leading to revised trade agreements on a larger scale.

Having Congress ratify such frameworks would be the best long-term option. The problem is that getting an agreement from two-thirds of the Senate for new treaties may not always be possible. Many of the products we consume come from countries that overwhelmingly rely on fossil fuels, so increasing the price of their imports through tariffs would impact American consumers. Deliberately making things more expensive is usually not politically advantageous.

It would likely fall to the president to make the tough political choices to unilaterally change trade policy through proclamation. It would allow for some progress, but the change could immediately reverse as soon as that president leaves office. Substantially changing trade policy would also come at a political cost that endangers the rest of the strategy. It may alienate support in Congress, especially if other nations respond in kind with their own restrictions

---

12 Reuters Staff, "France Says," August 23, 2019.

13 Carbon border adjustments were included in House Resolution 763 in 2019, but this bill was never enacted.

14 Colman, "Europe Threatens," December 13, 2019.

that harm our industries. In that light, altering trade is one of the trickier methods of approaching climate change. The president would need to be capable of executing change with impeccable nuance and sophistication. Given other competing priorities, that may not always be possible.

NATIONAL SECURITY

Another pillar of foreign policy is national security. Our priorities determine how and when we engage in conflicts and for what reasons. Climate change will naturally force a reassessment of our security posture. Declining material conditions in other nations will inevitably lead to instability and war, like what has already happened with the climate-exacerbated droughts and unrest in Syria and Sudan. These conflicts will not only impede our goals for a more global transition away from fossil fuels but have severe consequences for the people who are caught up in them, and those effects don't remain local.

Experience shows mass migrations will likely become more common in the future. Millions have sought to escape conflict over the past decade, primarily seeking refuge in more stable European countries. One of the side effects was the rise of reactionary movements across the continent. The politics of these groups often either deny climate change or use it as justification for repressing targeted populations.[15] Such deterioration of the political situation at home would only impede our ability to make progress, which means we have to end the conflicts that drive these societal disruptions before they even take place.

---

15   Walker, "Migration v Climate," December 2, 2019; Darby, "What is Eco-Fascism," August 7, 2019.

If we want to avoid a future of resource wars, we'll need to change how we engage with the rest of the world. You can't shoot your way out of climate change, so the majority of our defense budget is useless for the task ahead. We would have better spent the trillion dollars required to develop the F-35 on building a quarter-million wind turbines in this context.[16] If we take the national security threat posed by climate change seriously, we should not be afraid of resource reallocation. Instead of investing in weapons to fight future wars, we should redirect those billions of dollars to stopping climate change.

Part of this new foreign policy would entail more aid for building sustainable infrastructure in developing countries. In addition to better stabilizing the material conditions of those regions, broader decarbonization will lower the risk that future conflicts will arise. If we move quickly enough, this will substantially alter the global climate trajectory and help avert the worst impacts of climate change. If we don't, we'll become trapped in a never-ending cycle of violence.

As with trade, the best approach involves Congress. They have the authority to appropriate or redirect the funds necessary to accomplish these foreign policy goals. The president can make that easier by saving resources in other areas. They could, for example, stop pouring money, people, and equipment into wars of choice, as there is no legal obligation to be conducting military operations across almost half of the planet.[17] The president could unilaterally decide to cease those activities and switch to a soft power (i.e., nonmilitary)

16   Average wind turbine cost from: Windustry, "How Much," accessed September 20, 2020.

17   Savell and 5W Infographics, "This Map Shows," January/February 2019.

approach to diplomacy and engagement with the rest of the world.

In many respects, changing this status quo will face the same type of opposition as our transition from fossil fuels. The military-industrial complex President Eisenhower warned about is spread across every state, meaning a decrease in conflict is bad for the bottom lines of companies that manufacture weapons and other military gear. It will take a strong president to stand up to that power in addition to fossil fuel interests, but that's what it will take. A strong and focused leader who will take potentially controversial action to achieve the larger goal.

EXECUTIVE ACTION

Ending our present focus on conflict would also free the president to spend more of their time focusing on climate change. Much of the day-to-day responsibility will fall to political appointees, but an engaged leader will be required to keep everyone on track and working toward the same goals. Fewer distractions means more oversight, which, given how many powers are vested in various federal agencies, can only work to our benefit. Federal agencies will also need to know they have the cover to enact necessary polices. Whether they're creating new regulations, executing funds, or anything else, the people on the ground need to know they have a boss who has their back.

The president also has the bully pulpit, as Theodore Roosevelt put it. They have the ability to speak to the public and galvanize support for the needed transition. In times of crisis, a president's address can calm fears and call people to action. Franklin Roosevelt helped us navigate through the Great Depression by speaking to the people through his fireside chats and preparing the country for war after Pearl Harbor's attack. The president needs to do the same for climate change, to be a consistent and moral advocate for the work that needs doing.

A climate-engaged president also allows us to take action in a penultimate worst-case scenario. If Congress is completely unwilling to work in good faith, the strategy falls entirely to the executive branch. In such an event, our only recourse would be to have the president declare a national emergency and start using the resulting unilateral powers to take the necessary action.[18] The president would be able to divert money from military spending to building renewable infrastructure, halt fossil fuel extraction on federal lands, and enact new regulations on key sectors. In sum, it wouldn't completely solve the problem, but at least allow some progress to be made in a short period of time.

An emergency declaration isn't foolproof. Congress could rescind the declaration by law and reverse any changes made during its lifespan. Our best-case scenario remains one where Congress does its job to get this project underway. The ability to direct funding and fundamentally change the law is simply irreplaceable. Still, the threat of an emergency declaration may be enough to rouse Congress to action, so the option has to remain on the table.

STATE AND LOCAL GOVERNMENTS

The worst-case scenario for our strategy is one where there is no federal willpower to take on climate change. In this situation, both the president and Congress are unsympathetic

---

18   The National Emergencies Act of 1976; Mogensen, "What Could Happen," March 9, 2019.

to the immediacy of the need to act. This is not an unlikely situation, given our track record. If inaction persists, it will be the responsibility of the states to continue to take action. Several states are already ahead of the curve, and they've helped maintain momentum during the years the United States was absent from the Paris Agreement.

States have substantial leeway thanks to their ability to regulate the power sources within their borders. States like Iowa, Oregon, and New York have implemented power standards that necessitate building renewables within a set timeframe.[19] Absent federal involvement, enough states taking similar actions would essentially change the grid for us. The endeavor would just be slower, less coordinated, and less efficient. States can provide a fiscal stimulus for carbon sequestration as well. They could dramatically ease or cut property taxes altogether for farmland that's been returned to nature, in addition to further regulating how new land is developed.

Cities and towns are the lowest political rung in the United States, but nonetheless important partners for the transition. Ordinances can be updated to support greener behavior. Local money could be directed toward decarbonized transportation, like adding more public transit or electric vehicle charging stations. We could expedite zoning and permitting processes could be expedited to support renewable infrastructure development. Localities can even change their local building requirements to prioritize

---

19   NCSL, "State Renewable Portfolio," April 17, 2020.

decarbonization, like those in certain Californian cities that ban new construction from included natural gas.[20]

State and local efforts against climate change are not mutually exclusive with a federal response. Making taxes, zoning, and building codes work for us at all levels helps with any configuration of the transition. That means we have to get people elected at each level of government. We can't just stop at the White House and Congress. We need to fill every state legislature and county office with representatives who are onboard. Only with a groundswell that massive do we have a good chance of success.

***

The past two chapters are not an exhaustive explanation for every task the government has to do to mitigate this crisis. Bills and budgets routinely reach thousands of pages, and regulations fill bookshelves. The topics discussed here capture the most substantial bottlenecks for success, the things that will foremost stand in the way of change. Institutions like the Senate have traditions, but we cannot be afraid of changing them. Eliminating the filibuster goes against current precedent, but climate change is unprecedented. If we don't change them at the outset, we'll be stuck fighting unnecessary battles and wasting time.

SACRIFICE: FAITH IN SAVIORS

Scientists are critical for dealing with climate change. Making the new power grid and all its pieces work in harmony

---

20 Chappell, "California Gives," December 6, 2018; Ivanova, "Cities are Banning," updated December 6, 2019.

requires physicists, chemists, and all manner of engineers. Rebuilding ecosystems of all stripes requires the input of myriad biological scientists and environmental engineers. Our strategy cannot succeed without them, but we can't make them shoulder everything.

Many leaders are responsible for a lot of bad rhetoric around scientists. On one side, you have politicians using the fact they're not scientists as an excuse for not enacting climate change legislation.[21] The other side takes a superficially better stance by extolling people to listen to the scientists about the necessity of dealing with the problem. Both approaches are unhelpful as it allows those making the comments to abrogate responsibility. The first is obvious. It says: I'm not a scientist, so it isn't up to me to take any action. The other makes the same point, but in softer language: don't listen to me, let the scientists sort it out. In both cases, elected officials can use their nonscientist status as a rhetorical screen for removing themselves from the problem-solving effort. While the intentions may be different, the effect is the same in that it puts the burden on one group of people who don't actually have very much political power.

Our culture has historically put a lot of weight behind the opinion of someone in a lab coat. They're often portrayed as almost omniscient. Your Dr. Houses and Tony Starks are experts in so many things they can approach any given situation with immediate answers and correct courses of action. A natural reaction from some people upon hearing the need to listen to the scientists might be to put them in more positions of political authority. That worries me as someone who put in the time as a scientist to earn a doctorate. The truth is most

---

21 Atkin, "'I'm Not a Scientist,'" October 3, 2014.

scientists are very good at what they do (practicing science) but don't have a wider expertise beyond that.

There is nothing less akin to science than the political process. The complex machinery used to make policy is fundamentally arbitrary, while the laws of nature are not. There is no a priori requirement that the Supreme Court has nine justices, while the heat-absorbing properties of carbon dioxide are fundamental expressions of chemistry and physics. Navigating the political world requires expertise no less rigorous than any technical field. Few scientists have that capability, not because they are unintelligent or unwilling, but because they are not trained to do so. Just as we would not expect a lawyer to be able to operate a particle accelerator, we cannot assume that throwing scientists at political problems will make them go away.

That reality is okay. Climate change is such an all-encompassing problem we need to approach it as a team. All skill sets are relevant. Scientists certainly tell us what needs to happen and what our technical constraints are. Still, we need foreign affairs experts, political scientists, and legal scholars to tell us how to engage with governments and people to achieve our goals. Labor needs to be at the table to ensure a just transition. We'll need an army of managers and accountants to direct the resources of such a gargantuan undertaking. Fundamentally, every skill set has a role to play. In our hearts, we may wish for an authoritative genius to swoop in, take charge, and save us, but no one like that is coming.

Most importantly, we need empathetic leaders who possess the knowledge required to run the government and the conviction to do so. Leaders must be able to take a technical issue and put it in a moral framework that will resonate with people and provide the political foundation for the strategy.

A movement that does not energize the people will not work because we need broad societal buy-in to countervail the entrenched-interests that would preserve the status quo.[22]

A broad foundation is also critical because we don't need just one leader. We need many. We cannot simply focus only on the big contests like a presidential race and expect progress to happen. Passing a bill through Congress alone requires hundreds of people working toward the same goal. We need to elevate as many people as possible, including the thousands that work in statehouses and town halls across the country and from all parts of the population. Getting all of those legislators into power will require sacrifice by a massive movement. We must sacrifice our time, attention, and desire for superheroes who will solve our problems for us.

---

22 Moffitt, "The Trouble," February 14, 2020.

CHAPTER 16

YOU

—

The two words that filled me with the worst sense of dread in school were always *group project*. There were just too many ways for it to go wrong. Perhaps I wouldn't be able to find a group, and the teacher would have to assign me to one, a humiliating prospect. Even worse, what if my group sucked? I would be stuck with the burden of completing the majority of the project myself. That would just be inefficient, and we could cut out the middle man entirely if I could do the whole thing by myself on my terms and at my own speed.

Completing the project was never really the goal of those assignments. Working as part of a team, dysfunctional as it may be, is as much a lesson unto itself as a presentation on the pyramids or prion diseases. Figuring out how to accomplish something as a group is foundational to success outside of school, where every problem of consequence is greater than any single person. The need for group work is especially true for climate change.

Electing representatives at every level of government requires vast numbers of people working together in a common cause. We need to mobilize half of the electorate (plus one) to make any part of this strategy worthwhile. Because you are reading this book, I hope you are among them, but we need you for more than your vote. If we are to manifest change, we need your attention and activity. The first step is getting into the halls of power, which won't happen until there's enough people working for it.

A MOVEMENT

A question I was asked early in the process of writing this book was, "how can I change my behavior to help fight climate change?" Such a question is perfectly logical to ask if you care about the future. The activities they were looking for were all based on individual choice and action. It boiled down to changes in buying habits: how one eats, how one shops, and how one uses electricity. Basically, they were really asking the question, "how do I change my consumption?"

The choice of what we consume has become a proxy for the values we claim to have. Consumption is a performance meant to signal to others how we view ourselves and how we think others should view us. Your choice of a grocery store and restaurants, as an example, acts as a shorthand for your politics in the public eye. You might buy organic food, recycle, and install LED lightbulbs because you want to show concern for the environment. Partially, if you're like me, it's because you've internalized a sense of guilt, knowing you aren't making the optimal choices, and you have to atone for them somehow.

That individualism is illogical. *You* are not solely responsible for climate change. *We* are collectively responsible, as are the systems we put in place. Guilt over our consumption makes no sense when there is presently no moral consumption regarding climate change. When every product you can possibly buy is mined, processed, or manufactured in some way using fossil fuels, it is not possible. Herein is the illusion of choice you must see through if you want to make real change.

This realization goes against everything we are taught since birth. We are socialized to internalize the notion that any negative aspect of our lives is our fault. It makes us blind to the realities of overarching systems that have much more control over us than our personal decisions. We fault people for their health, even though social class determines access to health care. We categorize people by education, even though academic success is largely determined by zip code. We judge people's morality based on their consumption, even though your choices are predetermined by a market that gives the illusion of choice.

In the grand scheme of things, your choice to pick one product over another, avoid flying, or consume less meat does not matter. Carrying reusable bags for your entire lifetime will not offset a fraction of a fraction of a percent of a coal power plant's daily emissions. What does matter is the collective choices we make as a society. The question from the concerned citizen above should have been, "how can *we* change *our* behavior to solve climate change?"

The first step is to recognize your solidarity with those around you. Buying into false divisions only serves to make us easier to conquer by those with a vested interest in the status quo. We need to move from an individual mindset to one that recognizes the common good that will result from this strategy. Not only is a chorus of voices harder to ignore than a solo, but it is also easier to stay in tune when others are standing beside you. Doing so can only be made possible by abandoning our solitary and individualistic existences in favor of collective action. We must revive the civic mentality that served past movements so well in making this a better society. You must be willing to step outside of your bubble and join something greater than yourself. So, join a local group of similarly minded climate folks. If one doesn't exist, gather a few friends and start one. The key is to help build infrastructure at the local level because that's how you turn people out to vote when the time comes.

Expanding the movement will take evangelizing to recruit more people, but there isn't a universal way of doing that. As northern Wisconsin climate activist David Barnhill put succinctly to me, "what works in the cities will not work in rural areas." Beyond the ease of organizing, the material conditions are just fundamentally different. Talking about impending weather disasters won't matter as much in locations beset by more pressing economic issues. The messaging needs to adapt to the audience, and the one commonality that will most easily find footing is to frame the discussion of climate change in terms of jobs.

Everyone in this country is primed to talk about jobs, and every politician runs on their record of creating jobs. The Green New Deal had a just transition and jobs program precisely because that is the kind of messaging that always lands across the political spectrum. Good paying jobs, cleaner air, energy savings, and all the myriad side benefits of a transition appeal to the listeners' self-interest, regardless of their other politics. It also helps soften the blow of the sacrifices required if you can frame the discussion in positive terms. Instead of viewing climate change as a cost to society, present it as an opportunity to put people back to work and provide hope for a better future. It certainly worked during the Great Depression. Remember, Roosevelt was so popular he was elected President *four* times.

You also need to reiterate that more research and development are not necessary to solve this problem. Even when opponents do acknowledge climate change, they always frame potential solutions through this lens of needing new technologies to bring costs down.[1] As this book has endeavored to point out, technology is not the issue, the will to use it is. Thus, it is imperative to expand the number of people who accept that point, as they will, hopefully, be more willing to fight for change now. You need to spread the message that there is hope because we can solve the problem.

Providing hope must be part of the larger message. We can present the terrifying reality of climate change, but that won't incentivize much action if we don't simultaneously provide a way to avoid it. People will just give up and disengage. It's already happened for some of the generation younger than me, who have given in to being *doomers* waiting for the world to end.[2] We won't be able to build a successful movement if people voluntarily remove themselves from the process, and we need emotional responses beyond despair to bring them back.

The call to action will never reach some people. For whatever their personal reasons, there will be no way to convince everyone that taking action on climate change is imperative. It is necessary to know when to quit with a certain person and move on to the next because all the time and effort you expend on convincing someone who is inconvincible is wasted. Our goal should not be to make a movement including 100 percent of the population. Just like waiting for a technological silver bullet, this method will not help us.

1   Colman, "Gaetz Drafting," March 3, 2019.

2   Villarreal, "Meet the Doomers," September 21, 2020.

Focus instead on building the bare majority first: 50 percent of the population plus one.

Sustaining a movement requires energy, and one of the greatest sources of energy is anger. I want you to get angry about the trajectory of our future. I want you to get angry that the system and those in charge have failed to provide us the opportunity for a better, more hopeful future. I want you to get others angry they've been denied the benefits of a just transition. And I want you to use that anger to make sure something is done about climate change.

ACCOUNTABILITY

Our goal is to ensure our elected representatives are responsive to our needs. We live in a representative democracy, which means the first tactic is voting. People are single-issue voters on other concerns, so one option is to make climate change the overriding factor when making your vote. One would only support candidates if their climate bona fides are up to spec, but that's kindergarten stuff. Pulling a lever every couple of years is hardly a radical course of action or up to the task of fixing a problem like this, and you're probably doing it already if you're reading this book.

The real work is holding your elected officials accountable between elections. If you tune out after election night, you're only giving room to lobbyists who have no trouble being on top of their game every day to advocate on behalf of their patrons. You will have to fight against an ingrained inertia that directs your representatives to side with those interests, regardless of what they say on the campaign trail. President Obama admitted as much and reflected on this problem in his 2006 memoir, confirming that it's easy to lose track of the peoples' interests when you are surrounded by powerful persons.[3]

We cannot give our representatives a choice. Since we don't have the same influence, we need to hit them at a fundamental pressure point: their position itself. Nothing will make a politician take you more seriously than if you threaten their job. The way you do that is by working to remove them from office unless they do what you want.

Replacing unhelpful politicians is complicated by the dichotomy of the current system. Either party can run whoever they want and use the excuse to prevent the other side from winning, you must lineup behind them and vote for the least bad choice. We can't buy into that game but must demand their attention by threatening to walk away. You don't have to vote for the other side, but you don't have to vote for theirs either. That's how you take your power back, make them chose between losing or acquiescing to your preferred policies.

Such a tactic will no doubt result in much pearl clutching. It could mean risking other, non-climate related policy priorities that would otherwise receive support. While it is true no other policies will matter unless we solve this problem, it presents another opportunity for solidarity. Climate change intersects with healthcare, racial inequality, and myriad other issues. Joining forces with advocates in those spaces will serve to broaden the base of support for the transition to include other highly motivated persons. A large coalition focused on broad, systemic change will be better positioned to demand change.

---

3   Relevant passage quoted in: Schwarz, "Barack Obama," April 15, 2016.

If that doesn't work, we need to challenge underperformers directly. Instead of settling for whatever incumbent the party wants you to vote for, get involved with the primary process. Either run yourself or support someone who is running on a better climate platform. Do the groundwork of knocking on doors and reaching people one at a time. We need to be engaged at every level of the contest because that's how we gate who our representatives are.

The Republican Party's base is very good at doing this. They were able to coalesce around a couple of key issues, then force anyone out of office not seen as adequately pursuing those goals. For example, South Carolina Congressman Bob Inglis lost his seat in 2010 because he accepted the reality of climate change and wanted to do something about it.[4] Campaign donations and the incumbency advantage don't matter if there is a base of support primed and ready to act.

The Democratic party is only starting to come around to this strategy. One prominent success unrelated to climate change was the 2020 primary of Illinois Congressman Dan Lipinski over his views on women's rights.[5] An insurgent challenger with grassroots support was able to force-out a long-serving representative with dynastic roots in the district. This success was emulated later in the year when Massachusetts Senator Ed Markey defended his seat by running on his Green New Deal bona fides against Joe Kennedy III, another scion of a political dynasty.[6] It is possible to elect people on their climate platform if you focus on the issues and turn out the vote.

---

4   Rainey, "Bob Inglis," September 30, 2018.

5   Mutnick, "Rep. Dan Lipinski," April 18, 2020.

6   Murray, "Markey Overcomes," September 1, 2020.

Getting rid of a sitting politician is still not easy. The incumbency advantage is real, especially when the party establishment throws their weight against you.[7] Our two-party system exacerbates this problem quite a bit. The plethora of localities where one party is no longer viable means that anyone with political ambitions must at least adopt the guise of the one that can get elected, regardless of their actual beliefs.[8] It's how New York Representative Alexandria Ocasio-Cortez can accurately make the comment that two politicians who share a party in the United States wouldn't in Europe.[9] The offender need only survive the first primary to get the incumbency advantage and receive party support for the rest of their careers.

This is, again, mostly a problem with the Democrats, as the Republicans are very willing to call out politicians as Republicans in Name Only (RINOs) and primary them. Even though the Democratic Party is currently the one with a more substantial platform for addressing climate change, we need to be clear that just because someone has a D next to their name doesn't mean they're fully working towards those policies. California Governor Gavin Newsom can say he's concerned about climate change in an interview, but that appears to be in conflict with continued fracking and drilling going on in his state.[10] Power always reveals. Believe what politicians show you.

---

7   Cole, "Progressive House Democrats," April 1, 2019.

8   There are over a hundred Congressional districts where elections are routinely unopposed, per: Taibbi, "Far too Many," November 6, 2018.

9   Forgey, "AOC," updated January 6, 2020.

10   Nguyen, "Approvals for New," September 2, 2020.

Making parties more responsive can work in both directions. Polls show that young Republicans share the concern about climate change, which isn't reflected in current party leadership.[11] If that's you and you want a seat at the table crafting solutions, the same course of action still applies. You have to make your party reflect your views on this issue. Until that happens, any response to climate change will only occur when Democrats hold all the levers of government.[12]

Organizing an overhaul of a political party will take a long time. The recent behavior of Britain's Labour Party establishment, who documents indicate prioritized losing rather than having a Corbyn government, underlines the difficulty.[13] It might be years before enough people are in key positions to get things done. In the meantime, we can still take action to alter the course of decision-making already in motion.

INFLUENCING

Holding our representatives accountable is a cornerstone for the strategy, but it is not always the strongest one. While you, the reader of a book on climate change, may be inclined to regularly engage with politics, most people certainly are not. One statistic says that, since 2000, about one in twenty people don't even make up their minds about who they're voting for before Election Day, never mind the majority that doesn't vote.[14] It is not easy to make people understand

---

11   Smith-Schoenwalder, "Poll," November 25, 2019; Nawaguna, "Young Republicans," February 13, 2020.

12   Roberts, "This One Weird Trick," December 26, 2019.

13   Stone, "Anti-Corbyn Labour Officials," April 13, 2020.

14   Silver, "The Invisible," January 23, 2017.

something and do something about it, especially in the numbers required to mount a primary challenge. That means, even with a broader population that is willing to vote, we will have to rely on a smaller group of people to really push forward and do the grunt work. We need people who can fight, make deals, and work party systems for our benefit. A permanently engaged cohort of people can provide pressure much more continuously than sporadic elections.

Being an insider isn't the only way to go about influencing political parties. You have multiple constitutional rights you can put to use. The first amendment gives you the right to assemble with like-minded individuals, peacefully express yourself, and petition for policies you want to be enacted. The Sunrise Movement used their rights to great effect when pressuring House leadership during the introduction of the Green New Deal. Their sit-ins of Congressional offices drew attention to the resolution and likely drove the decision to bring it to a floor vote.

Flexing political muscle like this can have wide-ranging effects. The Sunrise Movement's endorsements of politicians and their policies now carry weight. It's all part of moving the Overton window—a measure of what is politically feasible—toward taking action. Getting out there and continuing to push these ideas in a public forum normalizes demanding action on climate change. Once more people with positions of power begin to adopt the talking points related to the strategy, it starts to become less controversial. Eventually, it will simply be the new normal.

Influencing politics like this will be frustrating. You will certainly experience more setbacks than successes, and you need to be prepared for that. However, this is a struggle worth the effort. You will just need to keep going because allowing yourself to retreat back into comfortable inaction means we are doomed.

✳✳✳

Saving the planet isn't really what we're trying to do with this strategy. To quote George Carlin, "the planet isn't going anywhere—we are." The Earth has already survived our worst-case scenario, where the poles completely melted, turned tropical, and flooded the continents. Life survived and was able to recover over time. Our choice is only whether or not we will still be here by preventing the flood in the first place.

The final thing you need to do is not give up. It is all too easy to give into a nihilistic despair when dealing with climate change. The problem is just so vast, and we are each so small. This book was me trying to deal with that unpleasantness, to prove to myself that there was still hope for us. I think there is. Nothing we've gone over has been technically insurmountable. The only barriers standing in our way are the arbitrary ones that society has erected against itself. It is much easier to change something arbitrary than alter the laws of physics, and we can't stop trying.

We have to stay focused on the end-state. Once climate change is dealt with, it will be done. Forever. There will be an escape from the continual anxiety it creates that will only grow worse if nothing is done. We will also reap the ancillary benefits of the transition once it is complete, from cleaner air and water to stability and protected biodiversity. You should always take heart knowing the effort is worth it.

That is the only way this works. No one is going to do this for us, so I want you to fight for it. Whatever time you can dedicate, dedicate it. Whatever passion you can muster, muster it. Whatever you can do, do it.

Please.

THE COMPILED
STRATEGY

—

We've covered a lot of ground throughout this book. It's easy to lose sight of the big picture when delving into so many different topics, especially when many of them don't end up contributing to the strategy. This final section is dedicated to pulling everything together and listing out, in brief, what the coherent actions for our strategy actually are. Listing these actions out in one place makes our goals and priorities clear and provides a to-do list we can follow and use to track our accomplishments. If we're really going to make progress on climate change and reach a complete solution, we'll need a quick reference like this to make sure we're on track for meeting our goals.

In addition to knowing what we're doing, it's helpful to know when we should be doing it. The pieces of the strategy are further delineated by the timeframe when they'll come into play. The broad strokes can fit into three distinct phases.

Phase one is where we set the stage for our efforts by getting started on energy projects that are critical but take a long time to complete. This phase also includes the structural changes in government necessary for any real progress to be made. In terms of a time frame, we should start phase one immediately, and we should complete it in no more than five years. Speed is of the essence, and the sooner we harvest the low-hanging fruit, the more of a buffer we have for averting catastrophe.

The next phase expands the energy transition effort and puts it into high gear. We'll be doing the heavy lifting during this time, and this is when we really eliminate fossil fuels as our primary energy source and begin to operate a wholly renewable grid throughout most of the country. Phase two is also where we start laying the groundwork for pulling carbon out of the atmosphere so we can restabilize the climate. On the government side, keeping the pressure on elected officials remains critical. Ideally, we'd be able to get this done within five to ten years after exiting phase one. We will complete some projects later than that, but time remains of the essence both for alleviating climate change and fortifying the new status quo.

The final phase is where the healing begins. Most of our economy will be decarbonized by this point, so that the priority will be returning the climate to normal. The timeframe for this one is a bit more open-ended. While we certainly want to pull carbon out as quickly as possible, it will take time for a draw-down based on restoring nature to really take effect. Let's be optimistic in our outlook and say phase three takes no longer than ten years. It's better to set an aggressive goal when the world is at stake since that will give us more drive and disincentivize complacency.

Starting today would put the fulfillment of the strategy at fifteen to twenty years in the future. That gives us enough time to avoid the worst effect of climate change, about a decade before the presently agreed-upon cutoff of 2050. It will be a monstrous effort, requiring sustained work for years longer than we are used to. However, the result of an aggressive strategy is safety and relief. After we solve this problem, we never have to deal with it again. There would be no reason to burn fossil fuels and warm the climate once we're done. It will be a highly satisfying and cathartic event at the end point, and I am very much looking forward to it.

Getting there will require the actions delineated in the following sections. They're broken up in the same order as the parts of the book. Each section has its own chart detailing what actions will take place in each phase, which is supplemented by a brief list of activities and a smidgeon of justification. Collectively, *this* is the strategy that will yield a complete solution.

ACTIONS FOR THE POWER GRID

The power grid will be rebuilt first. The top priority is taking fossil fuel power sources like coal and natural gas offline as quickly as possible. Energy storage is a top priority to avoid problems caused by intermittent renewables and their concomitant duck curve. The actions taken by the strategy are as follows:

- *Install photovoltaic cells on buildings.* Start with large commercial roofs in phase one, then expand to smaller installations in phase two. Priority will be given to regions with the most solar potential first, like the South and Southwest, to maximize efficiency. We will build no photovoltaic.

- *Install solar thermal facilities.* Desert installations in the Southwest take priority in phase one to begin building energy storage capacity. Phase two includes expansions along the gulf coast to provide heat for industrial processes, helping decarbonize that sector.
- *Deploy wind turbines.* Priority is given for offshore wind in phase one, given their higher energy production capacity and the population they would support along the coasts. Land-based turbines will supplement the power base for other regions that don't have other options for renewables, like the Plains and Midwest, starting in phase two.
- *Increase hydropower capacity.* Phase one starts with improving and electrifying existing dams to fully exploit already existing resources. Siting locations for ocean barrages and wave generations is also completed in phase one, which are constructed in subsequent phases.
- *Massively expand geothermal power.* Given the decade-long timescale required to build a geothermal plant, work on siting and construction begins immediately in phase one. As the only fully dispatchable renewable source, building these facilities is the top and overriding priority for resource commitment.
- *Maintain the existing nuclear base.* New reactors based on existing technology won't be built but will be kept running as long as possible. To support them, fuel-reprocessing infrastructure will be built in phase one and operated as long as necessary. If new reactor designs become available, they will be evaluated for their potential to support carbon sequestration.
- *Prioritize batteries for cars.* The lithium we mine will be necessary for decarbonizing the transportation sector for

the foreseeable future. We will install limited grid storage using banks of nickel-cadmium (NiCd) batteries.

- *Construct thermal storage.* We'll begin by converting fossil fuel power plants to thermal storage where applicable, along with standalone facilities as needed. Work will begin in phase one and continue until there is enough capacity to balance the grid.
- *Build pumped hydropower and compressed air storage.* Both will provide some longer-term energy storage. Phase one includes finding appropriate sites to be developed in phases two and three.
- *Use liquid fuels for seasonal energy storage.* We'll start by making air travel carbon neutral using biofuels in phase one. Phase two starts building the infrastructure for producing other liquid fuels by investing in green hydrogen capacity that will feed hydrocarbon production starting in phase three.
- *Capture and use trash gas.* Start by installing capture infrastructure in phase one and burning the collected methane for immediate use. That will be refined in phase two with gas storage capacity, allowing the gas to be kept for seasonal energy storage.

Power Grid Timeline

Energy Generation	Phase 1	Phase 2	Phase 3
Photovoltaics	Commercial Roofs		
	Small Roofs		
Solar Thermal	Desert with Storage		
		Industrial Heat	
Wind	Offshore Wind		
		Land Wind	
Water	Upgrade Dams		
	Site Coastal Locations	Build Ocean Power	
Geothermal	Plan and Construct		
Nuclear	Fuel Reprocessing		

Energy Storage

Batteries	Lithium for Cars		
	NiCd for Grid		
Thermal Storage	Retrofitting	New Construction	
Pumped Hydropower	Siting	Construction	
Compressed Air	Siting	Construction	
Liquid Fuels	Biomass for Aircraft		
		Hydrogen Infrastructure	
			Hydrocarbons
Trash Gas	Burn	Store	

ACTIONS FOR CARBON DRAWDOWN

Land restoration and rewilding, supplemented by some geologic storage, will primarily return the climate to normal. Sequestering carbon dioxide can only take place after the bulk of emitting sources have been mitigated, placing all activities no earlier than phase two. The actions taken by the strategy are as follows:

- *Restore critical environments.* Start by rebuilding wetlands both inland (bogs) and along the coast (mangroves and marshes) in phase two, then move to forests and grassland on rewilded land (e.g., from retired farmland) in phase three.
- *Capture carbon dioxide for sequestration.* Retrofit inherently emitting industries (e.g., cement manufacturing) to capture their concentrated effluent in phase two. Pull carbon out of the atmosphere in phase three by burning vegetation and capturing the emissions.
- *Sequester carbon underground with mineralization.* Begin a mass survey to find the sites with amendable geology in phase one, then start pumping the carbon dioxide captured from industry below ground in phase two and from plants in phase three.
- *Build with more wood.* Set the stage in phase one by updating building codes to allow for mass timber, then construct more new buildings with this material in subsequent phases.

Sequestration Timeline

	Phase 1	Phase 2	Phase 3
Environmental Restoration		Wetlands/ Ocean	
			Farmland
Carbon Dioxide Capture		Industrial Emissions	
			Burning Vegetation
Mineralization	Locate Sites	Develop and Sequester	
Buildings	Allow Mass Timber	Build with Wood	

ACTIONS FOR SOCIETY

A strategy for dealing with climate change has no chance if it does not use the political process to drive societal change. The underlying assumption throughout is that, before work begins, we have a large enough movement demanding action to enact the required policies. As a society, that also means we have the willpower to make uncomfortable demands and sacrifices of ourselves. The actions taken by the strategy are:

- *Build the movement.* Dedicate time and effort throughout each phase to recruit new people and organize.
- *Hold representatives accountable.* Make sure those who are elected are responsive to our needs. Use your vote, run primaries against them, and peacefully protest if they fail to take action.
- *Control the grid.* Our representatives need to nationalize the electric grid, bringing it under public control so a rapid restructuring may take place.

- *End the filibuster.* Prevent a climate-change-denying minority from stymying the strategy by eliminating the procedural tools they would use against it.
- *Align subsidies with climate change.* Immediately end fossil fuel subsidies and leases on government land, then redirect those resources to decarbonization. Subsidize practices like producing plant protein over animal meat and manufacturing long-lasting goods over disposable products to lower our carbon output. Starting in phase two, begin to subsidize rewilding in support of our sequestration activities.
- *Appointments.* Make sure that political appointees in the executive branch are executing the policies we need through their confirmations.
- *Change foreign policy.* Make our interactions with the rest of the world based primarily on mitigating climate change.
- *Invest in new jobs.* Build a base of popular support by increasing unionization within renewable industries, improving benefits, pay, and organizing. As fossil fuels are brought offline, help those displaced workers either retire or move into as similar jobs as possible in their area.
- *Limit air travel.* Help make the airline industry carbon neutral by flying less. To better decarbonize the grid, invest in a high-speed rail network.

Institutions Timeline

	Phase 1	Phase 2	Phase 3
The Movement	Recruit		
	Organize		
Government Accountability	Vote		
	Primary		
	Peacefully Protest		
Grid Control	Nationalize	Manage	
Filibuster	End It		
Subsidies for	Fossil Fuels No More		
	Plant Protein		
		Rewilding	
	Durable Goods		
Appointments	Confirm for Climate		
Foreign Policy	Center on Climate		
Jobs	Unionize Renewables		
	Retrain		
Air Travel	Fly Less	Build Rail	

ACKNOWLEDGMENTS

———

The genesis of this book can be traced to the Ladies, who encouraged me to put pen to paper and capture my ideas, climate change-related or not. Thank you for listening to my ramblings.

My writing process greatly benefited from the course offered by Prof. Eric Koester, who graciously invited me to join the class. The first rough draft of this book was a sprawling sea of word ejecta. Thanks to the profoundly helpful work of my developmental editor, Kimberly Dalton, it was almost entirely rewritten and made comprehensible. My marketing and revisions editor, Jason Chinchen, was also quite helpful in helping me further tighten-up the manuscript. My copy editor, Leah Pickett, helped with the final polish. I made additional revisions thanks to the feedback I received from early readers. I would like to thank them for their time and effort in helping me produce the final form of the book: Jon Brutlag, Ashley Gempp, Kathleen Goodman, Eric Grimsrud, Dick Hutchinson, Robert Ireland, Virginia Metzdorf, Karen Olson, Tom Rehm, and Henry Utschig.

I would also like to thank everyone who contributed to my fundraising campaign, without whom this book would not have been published: Ghidewon Arefe, Heather Bloemhard, Andrea Cantú, Colleen Courtney, Sarah Domnitz, Madison Gallipo, Ashley Gempp, Thomas Gempp Jr., Thomas Gempp Sr., Sandra Gempp, Brian Goodman, Kathleen Goodman, Michael Horecki, Eric Koester, Esha Mathew, Anthony May, Caitlyn McGuire, Virginia Metzdorf, Jaime Olson, Ivana Pelikan, Sharon Schlewitz, Douglas Stevenson, Erin Stevenson, Frederick Stevenson, Karen Stevenson, Margaret Stevenson, Susan Stevenson, Henry Utschig, Anna Whittlinger, Serena Zhang, and all those who made anonymous contributions.

Finally, I want to thank my wife, Ashley, for the constant encouragement throughout the process. I don't think I would have been able to accomplish this without you. Love you, babe!

APPENDIX

———

This section contains additional details about the numbers cited throughout the book. The intention is to provide the interested reader what they would need to repeat the calculations for themselves to better understand the process that led to the book's conclusions. Equations are presented in the order they appear in the chapters. The relevant citations are also reproduced here for convenience.

INTRODUCTION

The cube of carbon dioxide we emit every year was sized using the ideal gas law. This equation relates the volume a gas occupies (V) to its pressure (P), mass (m), temperature (T), molecular weight (M_w), and the ideal gas constant (R).[1] The side length of a cube (L) is equal to the cube root of its volume, resulting in the following equation:

$$L = V^{1/3} = \left[\frac{mRT}{M_w P}\right]^{1/3} = \left[\frac{(3.7 \cdot 10^{13} \text{ kg})\left(8.3145 \frac{\text{J}}{\text{molK}}\right)(300 \text{ K})}{\left(0.044 \frac{\text{kg}}{\text{mol}}\right)(10^5 \text{ Pa})}\right]^{1/3} = 2.7 \cdot 10^4 \text{ m}$$

———

1   Units used are kilograms (kg), moles (mol), degrees Kelvin (K), pascals (Pa), and meters (m). The value quoted in the chapter converts the length in meters to miles.

CHAPTER 3

I calculated the power output of a model solar farm based on the actual output of currently operating facilities. For each solar farm, its yearly energy output (E) was divided by its total area (A) to yield the total energy density (E_{pv}). The average E_{pv} of multiple installations (Solar Star, Rosamond, CA; Mount Signal Solar, Calexico, CA; and the Mesquite Solar Project, Arlington, AZ) was used to calculate the overall value of 330 terajoules per square kilometer (TJ/km²).[2] The same procedure was used for solar thermal facilities. An example calculation for Solar Star, which has a yearly output of approximately 5,800 TJ and an area of 13 km², is as follows:

$$E_{PV,Solar\ Star} = \frac{E}{A} = \frac{5,800\ TJ}{13\ km^2} = 448\ \tfrac{TJ}{km^2}$$

The energy storage capacity for molten salts and thermal oils was compared using their physical properties in a best-case scenario. The total thermal capacity (E) of each depends on their respective heat capacities (C_p) and temperature ranges (ΔT), where the temperature range is the difference between the maximum and minimum operating temperature for the material.[3] The quoted ratio, where salts have a 10 percent higher energy capacity, is derived from the following equation:

$$\frac{E_{salt}}{E_{oil}} = \frac{C_{P,salt} \cdot \Delta T_{salt}}{C_{P,oil} \cdot \Delta T_{oil}} = \frac{\left(1.5\ \tfrac{kJ}{kgK}\right)(585\ K - 290\ K)}{\left(2\ \tfrac{kJ}{kgK}\right)(400\ K - 200\ K)} = 1.1$$

---

2   Sunpower, "Solar Star Projects," 2016; Shugar, "Mount Signal 3," December 9, 2018; 8minute Solar Energy, "8minute Renewables," November 12, 2012; Misbrener, "8minutenergy Completes," July 11, 2018; Cassell, "Sempra Working," June 4, 2015; USEIA, "Electricity Data Browser," accessed December 24, 2020.

3   Units used are kilojoules (kJ), kilograms (kg), and degrees Kelvin (K).

The total energy provided in the scenario when every Costco is covered in solar panels (E_{Costco}) is derived from our previously calculated value for an ideal solar farm (E_{pv}). That number is multiplied by the area of a typical Costco roof (A) and the number of stores in the United States (N), as shown in the following equation:

$$E_{Costco} = A \cdot N \cdot E_{PV} = 0.013 \text{ km}^2 \cdot 770 \cdot 330 \frac{\text{TJ}}{\text{km}^2} = 3{,}400 \text{ TJ}$$

CHAPTER 4

The model wind turbine was defined using a similar procedure as the ideal solar farm. The average turbine output (E) for a given facility was estimated by dividing the yearly energy output of the entire wind farm (E_{WF}) by the total number of turbines (N_T). The value quoted in the chapter of 18 TJ per turbine is the average of multiple wind farms spread across the country (Alta Wind Energy Center, California; Bison Wind Energy Center, North Dakota; Buffalo Gap Wind Farm, Texas; Fowler Ridge Wind Farm, Indiana; Limon Wind Energy Center, Colorado; and Shepard's Flat Wind Farm, Oregon).[4] An example calculation for Shepard's Flat, which has a yearly output of approximately 6,038 TJ and across 338 turbines, is as follows:

$$E_{Shepard's \ Flat} = \frac{E_{WF}}{N_T} = \frac{6{,}038 \text{ TJ}}{338 \text{ turbines}} = 16 \frac{\text{TJ}}{\text{turbine}}$$

---

4   Power Technology, "Alta," accessed December 24, 2020; Minnesota Power, "Bison Wind," accessed December 24, 2020; Neville, "Top Plants," December 1, 2009; Caithness Energy, "Project Overview," accessed December 24, 2020; The Wind Power, "Wind Farms," accessed December 24, 2020; USEIA, "Electricity Data Browser," accessed December 24, 2020.

CHAPTER 5

The quoted change in ocean acidity is estimated based on the reported change in ocean pH due to climate change.[5] Because pH is defined as the negative logarithm of acid concentration ($[H^+]$), the relative change can be calculated with the following equation:

$$\frac{[H^+]_2}{[H^+]_1} = 10^{pH_1 - pH_2} = 10^{8.2 - 8.1} = 1.26$$

CHAPTER 7

Creating a model thermal storage facility was accomplished by defining the desired parameters and output. The total mass required (M_{salt}) depends on the total power output (P) and the desired duration (t), whose product is divided by the energy density for salts calculated in chapter 3 (E_{salt}). The resulting value has to be reduced because the energy conversion process is not completely efficient, which is captured by the overall estimated efficiency (η). The total power output was set at a gigawatt for a duration of eight hours, and the efficiency was conservatively estimated as 25 percent. Converting the resulting mass to volume (V_{salt}) requires dividing the total mass required by the molten salt density (ρ), as shown in the following equations:

$$M_{salt} = \eta \frac{P \cdot t}{E_{salt}} = 0.25 \frac{\left(10^6 \frac{kJ}{s}\right)(28{,}800 \text{ s})}{443 \frac{kJ}{kg}} = 2.6 \cdot 10^8 \text{ kg}$$

$$V_{salt} = \frac{M_{salt}}{\rho} = \frac{260{,}000 \text{ ton}}{1.5 \frac{ton}{m^3}} = 174{,}000 \text{ m}^3$$

---

5   USEPA, "Understanding the Science," accessed August 6, 2020.

Pumped hydropower has an energy storage potential based on how much water is moved and the height difference between the two reservoirs (h). On a per mass basis, this reduces down to the height difference multiplied by Earth's gravitational force (g). For water elevated 50 stories, the total energy density (E_{PS}) is given by the following equation:

$$E_{PS} = g \cdot h = \left(9.8 \tfrac{m}{s^2}\right)(200 \text{ m}) = 1{,}960 \tfrac{J}{kg}$$

The energy density for compressed air storage can be estimated by using the ideal gas law (see the cube of gas calculation above). The total energy storage per mass of air (E_{CA}) is calculated by integrating the function across the change in pressure, as shown in the following equation:

$$E_{CA} = \int_{P_1}^{P_2} V dP = \frac{RT}{M_W} \ln\left(\frac{P_2}{P_1}\right) = \frac{(8.3145 \tfrac{J}{molK})(300 \text{ K})}{0.02884 \tfrac{kg}{mol}} \ln\left[\frac{58 \text{ atm}}{1 \text{ atm}}\right] = 350 \tfrac{kJ}{kg}$$

CHAPTER 8

The energy released (ΔH_R) by a combustible fuel is calculated using the standard heats of formation for each species (ΔH_f).[6] For a generic, balanced chemical reaction, the calculation for the total energy storage capacity of a given fuel will take the following form:

$$aA + bB \longrightarrow cC + dD$$

$$\Delta H_R = \left(c\Delta H_{f,C} + d\Delta H_{f,D}\right) - \left(a\Delta H_{f,A} + b\Delta H_{f,B}\right)$$

---

6   Heats of reaction for this and subsequent calculations from: NIST, "NIST Chemistry WebBook," accessed August 28, 2020; Jessup and Prosen, "Heats of Combustion," April 1950.

If we model wood as 100 percent dry cellulose ($[C_6H_{10}O_5]$), the two equations look as follows:[7]

$$[C_6H_{10}O_5] + 6O_2 \longrightarrow 6CO_2 + 5H_2O$$

$$\Delta H_{R,W} = \frac{-1}{M_W}\left[\left(6\Delta H_{f,CO_2} + 5\Delta H_{f,H_2O}\right) - \left(1\Delta H_{f,[C_6H_{10}O_5]} + 6\Delta H_{f,O_2}\right)\right] =$$

$$-6.17\,\tfrac{mol}{kg}\left[\left(6\cdot-394\tfrac{kJ}{mol} + 5\cdot-242\tfrac{kJ}{mol}\right) - \left(-394\tfrac{kJ}{mol} + 6\cdot0\tfrac{kJ}{mol}\right)\right] = 16{,}100\,\tfrac{kJ}{kg}$$

The total energy density of wood in terms of land (E_W) is calculated by defining a model forest. Inputs were used based on a minimum viable tree, which might have a mass (m) of 180 kg and a planting density (ρ) of about 500 per acre. We also need to factor in the growing time (t), which, at a minimum, would be about six years for the fastest growing species. Finally, we also need to factor in the energy conversion efficiency of the power plant (η), which we will keep at 25 percent. Factoring in all those variables results in the following equation:

$$E_W = \eta\frac{\Delta H_{R,W}\cdot m\cdot \rho}{t} = 0.25\frac{\left(16{,}100\,\tfrac{kJ}{kg}\right)(180\,kg)\left(124{,}000\,\tfrac{1}{km^2}\right)}{6\,yr} = 15\,\tfrac{TJ}{km^2 yr}$$

The total energy released by burning ethanol (C_2H_6O) is provided by the following balanced chemical reaction and energy calculation:

$$C_2H_6O + 3O_2 \longrightarrow 2CO_2 + 3H_2O$$

$$\Delta H_{R,E} = -22\,\tfrac{mol}{kg}\left[\left(2\cdot-394\tfrac{kJ}{mol} + 3\cdot-242\tfrac{kJ}{mol}\right) - \left(-278\tfrac{kJ}{mol}\right)\right] = 26{,}800\,\tfrac{kJ}{kg}$$

The land energy density of ethanol (E_E) is calculated in a similar manner as the model forest above. The difference

---

7   Cellulose is a polymer, so the combustion reaction is based on one monomer unit. Other species in the reaction are oxygen (O_2), carbon dioxide (CO_2), and water (H_2O).

is that the density (ρ) in this equation represents the liquid density of ethanol, not the planting density, we use the area planted to grow corn for ethanol (A) is used instead of the tree growing time, and we substitute the yearly volume of ethanol produced (V) for the mass of a tree:

$$E_E = \eta \frac{\Delta H_{R,E} \cdot V \cdot \rho}{A} = 0.25 \frac{\left(26{,}800 \frac{kJ}{kg}\right)\left(54.5 \cdot 10^9 \frac{L}{yr}\right)\left(0.7893 \frac{kg}{L}\right)}{141{,}000 \text{ km}^2} = 2 \frac{TJ}{km^2 yr}$$

The minimum land for algae ponds that is required to fully meet our demand for airline fuel (A_{AL}) is derived from the ideal volume of fuel that can be produced per acre (V_{AL}) and the total aircraft fuel demand over the course of a year (V_{AF}):[8]

$$A_{AL} = \frac{V_{AF}}{V_{AL}} = \frac{70 \cdot 10^9 \frac{L}{yr}}{\left(5{,}000 \frac{gal}{acre\,yr}\right)\left(3.79 \frac{L}{gal}\right)\left(247 \frac{acre}{km^2}\right)} = 15{,}000 \text{ km}^2$$

The estimated energy density for synthetic hydrocarbons is provided using a model calculation for octane (C_8H_{18}). The balanced chemical reaction and resulting energy released upon burning are shown in the following equations:

$$C_8H_{18} + \tfrac{25}{2}O_2 \longrightarrow 8CO_2 + 9H_2O$$

$$\Delta H_{R,O} = -8.8 \frac{mol}{kg}\left[\left(8 \cdot -394 \frac{kJ}{mol} + 9 \cdot -242 \frac{kJ}{mol}\right) - \left(-250 \frac{kJ}{mol}\right)\right] = 44{,}500 \frac{kJ}{kg}$$

For reference, the combustion reaction for hydrogen (H_2) and the energy released is provided by the following equations:

$$H_2 + \tfrac{1}{2}O_2 \longrightarrow H_2O$$

$$\Delta H_{R,H} = -500 \frac{mol}{kg}\left[\left(-242 \frac{kJ}{mol}\right)\right] = 121{,}000 \frac{kJ}{kg}$$

---

8   USEIA, "As U.S. Airlines Carry," June 6, 2017; All About Algae, "FAQ," accessed August 29, 2020; ABO, "Algae and Land," April 30, 2020.

BIBLIOGRAPHY

———

INTRODUCTION

Allan, Tom. "Chernobyl: the Wildlife Haven Created when People Left." *The Guardian*, May 28, 2019. *https://www.theguardian.com/travel/2019/may/28/chernobyl-wildlife-haven-tour-belarus-created-nuclear-disaster-zone.*

Aton, Adam. "Once Again, Climate Change Cited as Trigger for Conflict." *E&E News*, June 9, 2017. *https://www.scientificamerican.com/article/once-again-climate-change-cited-as-trigger-for-war/.*

Barras, Colin. "The Chernobyl Exclusion Zone is Arguably a Nature Reserve." *BBC*, April 22, 2016. *http://www.bbc.com/earth/story/20160421-the-chernobyl-exclusion-zone-is-arguably-a-nature-reserve.*

BBC. "Australia Fires: A Visual Guide to the Bushfire Crisis." *BBC News*, January 31, 2020. *https://www.bbc.com/news/world-australia-50951043.*

Borunda, Alejandra. "Climate Change is Contributing to California's Fires." *National Geographic*, October 25, 2019. *https://www.nationalgeographic.com/science/2019/10/climate-change-california-power-outage/.*

Borunda, Alejandra. "See How Much of the Amazon is Burning, How it Compares to Other Years." *National Geographic*, August 29, 2019. *https://www.nationalgeographic.com/environment/2019/08/amazon-fires-cause-deforestation-graphic-map/.*

Cosgrove, Jaclyn. "These Are the Largest Wildfires Burning in California Now." *Los Angeles Times*, October 9, 2019. *https://www.latimes.com/ california/story/2019-09-10/fires-california-wildfire-season-now.*

Deutsch, Curtis A., Joshua J. Tewksbury, Michelle Tigchelaar, David S. Battisti, Scott C. Merrill, Raymond B. Huey, and Rosamond L. Naylor. "Increase in Crop Losses to Insect Pests in a Warming Climate." *Science* 361, no. 6405 (August 2018): 916–919. *https://doi.org/10.1126/ science.aat3466.*

Dorman, Sam. "House GOP Resolution Blasts 'Green New Deal' as Violating Nation's 'Bedrock Principles'." *Fox News*, May 22, 2019. *https:// www.foxnews.com/politics/house-gop-resolution-blasts-green-new-deal-as-violating-nations-bedrock-principles.*

Funk, Cary and Brian Kennedy. "How Americans See Climate Change and the Environment in 7 Charts." *Pew Research Center*, April 21, 2020. *https://www.pewresearch.org/fact-tank/2020/04/21/how-americans-see-climate-change-and-the-environment-in-7-charts/.*

Gleckman, Howard. "The Green New Deal would Cost a Lot of Green." *Forbes*, February 7, 2019. *https://www.forbes.com/sites/howardgleckman/2019/02/07/the-green-new-deal-would-cost-a-lot-of-green/#78f-2baad37cb.*

Goudarzi, Sara. "As Earth Warms, the Diseases That May Lie within Permafrost Become a Bigger Worry." *Scientific American*, November 1, 2016. *https://doi.org/10.1038/scientificamerican1116-11.*

Gray, Ellen. "Earth's Freshwater Future: Extremes of Flood and Drought" *NASA*, June 13, 2019. *https://climate.nasa.gov/news/2881/earths-freshwater-future-extremes-of-flood-and-drought/.*

Hannam, Peter. "How Bad is this Drought and Is It Caused by Climate Change?" *The Sydney Morning Herald*, November 4, 2019. *https://www. smh.com.au/environment/climate-change/how-bad-is-this-drought-and-is-it-caused-by-climate-change-20191024-p533xc.html.*

Harvey, Chelsea. "CO2 Emissions Reached an All-Time High in 2018." *E&E News*, December 6, 2018. *https://www.scientificamerican.com/ article/co2-emissions-reached-an-all-time-high-in-2018/.*

Intergovernmental Panel on Climate Change (IPCC). "Summary for Policymakers." In: *Global Warming of 1.5°C. An IPCC Special Report on the impacts of global warming of 1.5°C above pre-industrial levels and related global greenhouse gas emission pathways, in the context of strengthening the global response to the threat of climate change, sustainable development, and efforts to eradicate poverty.* 2018. *https://www.ipcc.ch/sr15/chapter/spm/.*

Irfan, Umair. "The Amazon Rainforest's Worst-Case Scenario is Uncomfortably Near." *Vox*, August 27, 2019. *https://www.vox.com/2019/8/27/20833275/amazon-rainforest-fire-wildfire-dieback.*

Isachenkov, Vladimir. "Putin Acknowledges Threats Posed by Climate Change." *Business Insider*, December 19, 2019. *https://www.businessinsider.com/putin-acknowledges-threats-posed-by-climate-change-2019-12.*

Klare, Michael. "If the US Military is Facing up to the Climate Crisis, Shouldn't we all?" *The Guardian*, November 12, 2019. *https://www.theguardian.com/commentisfree/2019/nov/12/us-military-pentagon-climate-crisis-breakdown-.*

Lieberman, Bruce. "Wildfires and Climate Change: What's the Connection?" *Yale Climate Connections*, July 2, 2019. *https://www.yaleclimateconnections.org/2019/07/wildfires-and-climate-change-whats-the-connection/.*

Loris, Nicolas. "The Green New Deal would Cost Trillions and Make not a Dime's Worth of Difference." *The Heritage Foundation*, May 29, 2019. *https://www.heritage.org/environment/commentary/the-green-new-deal-would-cost-trillions-and-make-not-dimes-worth-difference.*

Machemer, Theresa. "The Far-Reaching Consequences of Siberia's Climate-Change-Driven Wildfires." *Smithsonian Magazine*, July 9, 2020. *https://www.smithsonianmag.com/smart-news/siberian-wildfires-cause-record-pollution-send-smoke-us-180975275/.*

National Oceanic and Atmospheric Administration (NOAA). "Ocean Acidification." Updated April 2020 *https://www.noaa.gov/education/resource-collections/ocean-coasts/ocean-acidification.*

National Oceanic and Atmospheric Administration (NOAA). "Sea Level Rise Viewer." Accessed August 6, 2020. *https://coast.noaa.gov/slr/.*

Reuters Staff. "Australia's Leaders Unmoved on Climate Action after Devastating Bushfires." *Reuters*, January 7, 2020. *https://www.reuters.com/article/us-australia-bushfires-climatechange/australias-leaders-un-*

moved-on-climate-action-after-devastating-bushfires-idUSKBN-1Z6oIB.

Reuters Staff. "Brazil Foreign Minister Says 'There is no Climate Change Catastrophe'." *Reuters*, September 11, 2019. *https://www.reuters.com/ article/us-brazil-environment-araujo/brazil-foreign-minister-says-there-is-no-climate-change-catastrophe-idUSKCN1VW2S2.*

Rojas-Rocha, Xochitl. "Worsening Ocean Acidification Threatens Alaska Fisheries." *Science*, July 29, 2014. *https://www.sciencemag.org/ news/2014/07/worsening-ocean-acidification-threatens-alaska-fisheries.*

Sova, Chase. "The First Climate Change Conflict." *World Food Program USA*, November 30, 2017. *https://www.wfpusa.org/articles/the-first-climate-change-conflict/.*

Stone, Madeleine. "A Heat Wave Thawed Siberia's Tundra. Now It's on Fire," *National Geographic*, July 6, 2020. *https://www.nationalgeo-graphic.com/science/2020/07/heat-wave-thawed-siberia-now-on-fire/.*

Tharoor, Ishaan. "Bolsonaro, Trump and the Nationalists Ignoring Climate Disaster." *The Washington Post*, August 23, 2019. *https://www. washingtonpost.com/world/2019/08/23/bolsonaro-trump-national-ists-ignoring-climate-disaster/.*

The National Academies of Sciences Engineering and Medicine (NASEM). "Global warming is contributing to extreme weather events." Accessed August 6, 2020. *https://sites.nationalacademies.org/BasedOnScience/ climate-change-global-warming-is-contributing-to-extreme-weather-events/index.htm.*

Thompson, Andrea. "Yes, Climate Change Did Influence Australia's Unprecedented Bushfires." *Scientific American*, March 4, 2020. *https:// www.scientificamerican.com/article/yes-climate-change-did-influ-ence-australias-unprecedented-bushfires/.*

Treat, Jason, Matthew Twombly, Web Barr, Maggie Smith, National Geographic Magazine Staff, and Kees Veenenbos. "What the World would Look like if all the Ice Melted." *National Geographic*, September 2013. *https://www.nationalgeographic.com/magazine/2013/09/rising-seas-ice-melt-new-shoreline-maps/.*

Westerling, Anthony, Tim Brown, Tania Schoennagel, Thomas Swetnam, Monica Turner, and Thomas Veblen. "Briefing: Climate and Wildfire in Western U.S. Forests." USDA Forest Service RMRS-P-71, 2014. *https://www.fs.usda.gov/treesearch/pubs/46580.*

Woodward, Aylin. "The Amazon Rainforest Is Burning. Here's why there Are so Many Fires and what it All Means for the Planet." *Business Insider,* August 24, 2019. *https://www.businessinsider.com/ amazon-rainforest-fires-started-by-humans-worsened-by-climate-change-2019-8.*

CHAPTER 1. THE FOUNDATION

Colman, Zach. "Gaetz Drafting 'Green Real Deal' Climate Resolution." *Politico,* March 3, 2019. *https://www.politico.com/story/2019/03/22/gaetz-green-real-deal-1290463.*

Hackbarth, Sean. "Here's a Chart Showing that Fossil Fuels Will Be America's Top Energy Source for Decades." *U.S. Chamber of Commerce,* June 12, 2015. *https://www.uschamber.com/above-the-fold/heres-chart-showing-fossil-fuels-will-be-america-s-top-energy-source-decades.*

Harbert, Karen. "Clean Power Plan Was the Wrong Answer." *USA Today,* October 29, 2017. *https://www.usatoday.com/story/opinion/2017/10/29/ clean-power-plan-wrong-answer-editorials-debates/107143196/.*

International Energy Agency (IEA). "Energy Technology Perspectives 2020." July 2020. *https://www.iea.org/reports/clean-energy-innovation* (account required to download full report).

Kelly, Sharon. "After Calling for Climate Action, US Chamber of Commerce Pushes Pro-Fossil Fuel Agenda." *Desmog,* September 29, 2020. *https://www.desmogblog.com/2020/09/29/change-us-chamber-commerce-fossil-fuels-climate.*

Lamb, William F. "How 'Discourses of Delay' Are Used to Slow Climate Action." *Carbon Brief,* July 6, 2020. *https://www.carbonbrief.org/guest-post-how-discourses-of-delay-are-used-to-slow-climate-action.*

Roberts, David. "Many Technologies Needed to Solve the Climate Crisis are Nowhere near Ready." *Vox,* July 14, 2020. *https://www.vox.com/ energy-and-environment/2020/7/14/21319678/climate-change-renewable-energy-technology-innovation-net-zero-emissions.*

Roberts, David. "The Key to Tackling Climate Change: Electrify Everything." *Vox,* updated October 27, 2017. *https://www.vox.com/2016/9/19/12938086/electrify-everything.*

Roberts, David. "We Have to Accelerate Clean Energy Innovation to Curb the Climate Crisis. Here's How." *Vox*, September 16, 2020. *https://www. vox.com/energy-and-environment/21426920/climate-change-renew- able-energy-solar-wind-innovation-green-new-deal.*

Rumelt, Richard. *Good Strategy Bad Strategy.* New York: Currency, 2011.

U.S. Energy Information Administration (USEIA). "How Much Car- bon Dioxide Is Produced from U.S. Gasoline and Diesel Fuel Consumption?" May 20, 2020. *https://www.eia.gov/tools/faqs/faq. php?id=307&t=10.*

U.S. Environmental Protection Agency (USEPA). "Sources of Greenhouse Gas Emissions." Accessed August 1, 2020. *https://www.epa.gov/ghgem- issions/sources-greenhouse-gas-emissions.*

CHAPTER 2. THE FIRE

Andrew, Anthony. "Nuclear Fuel Reprocessing: U.S. Policy Development." Congressional Research Service Report RS22542. March 27, 2008. *https://www.everycrsreport.com/reports/RS22542.html.*

Appunn, Kerstine, Yannick Haas, and Yulian Wettengel. "Germany's Energy Consumption and Power Mix in Charts." *Clean Energy Wire*, August 21, 2020. *https://www.cleanenergywire.org/factsheets/germa- nys-energy-consumption-and-power-mix-charts.*

Bateman, Kate. "U.S. Public Opinion on Addressing State Fragility." *Cen- ter for a New American Security*, April 18, 2018. *https://www.cnas.org/ publications/reports/sustaining-u-s-public-opinion-to-address-the- challenge-of-fragile-states.*

Beaubien, Jason. "Whatever Happened to the Mysterious Kidney Dis- ease Striking Central America." *NPR*, August 26, 2019. *https://www. npr.org/sections/goatsandsoda/2019/08/26/753834371/whatever-hap- pened-to-the-mysterious-kidney-disease-striking-central-america.*

Buchholz, Katharina. "How Fukushima Changed Japan's Energy Mix." *Statista*, March 10, 2020. *https://www.statista.com/chart/18679/elec- tricity-generated-in-japan-by-source/.*

Depersio, Greg. "How Does the Price of Oil Affect Venezuela's Economy?" *Investopedia*, Updated June 25, 2019. *https://www.investopedia.com/ ask/answers/032515/how-does-price-oil-affect-venezuelas-economy.asp.*

Environmental and Energy Study Institute (EESI). "The National Security Impacts of Climate Change." December 2017. *https://www.eesi.org/ files/IssueBrief_Climate_Change_Security_Implications.pdf.*

Ghoshal, Devjyot. "Heatwaves could Turn Parts of India and Pakistan Uninhabitable by the End of the Century." *Quartz India*, August 10, 2017. *https://qz.com/india/1049730/heatwaves-could-turn-parts-of-india-and-pakistan-uninhabitable-by-the-end-of-the-century/.*

Gubash, Charlene. "Searing Heat could Make Countries in North Africa and along the Persian Gulf Unlivable." *NBC News*, August 12, 2018. *https://www.nbcnews.com/news/world/searing-heat-made-could-make-countries-north-africa-along-persian-n899921.*

Institute for Energy Research (IER). "The United States Was Energy Independent in 2019 for the First Time Since 1957." March 11, 2020. *https://www.instituteforenergyresearch.org/fossil-fuels/gas-and-oil/the-united-states-was-energy-independent-in-2019-for-the-first-time-since-1957/.*

International Energy Agency (IEA). "Japan." Accessed August 28, 2020 *https://www.iea.org/countries/japan.*

Kiger, Patrick J. "How Venezuela Fell from the Richest Country in South America into Crisis." *History*, May 9, 2019. *https://www.history.com/news/venezuela-chavez-maduro-crisis.*

Krikorian, Shant. "France's Efficiency in the Nuclear Fuel Cycle: What can 'Oui' Learn?" *International Atomic Energy Agency*, September 4, 2019. *https://www.iaea.org/newscenter/news/frances-efficiency-in-the-nuclear-fuel-cycle-what-can-oui-learn.*

Martin, Richard. *Super Fuel: Thorium, The Green Energy Source for the Future.* London: St. Martin's Press, 2012.

McBride, James. "How Does the U.S. Spend its Foreign Aid?" *Council on Foreign Relations*, October 1, 2018. *https://www.cfr.org/backgrounder/how-does-us-spend-its-foreign-aid.*

McCurry, Justin. "Japan Should Scrap Nuclear Reactors after Fukushima, Says New Environment Minister." *The Guardian*, September 12, 2019. *https://www.theguardian.com/world/2019/sep/12/japan-should-scrap-nuclear-reactors-after-fukushima-says-new-environment-minister.*

Oberhaus, Daniel. "Germany Rejected Nuclear Power—and Deadly Emission Spiked." *Wired*, January 23, 2020. *https://www.wired.com/story/germany-rejected-nuclear-powerand-deadly-emissions-spiked/*.

Parkinson, Giles. "Solar Meets 100 per cent of South Australia Demand for First Time." *Renew Economy*, October 12, 2020. *https://reneweconomy.com.au/solar-meets-100-per-cent-of-south-australia-demand-for-first-time-78279/*.

Planete Energies, "France's Overall Energy Mix, 2018," August 27, 2018. *https://www.planete-energies.com/en/medias/close/france-s-overall-energy-mix*.

Rooney, Katharine. "Eight Years after Fukushima, Nuclear Power is Making a Comeback." *World Economic Forum*, December 11, 2019. *https://www.weforum.org/agenda/2019/12/japan-nuclear-power-reactor-fukushima/*.

The Observatory of Economic Complexity; accessed August 28, 2020. *https://oec.world/en*.

U.S. Department of Defense (USDOD). "National Security Implications of Climate-Related Risks and a Changing Climate." July 23, 2015. *https://archive.defense.gov/pubs/150724-congressional-report-on-national-implications-of-climate-change.pdf*.

U.S. Energy Information Administration (USEIA). "California State Energy Profile." Updated January 16, 2020. *https://www.eia.gov/state/print.php?sid=CA*.

U.S. Energy Information Administration (USEIA). "Electricity Explained." Updated March 19, 2020. *https://www.eia.gov/energyexplained/electricity/electricity-in-the-us-generation-capacity-and-sales.php*.

U.S. Energy Information Administration (USEIA). "How Much Electricity Does a Nuclear Power Plant Generate?" Updated December 30, 2019. *https://www.eia.gov/tools/faqs/faq.php?id=104&t=3*.

U.S. Energy Information Administration (USEIA). "How Much Electricity Does an American Home Use?" Updated October 9, 2020. *https://www.eia.gov/tools/faqs/faq.php?id=97&t=3*.

U.S. Energy Information Administration (USEIA). "U.S. Energy Facts Explained." Updated May 7, 2020. *https://www.eia.gov/energyexplained/us-energy-facts/*.

U.S. Energy Information Administration (USEIA). "What is the Status of the U.S. Nuclear Industry?" Updated April 15, 2020. *https://www.eia.gov/energyexplained/nuclear/us-nuclear-industry.php.*

U.S. Energy Information Administration (USEIA). "What is U.S. Electricity Generation by Energy Source?" Updated February 27, 2020. *https://www.eia.gov/tools/faqs/faq.php?id=427&t=3.*

U.S. Government Accountability Office (USGAO). "Disposal of High-Level Nuclear Waste." Accessed August 1, 2020. *https://www.gao.gov/key_issues/disposal_of_highlevel_nuclear_waste/issue_summary.*

Union of Concerned Scientists (UCS). "Coal Power Impacts." Updated July 9, 2019. *https://www.ucsusa.org/resources/coal-power-impacts.*

Union of Concerned Scientists (UCS). "Each Country's Share of CO_2 Emissions." Updated August 12, 2020. *https://www.ucsusa.org/resources/each-countrys-share-co2-emissions.*

United Nations (UN). "Adoption of the Paris Agreement." 2015 *https://unfccc.int/files/essential_background/convention/application/pdf/english_paris_agreement.pdf.*

Welch, Craig. "Climate Change Helped Spark Syrian War, Study Says." *National Geographic,* March 2, 2015. *https://www.nationalgeographic.com/news/2015/3/150302-syria-war-climate-change-drought/.*

World Nuclear Association. "Nuclear Power in Japan." Updated September 2020. *https://www.world-nuclear.org/information-library/country-profiles/countries-g-n/japan-nuclear-power.aspx.*

Worldometer. "GDP by Country." Accessed August 28, 2020. *https://www.worldometers.info/gdp/gdp-by-country/.*

CHAPTER 3. THE SUN

8minute Solar Energy. "8minute Renewables 266 MW Mount Signal Solar Farm Starts Construction." November 12, 2012. *https://www.8minute.com/2012/11/8minute-renewables-266-mw-mount-signal-solar-farm-starts-construction/.*

African Development Bank. "Ouarzazate Solar Complex Project—Phase II (NOORo II and NOORo III Power Plants." Project Appraisal Report. November 2014. *https://www.afdb.org/fileadmin/uploads/afdb/Documents/Project-and-Operations/MOROCCO-AR_-_Ouarzazate_Solar_Complex_Project-_Phase_II_-_12_2014.pdf.*

Aratani, Lauren. "Buildings Are Killing up to 1bn Birds a Year in US, Scientists Estimate." *The Guardian*, April 7, 2019. *https://www. theguardian.com/environment/2019/apr/07/how-many-birds-killed-by-skyscrapers-american-cities-report.*

California Energy Commission. "Mojave Solar Project." Accessed December 24, 2020. *https://ww2.energy.ca.gov/sitingcases/abengoa/index. html.*

Cassell, Barry. "Sempra Working on 150-MW Part 2 to Mesquite Solar Project in Arizona." June 4, 2015. *https://www.transmissionhub.com/ articles/2015/06/sempra-working-on-150-mw-part-2-to-mesquite-solar-project-in-arizona.html.*

Codomo, Derrick. "File:PNGedUSoutline.png." *Wikimedia Commons*, May 20, 2006. *https://commons.wikimedia.org/wiki/File:PNGedU-Soutline.png.*

Deign, Jason. "Germany's Maxed-Out Grid Is Causing Trouble Across Europe." *Greentech Media*, March 31, 2020. *https://www.greentech-media.com/articles/read/germanys-stressed-grid-is-causing-trouble-across-europe.*

Dieterich, Robert. "24-Hour Solar Energy: Molten Salt Makes it Possible and Prices Are Falling Fast." *Inside Climate News*, January 16, 2018. *https://insideclimatenews.org/news/16012018/csp-concentrated-so-lar-molten-salt-storage-24-hour-renewable-energy-crescent-dunes-ne-vada.*

Field, Kyle. "First Solar Breaks Down Its Plans for Solar Module Recycling." *CleanTechnica*, December 4, 2018. *https://cleantechnica. com/2018/12/04/first-solar-breaks-down-its-plans-for-solar-module-recycling-spi2018/.*

First Solar. "First Solar Becomes Largest PV Module Manufacturer in the Western Hemisphere." *GlobeNewswire*, October 24, 2019. *https:// www.globenewswire.com/news-release/2019/10/24/1935036/0/en/ First-Solar-Becomes-Largest-PV-Module-Manufacturer-in-the-West-ern-Hemisphere.html.*

First Solar. "Topaz Solar Farm." April 15, 2011. *http://slocounty.granicus. com/MetaViewer.php?view_id=6&clip_id=1074&meta_id=211661.*

Glatzmaier, G. "Summary Report for Concentrating Solar Power Thermal Storage Workshop." Technical Report NREL/TP-5500-52134. August 2011. *https://www.nrel.gov/docs/fy11osti/52134.pdf.*

Gomez-Vidal, Judith, and Alan Kruizenga, "Technology Pathway Molten Salt." February 1, 2017. *https://www.energy.gov/sites/prod/files/2017/02/f34/Gen3%20Workshop_Liquid%20Overview_Vidal.pdf.*

Goodman, Samuel M., Vivek Singh, Josep Casamada Ribot, Anushree Chatterjee, and Prashant Nagpal. "Multiple Energy Exciton Shelves in Quantum-dot–DNA Nanobioelectronics." *The Journal of Physical Chemistry Letters* 5, no. 21 (October 2014): 3909–3913 *https://dx.doi.org/10.1021/jz502058y.*

Hoen, Ben, Joseph Rand, and Salma Elmallah. "Commercial PV Property Characterization: An Analysis of Solar Deployment Trends in Commercial Real Estate." *Lawrence Berkeley National Laboratory*, October 2019. *https://emp.lbl.gov/publications/commercial-pv-property.*

Hydrogen Europe. "Project HYDROSOL-PLANT." August 28, 2020. *https://hydrogeneurope.eu/project/hydrosol-plant.*

Kerlin, Kat. "Can Solar Energy and Wildlife Coexist?" *The Washington Post*, September 9, 2018. *https://www.washingtonpost.com/brand-studio/wp/2018/09/09/feature/can-solar-energy-and-wildlife-coexist/?utm_term=.9745144b3763.*

Latham, Saundra. "Costco by the Numbers: 22 Surprising Stats." *Cheapism*, September 25, 2017. *https://blog.cheapism.com/costco-numbers-18090.*

Misbrener, Kelsey. "8minutenergy Completes Two Phases of Mount Signal 3 Solar Project." *Solar Power World*, July 11, 2018. *https://www.solarpowerworldonline.com/2018/07/8minutenergy-completes-two-phases-of-mount-signal-3-solar-project/.*

National Renewable Energy Laboratory (NREL). "Best Research-Cell Efficiency Chart." Accessed August 3, 2020. *https://www.nrel.gov/pv/cell-efficiency.html.*

National Renewable Energy Laboratory (NREL). "Genesis Solar Energy Project." April 25, 2014. *https://solarpaces.nrel.gov/genesis-solar-energy-project.*

National Renewable Energy Laboratory (NREL). "Solar Resource Data, Tools, and Maps." Accessed January 14, 2021. *https://www.nrel.gov/gis/solar.html.*

Nevada Fish and Wildlife Office. "Threats to Desert Tortoises." Updated April 16, 2014. *https://www.fws.gov/nevada/desert_tortoise/dt/dt_threats.html.*

Noh, Hyunwoo, Samuel M. Goodman, Praveena Mohan, Andrew P. Goodwin, Prashant Nagpal, and Jennifer N. Cha. "Direct Conjugation of DNA to Quantum Dots for Scalable Assembly of Photoactive Thin Films." *RSC Advances* 4, no. 16 (January 2014): 8064–8071. *https://dx.doi.org/10.1039/c3ra47689h.*

Peltier, Robert. "Top Plant: Solana Generating Station, Maricopa County, Arizona." *Power Magazine*, December 1, 2014. *https://www.powermag.com/solana-generating-station-maricopa-county-arizona/.*

Perret, Robert. "Solar Thermochemical Hydrogen Production Research (STCH): Thermochemical Cycle Selection and Investment Priority." Sandia Report SAND2011-3622. May 2011. *https://www.energy.gov/sites/prod/files/2014/03/f9/solar_thermo_h2.pdf.*

Philipps, Simon, and Werner Warmuth. "Photovoltaics Report." *Fraunhofer Institute for Solar Energy Systems*, updated September 16, 2020. *https://www.ise.fraunhofer.de/en/publications/studies/photovoltaics-report.html.*

Price, Austin. "Massive Solar Farm Clears a Path Through the Mojave Desert." *Earth Island Journal*, January 30, 2020. *https://www.earthisland.org/journal/index.php/articles/entry/massive-solar-farm-clears-a-path-through-the-mojave-desert/.*

Reddy, Ramana G. "Molten Salts: Thermal Energy Storage and Heat Transfer Media." *Journal of Phase Equilibria and Diffusion* 32, (July 2011): 269. *https://link.springer.com/article/10.1007/s11669-011-9904-z.*

Shugar, Dan. "Mount Signal 3 Solar Farm Roars to Life." *Nextracker*, December 9, 2018. *https://www.nextracker.com/2018/12/mount-signal-3-solar-farm-roars-to-life/.*

Sommer, Lauren. "Whales Get a Break as Pandemic Creates Quieter Oceans." *NPR*, July 20, 2020. *https://www.npr.org/2020/07/20/891854646/whales-get-a-break-as-pandemic-creates-quieter-oceans.*

Stewart, Jessica. "Bridges for Animals to Safely Cross Freeways Are Popping up Around the World." *My Modern Met*, February 9, 2017. *https://mymodernmet.com/wildlife-crossings/.*

Strauss, Mark. "Take a Look at the World's Largest Solar Thermal Farm." *Smithsonian Magazine*, November 2012. *https://www.smithsonianmag.com/science-nature/take-a-look-at-the-worlds-largest-solar-thermal-farm-91577483/*.

Sunpower. "Solar Star Projects." 2016. *https://us.sunpower.com/sites/default/files/cs-solar-star-projects-fact-sheet_0.pdf*.

U.S. Energy Information Administration (USEIA). "EIA Projects Nearly 50% Increase in World Energy Usage by 2050, led by Growth in Asia." September 24, 2019. *https://www.eia.gov/todayinenergy/detail.php?id=41433*.

U.S. Energy Information Administration (USEIA). "Electricity Data Browser." Accessed December 24, 2020. *https://www.eia.gov/electricity/data/browser/*.

U.S. Energy Information Administration (USEIA). "In 2018, the United States consumed more energy than ever before." April 16, 2019. *https://www.eia.gov/todayinenergy/detail.php?id=39092*.

U.S. Energy Information Administration (USEIA). "Use of energy explained." Updated September 28, 2018. *https://www.eia.gov/energyexplained/index.php?page=us_energy_commercial*.

U.S. Geological Society (USGS). "Tellurium." Mineral Commodity Summaries. January 2020. *https://www.usgs.gov/centers/nmic/selenium-and-tellurium-statistics-and-information*.

University of Tennessee Institute of Agriculture (UTIA). "The Sun's Energy." Accessed July 21, 2020. *https://ag.tennessee.edu/solar/Pages/What%20Is%20Solar%20Energy/Sun%27s%20Energy.aspx*.

CHAPTER 4. THE WIND

American Wind Energy Association (AWEA). "Agriculture." Accessed July 6, 2020. *https://www.awea.org/wind-101/benefits-of-wind/wind-in-my-community/agriculture*.

Anderson, Dave. "Trump's False Claim about Windmills, Noise and Cancer Defended by Koch-Backed Blog." *Energy and Policy Institute*, April 17, 2019. *https://www.energyandpolicy.org/trump-anti-wind-koch/*.

BBC. "Donald Trump Loses Wind Farm Legal Challenge." *BBC News*, December 16, 2015. *https://www.bbc.com/news/uk-scotland-north-east-orkney-shetland-35106581.*

Caithness Energy. "Project Overview." Accessed December 24, 2020. *https://caithnessshepherdsflat.com/project-overview-2/.*

California Energy Commission. "Visualization of Seasonal Variation in California Wind Generation." Accessed October 17, 2020. *https://www.energy.ca.gov/data-reports/energy-almanac/california-electricity-data/visualization-seasonal-variation-0.*

Codomo, Derrick. "File:PNGedUSoutline.png." *Wikimedia Commons*, May 20, 2006. *https://commons.wikimedia.org/wiki/File:PNGedU-Soutline.png.*

Conte, Frank. "Cape Wind has Powerful Critics, Supporters." *The Heartland Institute*, September 1, 2006. *https://www.heartland.org/news-opinion/news/cape-wind-has-powerful-critics-supporters?-source=policybot.*

Doyle, Tim. "Koch's New Fight." *Forbes*, September 21, 2006. *https://www.forbes.com/2006/09/21/koch-gordon-nantucket-biz_cz_td_06rich400_0921nantucket.html#c73282f108a5.*

Federal Aviation Administration (FAA). "FAA Updates Airspace Obstructions Standards." December 8, 2015. *https://www.faa.gov/news/updates/?newsId=84336.*

Fraunhofer Institute for Solar Energy Systems (Fraunhofer). "Distance to Shore and Water Depth." Accessed July 20, 2020. *http://windmonitor.iee.fraunhofer.de/windmonitor_en/4_Offshore/2_technik/2_Kuestenentfernung_und_Wassertiefe/.*

GE Renewable Energy. "Haliade-X Offshore Wind Turbine Platform." Accessed July 6, 2020. *https://www.ge.com/renewableenergy/wind-energy/offshore-wind/haliade-x-offshore-turbine.*

Kennedy, Robert F., Jr. "An Ill Wind off Cape Cod." *The New York Times*, December 16, 2005. *https://www.nytimes.com/2005/12/16/opinion/an-ill-wind-off-cape-cod.html.*

McKenna, Phil. "America's First Offshore Wind Energy Makes Landfall in Rhode Island." *Inside Climate News*, May 1, 2017. *https://insideclimatenews.org/news/28042017/block-island-wind-farm-deepwater-wind-renewable-energy-climate-change.*

Minnesota Power. "Bison Wind Energy Center." Accessed December 24, 2020. *https://www.mnpower.com/environment/wind.*

National Renewable Energy Laboratory (NREL). "Wind Resource Data, Tools, and Maps." Accessed July 6, 2020. *https://www.nrel.gov/gis/ wind.html.*

National Research Council (NRC). *Environmental Impacts of Wind-Energy Projects.* Washington, DC: The National Academies Press, 2007. *https://doi.org/10.17226/11935.*

Neville, Angela. "Top Plants: Fowler Ridge Wind Farm, Benton County, Indiana." *Power Magazine,* December 1, 2009. *https://www.powermag. com/top-plants-fowler-ridge-wind-farm-benton-county-indiana/.*

Pelzer, Jeremy. "Nuclear Bailout Bill Passes Ohio Legislature, Signed by Gov. Mike DeWine." *Cleveland.com,* updated July 23, 2019. *https:// www.cleveland.com/open/2019/07/nuclear-bailout-bill-passes-ohio-leg- islature.html.*

Power Technology. "Alta Wind Energy Center (AWEC), California." Accessed December 24, 2020. *https://www.power-technology.com/ projects/alta-wind-energy-center-awec-california/.*

Rubin, G. James, Miriam Burns, and Simon Wessely. "Possible Psychological Mechanisms for 'Wind Turbine Syndrome.' On the Windmills of your Mind." *Noise and Health* 16, no. 69 (May 2014):116–122. *https:// doi.org/10.4103/1463-1741.132099.*

Schoetz, David. "Wind Farm? Not Off My Back Porch." *ABC News,* August 12, 2008. *https://abcnews.go.com/US/story?id=2995334&page=1.*

The Wind Power. "Wind Farms." Accessed December 24, 2020. *https:// www.thewindpower.net/windfarms_list_en.php.*

U.S. Energy Information Administration (USEIA). "DOE Provides Detailed Offshore Wind Resource Maps." January 30, 2012. *https:// www.eia.gov/todayinenergy/detail.php?id=4770.*

U.S. Energy Information Administration (USEIA). "Electricity Data Browser." Accessed December 24, 2020. *https://www.eia.gov/elec- tricity/data/browser/.*

U.S. Energy Information Administration (USEIA). "Where Wind Power is Harnessed." Updated March 24, 2020. *https://www.eia.gov/energy- explained/index.php?page=wind_where.*

Waters, Michael. "Anti-Wind Farm Activism Is Sweeping Europe—and the U.S. Could be Next." *Gizmodo*, October 9, 2018. *https://earther. gizmodo.com/anti-wind-farm-activism-is-sweeping-europe-and-the-us-c-1829627812*.

Weston, David. "London Array Breaks Offshore Production Record." *Wind Power Monthly*, January 8, 2016. *https://www.windpowermonthly. com/article/1378756/london-array-breaks-offshore-production-record*.

Wind Europe. "Offshore Wind in Europe: Key Trends and Statistics 2019." February 6, 2020. *https://windeurope.org/about-wind/statistics/offshore/european-offshore-wind-industry-key-trends-statistics-2019/*.

Zipp, Kathie. "To be precise, the FAA has not 500-ft limit on turbine towers." *Windpower Engineering & Development*, April 6, 2012. *https:// www.windpowerengineering.com/construction/to-be-precise-the-faa-has-no-500-ft-limit-on-turbine-towers/*.

CHAPTER 5. THE WATER

Bonifacio, Emmanuel. "Wave Energy." October 24, 2010. *http://large. stanford.edu/courses/2010/ph240/bonifacio1/*.

National Oceanic and Atmospheric Administration (NOAA). "New Study: Climate Change to Shift Many Fish Species North." May 17, 2018. *https://www.fisheries.noaa.gov/feature-story/new-study-climate-change-shift-many-fish-species-north*.

Patel, Sonal "Sihwa Lake Tidal Power Plant, Gyeonggi Province, South Korea." *Power*, December 1, 2015. *https://www.powermag.com/sihwa-lake-tidal-power-plant-gyeonggi-province-south-korea/*.

Power Technology. "Tidal Giants—the World's Five Biggest Tidal Power Plants." Updated July 14, 2020. *https://www.power-technology.com/ features/featuretidal-giants-the-worlds-five-biggest-tidal-power-plants-4211218/*.

Seenan, Gerard. "Islay Pioneers Harnessing of Wave Power." *The Guardian*, September 13, 2000. *https://www.theguardian.com/environment/2000/sep/14/energy.renewableenergy*.

Selin, Noelle E. "Tidal Power." *Britannica*, accessed September 14, 2020. *https://www.britannica.com/science/tidal-power*.

Trosper, Jaime. "How an Infamous Hydroelectric Dam Changed Earth's Rotation." *Futurism*, October 1, 2013. *https://futurism.com/how-infamous-hydroelectric-dam-changed-earths-rotation.*

U.S. Department of Energy (USDOE). "Hydropower Vision: A New Chapter for America's 1st Renewable Electricity Source." July 26, 2016. *https://www.energy.gov/eere/water/articles/hydropower-vision-new-chapter-america-s-1st-renewable-electricity-source.*

U.S. Department of Energy (USDOE). "Tapping into Wave and Tidal Ocean Power: 15% Water Power by 2030." January 27, 2012. *https://www.energy.gov/articles/tapping-wave-and-tidal-ocean-power-15-water-power-2030.*

U.S. Department of Energy (USDOE). "The National Hydropower Map." June 2018. *https://www.energy.gov/eere/water/downloads/national-hydropower-map.*

U.S. Department of The Interior (USDOI). "What is the Biggest Dam in the World?" Updated March 12, 2015. *https://www.usbr.gov/lc/hooverdam/history/essays/biggest.html.*

U.S. Energy Information Administration (USEIA). "U.S. Hydropower Output Varies Dramatically from Year to Year." August 15, 2011. *https://www.eia.gov/todayinenergy/detail.php?id=2650.*

U.S. Environmental Protection Agency (USEPA). "Understanding the Science of Ocean and Coastal Acidification." Accessed August 6, 2020. *https://www.epa.gov/ocean-acidification/understanding-science-ocean-and-coastal-acidification.*

CHAPTER 6. THE EARTH

Biello, David. "Where did the Carter White House's Solar Panels Go?" *Scientific American*, August 6, 2010. *https://www.scientificamerican.com/article/carter-white-house-solar-panel-array/.*

California Energy Commission. "California Geothermal Energy Statistics and Data." Accessed February 14, 2021. *https://ww2.energy.ca.gov/almanac/renewables_data/geothermal/index_cms.php.*

City of Boise "Geothermal." Accessed August 6, 2020. *https://www.cityofboise.org/departments/public-works/geothermal/.*

Codomo, Derrick. "File:PNGedUSoutline.png." *Wikimedia Commons*, May 20, 2006. *https://commons.wikimedia.org/wiki/File:PNGedU-Soutline.png.*

Conradt, Stacy. "This App Keeps Icelanders from Dating their Relatives." *Mental Floss*, March 2, 2016. *https://www.mentalfloss.com/article/76323/app-keeps-icelanders-dating-their-relatives.*

Geothermal Steam Act of 1970, Pub. L. 91–581, 84 Stat. 1566. *https://www.fs.fed.us/sites/default/files/media_wysiwyg/geothermal-steam-act-of-1970.pdf.*

Hall, Shannon. "Yellowstone Supervolcano Could Be an Energy Source. But Should It?" *National Geographic*, August 8, 2018. *https://www.nationalgeographic.com/science/2018/08/news-yellowstone-supervolcano-geothermal-energy-debate-iceland-hawaii/.*

Jacobs, Ryan. "Why so Many Icelanders Still Believe in Invisible Elves." *The Atlantic*, October 29, 2013. *https://www.theatlantic.com/international/archive/2013/10/why-so-many-icelanders-still-believe-in-invisible-elves/280783/.*

Johnston, Hamish. "Radioactive Decay Accounts for Half of Earth's Heat." *Physics World*, July 19, 2011. *https://physicsworld.com/a/radioactive-decay-accounts-for-half-of-earths-heat/.*

National Park Service. "Hydrothermal Systems." August 6, 2019. *https://www.nps.gov/yell/learn/nature/hydrothermal-systems.htm.*

NS Energy Staff Writer. "Profiling the Top Geothermal Power Producing Countries in the World." *NS Energy*, January 8, 2020. *https://www.nsenergybusiness.com/features/top-geothermal-power-producing-countries/.*

Orkustofnun National Energy Authority. "Direct Use of Geothermal Resources." Accessed July 31, 2020. *https://nea.is/geothermal/.*

Orkustofnun National Energy Authority. "Industrial Users." Accessed July 31, 2020. *https://nea.is/geothermal/direct-utilization/industrial-uses/.*

U.S. Department of Energy (USDOE). "Geothermal Power Plants—Minimizing Land Use and Impact." Accessed February 9, 2021. *https://www.energy.gov/eere/geothermal/geothermal-power-plants-minimizing-land-use-and-impact.*

U.S. Department of Energy (USDOE). "GeoVision: Harnessing the Heat Beneath our Feet." 2019. *https://www.energy.gov/eere/geothermal/downloads/geovision-harnessing-heat-beneath-our-feet.*

U.S. Energy Information Administration (USEIA). "Nearly Half of U.S. Geothermal Power Capacity Came Online in the 1980s." November 20, 2019. *https://www.eia.gov/todayinenergy/detail.php?id=42036.*

CHAPTER 7. THE MOON

All Oil Tank. "Crude Oil Storage Tanks." Accessed August 26, 2020. *http://alloiltank.com/crude-oil-storage-tanks/.*

Asokan, Akshaya. "Massive Botnet Attack Used More than 400,000 IoT Devices." *Bank Info Security*, July 26, 2019. *https://www.bankinfosecurity.com/massive-botnet-attack-used-more-than-400000-iot-devices-a-12841.*

Bush, Joseph. "Closing the Loop on Energy Storage Materials." *T&D World*, January 21, 2019. *https://www.tdworld.com/distributed-energy-resources/energy-storage/article/20972149/closing-the-loop-on-energy-storage-materials.*

Deign, Jason. "Germany Looks to Put Thermal Storage into Coal Plants." *Greentech Media*, March 18, 2019. *https://www.greentechmedia.com/articles/read/germany-thermal-storage-into-coal-plants.*

Emilio, Maurizio Di Paolo. "Smart Grid for Electric Vehicles." *EE Times*, September 5, 2019. *https://www.eetimes.com/smart-grid-for-electric-vehicles/.*

Energy Storage World Forum. "Are Energy Storage Systems Facing a Battery Recycling and Disposal Crisis?" Accessed April 22, 2020. *https://energystorageforum.com/news/energy-storage/energy-storage-systems-facing-battery-recycling-disposal-crisis.*

Epec. "Battery Cell Comparison." Accessed August 6, 2020. *https://www.epectec.com/batteries/cell-comparison.html.*

Fruhlinger, Josh. "The Mirai Botnet Explained: How Teen Scammers and CCTV Cameras almost Brought Down the Internet." *CSO*, March 9, 2018. *https://www.csoonline.com/article/3258748/the-mirai-botnet-explained-how-teen-scammers-and-cctv-cameras-almost-brought-down-the-internet.html.*

Hogg, Stefan. "Batteries Need to Be 'Renewable' Too: Why Recycling Matters Now." *Energy Storage News*, September 30, 2019. *https://www.energy-storage.news/blogs/batteries-need-to-be-renewable-too-why-recycling-matters-now.*

Hunt, Julian D., Edward Byers, Yoshihide Wada, Simon Parkinson, David E. H. J. Gernaat, Simon Langan, Detlef P. van Vuuren, and Keywan Riahi. "Global Resource Potential of Seasonal Pumped Hydropower Storage for Energy and Water Storage." *Nature Communications* 11 (February 2020): 947. *https://doi.org/10.1038/s41467-020-14555-y.*

International Cadmium Association (ICdA). "Collection and Recycling of Nickel-Cadmium (NiCd) Batteries." Accessed May 5, 2020. *https://www.cadmium.org/collection-and-recycling-of-nickelcadmium-nicd-batteries.*

Komando, Kim. "You're Not Paranoid: Your Phone Really is Listening in." *USA Today*, December 19, 2019. *https://www.usatoday.com/story/tech/columnist/2019/12/19/your-smartphone-mobile-device-may-recording-everything-you-say/4403829002/.*

Molla, Rani. "Your Smart Devices Listening to You, Explained." *Vox*, September 20, 2019. *https://www.vox.com/recode/2019/9/20/20875755/smart-devices-listening-human-reviewers-portal-alexa-siri-assistant.*

Neuhauser, Alan. "Where Batteries are Replacing Power Plants." *U.S. News & World Report*, May 21, 2019. *https://www.usnews.com/news/national-news/articles/2019-05-21/why-california-nixed-a-natural-gas-power-plant-in-favor-of-batteries.*

Pacific Northwest National Laboratory (PNNL). "Compressed Air Energy Storage." August 2019. *https://caes.pnnl.gov/.*

Paul, Fredric. "IoT Has an Obsolescence Problem." *Network World*, June 11, 2018. *https://www.networkworld.com/article/3279729/iot-has-an-obsolescence-problem.html.*

Pegues, Jeff. "Feds Tracking Down Hacker Who Tried to Poison Florida Town's Water Supply." *CBS News*, February 9, 2021. *https://www.cbsnews.com/news/florida-water-hack-oldsmar-treatment-plant/.*

Seltzer, Molly A. "Why Salt is this Power Plant's Most Valuable Asset." *Smithsonian Magazine*, August 4, 2017. *https://www.smithsonianmag.com/innovation/salt-power-plant-most-valuable-180964307/.*

Sobczak, Blake. "Report Reveals Play-by-play of first U.S. Grid Cyber-attack." *E&E News*, September 6, 2019. *https://www.eenews.net/stories/1061111289.*

Spector, Julian "Montana Developer Ready to Build Modern-Day Pumped Hydro Storage." *Greentech Media*, August 13, 2019. *https://www.greentechmedia.com/articles/read/montana-developer-ready-to-build-first-us-pumped-hydro-storage-in-years.*

Spector, Julian. "The Biggest Batteries Coming Soon to a Grid Near You." *Greentech Media*, September 3, 2019. *https://www.greentechmedia.com/articles/read/the-biggest-batteries-coming-soon-to-a-grid-near-you.*

U.S. Department of Energy (USDOE). "Pumped-Storage Hydropower." Accessed August 27, 2020. *https://www.energy.gov/eere/water/pumped-storage-hydropower.*

U.S. Department of Energy (USDOE). "What is the Smart Grid?" Accessed August 23, 2020. *https://www.smartgrid.gov/the_smart_grid/.*

U.S. Energy Information Administration (USEIA). "Battery Storage in the United States: an Update on Market Trends." July 15, 2020. *https://www.eia.gov/analysis/studies/electricity/batterystorage/.*

U.S. Energy Information Administration (USEIA). "Most Pumped Storage Electricity Generators in the U.S. Were Built in the 1970s." October 31, 2019. *https://www.eia.gov/todayinenergy/detail.php?id=41833.*

U.S. Energy Information Administration (USEIA). "U.S. Energy Mapping System." Accessed September 14, 2020. *https://www.eia.gov/state/maps.php.*

U.S. Geological Survey (USGS). "Cadmium." Mineral Commodity Summaries. January 2020. *https://www.usgs.gov/centers/nmic/cadmium-statistics-and-information.*

U.S. Geological Survey (USGS). "Lithium." Mineral Commodity Summaries. January 2020. *https://www.usgs.gov/centers/nmic/lithium-statistics-and-information.*

U.S. Geological Survey (USGS). "Nickel." Mineral Commodity Summaries. January 2020. *https://www.usgs.gov/centers/nmic/nickel-statistics-and-information.*

U.S. Geological Survey (USGS). "Nitrogen (Fixed)–Ammonia." Mineral Commodity Summaries. January 2020. *https://www.usgs.gov/centers/nmic/nitrogen-statistics-and-information.*

Wang, Jidai, Kunpeng Lu, Lan Ma, Jihong Wang, Mark Dooner, Shihong Miao, Jian Li, and Dan Wang. "Overview of Compressed Air Energy Storage and Technology Development." *Energies* 10, no. 7 (May 2017): 991. *https://doi.org/10.3390/en10070991.*

CHAPTER 8. THE WINTER

Algae Biomass Organization (ABO). "Algae and Land: a Few Acres Yield a lot of Fuel." April 30, 2020. *https://algaebiomass.org/blog/3286/algae-and-land-a-few-acres-yield-a-lot-of-fuel-2/.*

All About Algae. "FAQ: Biofuels: History, Demonstrations, End-Products, Production Process, Costs." Accessed August 29, 2020. *http://allaboutalgae.com/faq-history/.*

Beeler, Carolyn and James Morrison. "The UK's Move away from Coal Means They're Burning Wood from the US." *The World*, July 20, 2018. *https://www.pri.org/stories/2018-06-20/uk-s-move-away-coal-means-they-re-burning-wood-us.*

Clean Energy Institute. "Lithium-Ion Battery." Accessed September 14, 2020. *https://www.cei.washington.edu/education/science-of-solar/battery-technology/.*

Cooke, "Americans Have Stopped Relocating, and it could Dramatically Affect Society." *Quartz*, December 7, 2019. *https://qz.com/1761630/why-americans-have-stopped-moving-geographically-even-for-work/.*

Dart, Tom. "The Dirty Little Secret behind 'Clean Energy' Wood Pellets." *The Guardian*, June 30, 2018. *https://www.theguardian.com/environment/2018/jun/30/wood-pellets-biomass-environmental-impact.*

De Luna, Phil, Christopher Hahn, Drew Higgins, Shaffiq A. Jaffer, Thomas F. Jaramillo, Edward H. Sargent. "What Would it Take for Renewably Powered Electrosynthesis to Displace Petrochemical Processes?" *Science* 364, no. 6438 (April 2019): eaav3506. *http://dx.doi.org/10.1126/science.aav3506.*

Federal Reserve Bank of St. Louis. "All Employees, Coal Mining." Accessed September 14, 2020. *https://fred.stlouisfed.org/series/CES1021210001.*

Federal Reserve Bank of St. Louis. "Full-time and Part-time Employees: Domestic Private Industries: Coal Mining (J4209CoA173JBEA)." Accessed September 14, 2020. *https://fred.stlouisfed.org/series/J4209CoA173NBEA.*

Gander, Kashmira. "'Deaths of Despair': U.S. Life Expectancy Has Been Falling since 2014, with Biggest Impacts in Rust Belt and Ohio Valley." *Newsweek*, November 26, 2019. *https://www.newsweek.com/deaths-despair-u-s-life-expectancy-falling-since-2014-1473848.*

Gofman. Evelyn. "Energy Density of Aviation Fuel." *The Physics Factbook*, accessed September 14, 2020. *https://hypertextbook.com/facts/2003/EvelynGofman.shtml.*

Goldstein, Amy. *Janesville: An American Story.* New York: Simon & Schuster, 2017.

Howe, Frances. "Don't Believe the Hype: Biomass is an Environmental Disaster." *Red Pepper*, April 17, 2018. *https://www.redpepper.org.uk/dont-believe-the-hype-biomass-is-an-environmental-disaster/.*

International Energy Administration (IEA). "Outlook for Biogas and Biomethane: Prospects for Organic Growth." March 2020. *https://www.iea.org/reports/outlook-for-biogas-and-biomethane-prospects-for-organic-growth* (login required).

Irfan, Umair. "The Green New Deal is Fracturing a Critical Base for Democrats: Unions." *Vox*, June 19, 2019. *https://www.vox.com/2019/5/22/18628299/green-new-deal-labor-union-2020-democrats.*

Jessup, Ralph S. and Edward J. Prosen. "Heats of Combustion and Formation of Cellulose and Nitrocellulose (Cellulose Nitrate)." U.S. Department of Commerce Research Paper RP2086. April 1950 *https://nvlpubs.nist.gov/nistpubs/jres/44/jresv44n4p387_A1b.pdf.*

Kelley, Alexandra. "Biden Tells Coal Miners to 'Learn to Code'." *The Hill*, December 31, 2019. *https://thehill.com/changing-america/enrichment/education/476391-biden-tells-coal-miners-to-learn-to-code.*

Le Feuvre, Pharoah. "Are Aviation Biofuels Ready for Take off?" *International Energy Agency*, March 18, 2019. *https://www.iea.org/commentaries/are-aviation-biofuels-ready-for-take-off.*

National Institute of Standards and Technology (NIST). "NIST Chemistry WebBook." Accessed August 28, 2020. *https://doi.org/10.18434/T4D303.*

Princeton University. "A More Potent Greenhouse Gas than Carbon Dioxide, Methane Emissions Will Leap as Earth Warms." *Science Daily*, March 27, 2014. *https://www.sciencedaily.com/releases/2014/03/140327111724.htm.*

Reddy, Chris and Greg O'Neil, "Jet Fuel from Algae? Scientists Probe Fuel Potential in Common Ocean Plant." *Oceanus*, January 28, 2015. *https://www.whoi.edu/oceanus/feature/jet-fuel-from-algae/.*

Rodgers, Lucy. "Climate Change: The Massive CO2 Emitter You May Not Know About." *BBC News*, December 17, 2018. *https://www.bbc.com/news/science-environment-46455844.*

Selyukh, Alina. "What Gets to Be a 'Burger'? States Restrict Labels on Plant-Based Meat," *NPR*, July 23, 2019. *https://www.npr.org/sections/thesalt/2019/07/23/744083270/what-gets-to-be-a-burger-states-restrict-labels-on-plant-based-meat.*

Timperley, Jocelyn. "Q&A: Why Cement Emission Matter for Climate Change." *Carbon Brief*, September 13, 2018. *https://www.carbonbrief.org/qa-why-cement-emissions-matter-for-climate-change.*

U.S. Department of Agriculture (USDA). "2017 Census of Agriculture Highlights: Farm Producers." April 2019. *https://www.nass.usda.gov/Publications/Highlights/2019/2017Census_Farm_Producers.pdf.*

U.S. Department of Energy (USDOE). "Hydrogen production: Thermochemical Water Splitting." Accessed August 30, 2020. *https://www.energy.gov/eere/fuelcells/hydrogen-production-thermochemical-water-splitting.*

U.S. Energy Information Administration (USEIA). "As U.S. Airlines Carry More Passengers, Jet Fuel Use Remains Well Below Its Previous Peak." June 6, 2017. *https://www.eia.gov/todayinenergy/detail.php?id=31512.*

U.S. Energy Information Administration (USEIA). "U.S. Ethanol Production Capacity Continues to Increase." June 28, 2017. *https://www.eia.gov/todayinenergy/detail.php?id=31832.*

CHAPTER 9. THE SEA

Abrams, Lindsay. "Does Russ George Deserve a Nobel Price or a Prison Sentence?" *Salon*, updated November 4, 2013. *https://www.salon.com/*

test2/2013/08/30/does_millionaire_russ_george_deserve_a_nobel_
prize_or_a_prison_sentence/.

Bruckner, Monica. "The Gulf of Mexico Dead Zone." *Microbial Life*,
accessed September 2, 2020. *https://serc.carleton.edu/microbelife/
topics/deadzone/index.html.*

Convention on Biological Diversity. "Climate-Related Geoengineering
and Biodiversity," Accessed September 14, 2020. *https://www.cbd.int/
climate/geoengineering/.*

Cummins, Eleanor. "The Price of Solar Panels Just Went up—Here's what
that Means for You." *Popular Science*, June 8, 2018. *https://www.popsci.
com/solar-panel-tariff-effects/.*

Dopyera, Caroline. "The Iron Hypothesis." *Earth Magazine*, October
1996. *http://www.homepages.ed.ac.uk/shs/Climatechange/Carbon%20
sequestration/Martin%20iron.htm.*

Falconer, Bruce. "Can Anyone Stop the Man who Will Try Just about Anything to Put an End to Climate Change." *Pacific Standard*, updated
January 16, 2018. *https://psmag.com/social-justice/battlefield-earth-
can-anyone-stop-man-will-try-just-anything-fix-climate-78957.*

Homer, Marianne. "Underwater Meadows of Seagrass could be the Ideal
Carbon Sinks." *Smithsonian Magazine*, November 1, 2018. *https://
www.smithsonianmag.com/science-nature/underwater-meadows-sea-
grass-could-be-ideal-carbon-sinks-180970686/.*

Keim, Brandon. "Ocean Fertilization Works—Unless it Doesn't." *Wired*,
January 29, 2009. *https://www.wired.com/2009/01/oceaniron/.*

Lampitt, R.S., E.P. Achterberg, T.R. Anderson, J.A. Hughes, M.D. Igle-
sias-Rodriguez, B.A. Kelly-Gerreyn, M. Lucas, E.E. Popova, R.
Sanders, J.G. Sheperd, D. Smythe-Wright, and A. Yool. "Ocean Fertilization: a Potential Means of Geoengineering." *Philosophical Trans-
actions of the Royal Society A* 366, no. 1882 (August 2008): 3919–3945.
https://doi.org/10.1098/rsta.2008.0139.

Li, Qian, Louis Legendre, and Nianzhi Jiao. "Phytoplankton Response to
Nitrogen and Iron Limitation in the Tropical and Subtropical Pacific
Ocean." *Journal of Plankton Research* 37, no. 2 (February 2015): 306–
319. *https://doi.org/10.1093/plankt/fbv008.*

Macreadie, Peter I., Q.R. Ollivier, J.J. Kelleway, O. Serrano, P.E. Carnell,
C.J. Ewers Lewis, T.B. Atwood, J. Sanderman, J. Baldock, R.M. Con-

nolly, C.M. Duarte, P.S. Lavery, A. Steven, and C.E. Lovelock. "Carbon Sequestration by Australian Tidal Marshes." *Scientific Reports* 7 (March 2017): 44071. *https://doi.org/10.1038/srep44071.*

National Oceanic and Atmospheric Administration (NOAA). "Carbon Cycle." February 2019. *https://www.noaa.gov/education/resource-collections/climate/carbon-cycle.*

National Oceanic and Atmospheric Administration (NOAA). "NOAA Forecasts very large 'Dead Zone' for Gulf of Mexico." June 12, 2019. *https://www.noaa.gov/media-release/noaa-forecasts-very-large-dead-zone-for-gulf-of-mexico.*

Romañach, Stephanie S., Donald L. DeAngelis, Hock Lye Koh, Yuhong Li, Su Yean Teh, Raja Sulaiman Raja Barizan, and Lu Zhai. "Conservation and Restoration of Mangroves: Global Status, Perspectives, and Prognosis." *Ocean & Coastal Management* 154 (March 2018): 72–82. *https://doi.org/10.1016/j.ocecoaman.2018.01.009.*

Runwal, Priyanka. "Tracking Carbon Stored in Revived Bay Area Salt Marshes." Lawrence *Berkeley National Laboratory*, September 27, 2019. *https://eesa.lbl.gov/tracking-carbon-stored-in-restored-bay-area-salt-marshes/.*

Schiermeier, Quirin. "Ocean Fertilization: Dead in the Water?" *Nature* 457, no. 7228 (January 2009): 520–521. *https://doi.org/10.1038/457520b.*

Scott, Robert E. "We Can Reshore Manufacturing Jobs, but Trump Hasn't Done it." *Economic Policy Institute*, August 10, 2020. *https://www.epi.org/publication/reshoring-manufacturing-jobs/.*

Selin, Henrik and Rebecca Cowing. "Cargo Ships are Emitting Boatloads of Carbon, and Nobody Wants to Take the Blame." *Phys Org*, December 18, 2018. *https://phys.org/news/2018-12-cargo-ships-emitting-boatloads-carbon.html.*

Stecker, Tiffany. "Restoring Mangroves May Prove Cheap way to Cool Climate." *Scientific American*, July 31, 2012. *https://www.scientificamerican.com/article/restoring-mangroves-may-prove-cheap-way-to-cool-climate/.*

UN Environment Programme. "Seagrass–Secret Weapon in the Fight Against Global Heating." Accessed September 14, 2020. *https://www.unenvironment.org/news-and-stories/story/seagrass-secret-weapon-fight-against-global-heating.*

Underwood, Emily. "The Complicated Role of Iron in Ocean Health and Climate Change." *Smithsonian Magazine*, January 3, 2020. *https:// www.smithsonianmag.com/science-nature/complicated-role-iron- ocean-health-and-climate-change-180973893/.*

Worthington, Thomas and Mark Spalding. "Mangrove Restoration Potential: A Global Map Highlighting a Critical Opportunity." *International Union for Conservation of Nature*, 2018. *https://oceanwealth. org/applications/mangrove-restoration/.*

CHAPTER 10. THE LAND

Ahmed, Amal. "How Texas Prairies Could Help Combat Climate Change." *The Texas Observer*, September 6, 2019. *https://www.texasobserver.org/ climate-change-texas-prairie-grass-carbon-sink/.*

Barrett, Sully. "How the Impossible Burger is Changing the Debate over GMO Foods." *CNBC*, February 13, 2020. *https://www.cnbc. com/2020/02/13/how-the-impossible-burger-is-changing-the-debate- over-gmo-foods.html.*

Barthelmes, Alexandra, John Couwenberg, Mette Risager, Cosima Tegetmeyer, and Hans Joosten. "Peatlands and Climate in a Ramsar Context: A Nordic-Baltic Perspective." TemaNord 2015:544. 2015. *http:// norden.diva-portal.org/smash/get/diva2:814147/FULLTEXT02.pdf.*

Bromwich, Jonah Engel and Sanam Yar. "The Fake Meat War." *The New York Times*, July 25, 2019. *https://www.nytimes.com/2019/07/25/style/ plant-based-meat-law.html.*

Cassidy, Emily S., Paul C. West, James S. Gerber, and Jonathan A. Foley. "Redefining Agricultural Yields: From Tonnes to People Nourished per Hectare." *Environmental Research Letters* 8, no. 3 (August 2013): 034015. *https://iopscience.iop.org/article/10.1088/1748-9326/8/3/034015/ meta.*

Central Minnesota Regional Sustainable Development Partnership (CMRSDP). "A Landowner's Guide to Carbon Sequestration Credits." October 2009. *http://www.myminnesotawoods.umn.edu/wp-content/ uploads/2009/10/landowner-guide-carbon-seq1-5-12.pdf.*

Fargione, Joseph E., Steven Bassett, Timothy Boucher, Scott D. Bridgham, Richard T. Conant, Susan C. Cook-Patton, Peter W. Ellis, Alessandra Falucci, James W. Fourqurean, Trisha Gopalakrishna, Huan

Gu, Benjamin Henderson, Matthew D. Hurteau, Kevin D. Kroeger, Timm Kroeger, Tyler J. Lark, Sara M. Leavitt, Guy Lomax, Robert I. McDonald, J. Patrick Megonigal, Daniela A. Miteva, Curtis J. Richardson, Jonathan Sanderman, David Shoch, Seth A. Spawn, Joseph W. Veldman, Christopher A. Williams, Peter B. Woodbury, Chris Zganjar, Marci Baranski, Patricia Elia, Richard A. Houghton, Emily Landis, Emily McGlynn, William H. Schlesinger, Juha V. Siikamaki, Ariana E. Sutton-Grier, and Bronson W. Griscom. "Natural Climate Solutions for the United States." *Science Advances* 4, no. 11 (November 2018): eaat1869. *dx.doi.org/10.1126/sciadv.aat1869.*

Foley, Jonathan. "A Five-Step Plan to Feed the World." *National Geographic*, May 2014. *https://www.nationalgeographic.com/foodfeatures/ feeding-9-billion/.*

Food and Agriculture Organization of the United Nations (UNFAO). "Key Facts and Findings." Accessed September 14, 2020. *http://www. fao.org/news/story/en/item/197623/icode/.*

Food and Agriculture Organization of the United Nations (UNFAO). "The State of Food Security and Nutrition in the World." 2020. *http:// www.fao.org/documents/card/en/c/ca9692en.*

Frank, Robert. "Why Does the Govt. Pay Farmers to Not Grow Crops." *PBS News Hour*, August 4, 2009. *https://www.pbs.org/newshour/econ-omy/why-does-the-govt-pay-farmers.*

Gewin, Virginia. "How Peat Could Protect the Planet." *Nature* 578, no. 7794 (February 2020): 204–208. *https://doi.org/10.1038/d41586-020-00355-3.*

Hoover, William L. "Financial and Tax Aspects of Tree Planting." Purdue Agriculture FNR-214-W. 2004. *https://www.extension.purdue.edu/ extmedia/fnr/fnr-214-w.pdf.*

Kendall, Erika Nicole. "The Impossible Burger and Beyond Meat Aren't healthier. Fast Food's Meatless Marvels Are Just P.R." *Think*, September 8, 2019. *https://www.nbcnews.com/think/opinion/impossible-burger-or-beyond-meat-aren-t-healthy-fast-food-ncna1050911.*

Khan, Rina Saeed. "As a 'Green Stimulus' Pakistan sets Virus-Idled to Work Planting Trees." *Reuters*, April 28, 2020. *https://www.reuters. com/article/us-health-coronavirus-pakistan-trees-fea/as-a-green-stimulus-pakistan-sets-virus-idled-to-work-planting-trees-idUSKC-N22A369.*

Maslin, Mark and Simon Lewis. "Yes, We Can Reforest on a Massive Scale—but it's no Substitute for Slashing Emissions." *Climate Home News*, May 7, 2019. *https://www.climatechangenews.com/2019/07/05/ yes-can-reforest-massive-scale-no-substitute-slashing-emissions/.*

Niiler, Eric. "Tiny Country Cuts Carbon Emissions by Planting Bogs." *National Geographic*, August 4, 2017. *https://www.nationalgeo-graphic.com/news/2017/08/estonia-reduces-carbon-emissions-plant-ing-peat-bogs/.*

Schuetz, Jenny. "To Improve Housing Affordability, We Need Better Alignment of Zoning, Taxes, and Subsidies." *Brookings*, January 7, 2020. *https://www.brookings.edu/policy2020/bigideas/ to-improve-housing-affordability-we-need-better-alignment-of-zon-ing-taxes-and-subsidies/.*

Siegler, Kirk. "Small-Town Hospitals Are Closing Just as Coronavirus Arrives in Rural America." *NPR Weekend Edition Sunday*, April 9, 2020. *https://www.npr.org/2020/04/09/829753752/small-town-hospitals-are-closing-just-as-coronavirus-arrives-in-rural-america.*

Sommer, Lauren. "To Manage Wildfire, California Looks to what Tribes Have Known all Along." *NPR*, August 24, 2020. *https://www.npr. org/2020/08/24/899422710/to-manage-wildfire-california-looks-to-what-tribes-have-known-all-along.*

Soper, E.K. and C.C. Osbon. "The Occurrence and Uses of Peat in the United States." Department of the Interior Bulletin 728. 1922. *https:// pubs.usgs.gov/bul/0728/report.pdf.*

The National Academies of Sciences Engineering and Medicine (NASEM). *Genetically Engineered Crops: Experiences and Prospects*. Washington, DC: The National Academies Press, 2016. *https://doi.org/10.17226/23395.*

The Ontario Tallgrass Prairie and Savanna Association (TgO). "Tallgrass Prairie and Carbon Sequestration." Accessed September 4, 2020. *https://tallgrassontario.org/wp-site/carbon-sequestration/.*

Trembath, Alex. "Food Activists Angry About the Processed Nature of New Plant-Based Meats are Missing the Point." August 12, 2019. *https://onezero.medium.com/the-fake-backlash-to-fake-meat-f53098b-fb71b.*

UC Davis. "Grasslands More Reliable Carbon Sink than Trees." *Phys Org*, July 9, 2018. *https://phys.org/news/2018-07-grasslands-reliable-carbon-trees.html.*

U.S. Department of Agriculture (USDA). "Conservation Programs." Accessed December 29, 2020. *https://www.fsa.usda.gov/programs-and-services/conservation-programs/.*

U.S. Department of Agriculture (USDA). "Farms and Land in Farms 2018 Summary." April 2019. *https://www.nass.usda.gov/Publications/Todays_Reports/reports/fnlo0419.pdf.*

Urry, Amelia. "Our Crazy Farm Subsidies, Explained." *Grist*, April 20, 2015. *https://grist.org/food/our-crazy-farm-subsidies-explained/.*

Votteler, Todd H. and Thomas A. Muir. "Wetland Protection Legislation." U.S. Geological Survey Water Supply Paper 2425. January 29, 2002. *https://water.usgs.gov/nwsum/WSP2425/legislation.html.*

Wang, Jim J. and Syam K. Dodla. "Wetland Soil Carbon Sequestration." *Louisiana State University*, July 29, 2013. *https://www.lsuagcenter.com/portals/communications/publications/agmag/archive/2013/spring/wetland-soil-carbon-sequestration.*

CHAPTER 11. THE STONE

Bhambhani, Dipka. "Everyone Wants Carbon Capture and Sequestration—Now How to Make it a Reaility?" *Forbes*, November 21, 2019. *https://www.forbes.com/sites/dipkabhambhani/2019/11/21/washington-to-wall-street-hears-harmony-on-ccs-to-address-climate-change/#5c-2e282c35da.*

Biniek, Krysta, Kimberly Henderson, Matt Rogers, and Gregory Santoni. "Driving CO2 Emissions to Zero (and Beyond) with Carbon Capture, Use, and Storage." *McKinsey Quarterly*, July 30, 2020. *https://www.mckinsey.com/business-functions/sustainability/our-insights/driving-co2-emissions-to-zero-and-beyond-with-carbon-capture-use-and-storage.*

Center for Climate and Energy Solutions (C2ES). "Carbon Capture." Accessed September 6, 2020. *https://www.c2es.org/content/carbon-capture/.*

De Clercq, Geert. "Europe's First Solar Panel Recycling Plant Opens in France." *Reuters*, June 25, 2018. *https://www.reuters.com/article/*

us-solar-recycling/europes-first-solar-panel-recycling-plant-opens-in-france-idUSKBN1JL28Z.

Feulner, Georg. "Formation of Most of Our Coal Brought Earth Close to Global Glaciation." *Proceedings of the National Academy of Sciences* 114, no. 43 (October 2017): 11333–11337. *https://doi.org/10.1073/pnas.1712062114.*

Goode, Lauren. "Right-to-Repair Groups Don't Buy Apple's Answers to Congress." *Wired*, November 27, 2019. *https://www.wired.com/story/right-to-repair-apple-answers-congress/.*

Hadhazy, Adam. "Here's the Truth about the 'Planned Obsolescence' of Tech." *BBC Future*, June 12, 2016. *https://www.bbc.com/future/article/20160612-heres-the-truth-about-the-planned-obsolescence-of-tech.*

Huffman, Tom. "Boots Theory of Socioeconomic Unfairness." *MoneyWise*, December 11, 2019. *https://moneywise.com/a/boots-theory-of-socioeconomic-unfairness.*

Johnson, Jeff. "Capturing Carbon: Can it Save Us?" *C&EN*, February 25, 2019. *https://cen.acs.org/environment/greenhouse-gases/Capturing-carbon-save-us/97/i8.*

Kelemen, Peter, Sally M. Benson, Hélèn Pilorge, Peter Psarras, and Jennifer Wilcox. "An Overview of the Status and Challenges of CO_2 Storage in Minerals and Geological Formation." *Frontiers in Climate* 1 (November 2019). *https://doi.org/10.3389/fclim.2019.00009.*

McFall-Johnsen, Morgan. "The Fashion Industry Emits More Carbon than International Flights and Maritime Shipping Combined. Here Are the Biggest Ways it Impacts the Planet." *Business Insider*, October 21, 2019. *https://www.businessinsider.com/fast-fashion-environmental-impact-pollution-emissions-waste-water-2019-10.*

O'Callaghan, Jonathan. "Storing CO_2 Underground Can Curb Carbon Emissions, but Is it Safe?" *Horizon*, November 27, 2018. *https://horizon-magazine.eu/article/storing-co2-underground-can-curb-carbon-emissions-it-safe.html.*

Robbins, Jim. "As Mass Timber Takes Off, How Green Is this New Building Material?" *Yale Environment 360*, April 9, 2019. *https://e360.yale.edu/features/as-mass-timber-takes-off-how-green-is-this-new-building-material.*

Schwartz, Thomas J., Samuel M. Goodman, Christian M. Osmundsen, Esben Taarning, Michael D. Mozuch, Jill Gaskell, Daniel Cullen, Philip J. Kersten, and James A. Dumesic. "Integration of Chemical and Biological Catalysis: Production of Furylglycolic Acid from Glucose via Cortalcerone." *ACS Catalysis* 3, no. 12 (October 2013): 2689–2693. *https://doi.org/10.1021/cs400593p.*

Service, Robert F. "New Way to Turn Carbon Dioxide into Coal Could 'Rewind the Emissions Clock'." *Science*, February 26, 2019. *https://doi. org/10.1126/science.aax1527.*

Snæbjörnsdóttir Sandra Ó, Bergur Sigfússon, Chiara Marieni, David Goldberg, Sigurður R. Gislason, and Eric H. Oelkers, "Carbon Dioxide Storage Through Mineral Carbonation." *Nature Reviews Earth & Environment* 1, no. 1 (January 2020): 90–102. *https://doi.org/10.1038/ s43017-019-0011-8.*

U.S. Geological Survey (USGS). "Making Minerals—How Growing Rocks Can Help Reduce Carbon Emissions." March 8, 2019. *https://www. usgs.gov/news/making-minerals-how-growing-rocks-can-help-reduce- carbon-emissions.*

von Hippel, Ted. "Thermal Removal of Carbon Dioxide from the Atmosphere: Energy Requirements and Scaling Issues." *Climatic Change* 148, no. 1–2 (May 2018): 491–501. *https://doi.org/10.1007/s10584-018- 2208-0.*

CHAPTER 12. THE SKY

Appalachian Magazine. "200 Years Ago: The Year Without a Summer." *Appalachian Magazine*, May 20, 2016. *http://appalachianmagazine. com/2016/05/20/200-years-ago-the-year-without-a-summer/.*

Appelbaum, Binyamin. *The Economists Hour: False Prophets, Free Markets, and the Fracture of Society.* Boston: Little, Brown and Company, 2019.

Calma, Justine. "As a Last Resort, Andrew Yang Proposes Space Mirrors to Save the Planet." *The Verge*, August 26, 2019. *https://www.theverge. com/2019/8/26/20833928/andrew-yang-climate-change-nuclear-car- bon-capture-geoengineering-2020-elections.*

G., Leonard. "File:AlbertaSulfurAtVancouverBC.jpg." *Wikimedia Commons*, July 10, 2005. *https://commons.wikimedia.org/wiki/File:AlbertaSulfurAtVancouverBC.jpg.*

Irfan, Umair. "Air Travel is a Huge Contributor to Climate Change. A New Global Movement Wants You to Be Ashamed to Fly." *Vox*, November 30, 2019. *https://www.vox.com/the-highlight/2019/7/25/8881364/greta-thunberg-climate-change-flying-airline.*

Kaufman, Rachel. "Could Space Mirrors Stop Global Warming?" *Live Science*, August 8, 2012. *https://www.livescience.com/22202-space-mirrors-global-warming.html.*

Kennedy, Tristan. "I Quit Flying for Good. Here's How it Changed my Life." *Vice*, November 29, 2019. *https://www.vice.com/en_uk/article/43kjvp/quit-flying-change-life-flight-free.*

Khoo, Anna. "Coronavirus Lockdown Sees Air Pollution Plummet across UK." *BBC News*, April 8, 2020. *https://www.bbc.com/news/uk-england-52202974.*

Lee, Timothy B. "Watch American Passenger Rail Shrivel Up and Die in this Animated Map." *Vox*, March 11, 2015. *https://www.vox.com/2015/3/11/8192499/amtrak-passenger-train-decline.*

Milman, Oliver. "US Greenhouse Gas Emission Fell 10% in 2020 as Covid Curbed Travel." *The Guardian*, January 12, 2021. *https://www.theguardian.com/environment/2021/jan/12/us-greenhouse-gas-emissions-fell-2020-covid-curbed-travel.*

National Aeronautics and Space Administration (NASA). "Aerosols and Incoming Sunlight (Direct Effects)." November 2, 2010. *https://earthobservatory.nasa.gov/features/Aerosols/page3.php.*

Peshin, Akash. "Why Is the Sky Blue?" *Science ABC*, updated April 10, 2019. *https://www.scienceabc.com/nature/why-is-the-sky-blue.html.*

Petchenik, Ian. "Then and Now: Visualizing COVID-19's Impact on Air Traffic." *Flight Radar 24*, April 7, 2020. *https://www.flightradar24.com/blog/then-and-now-visualizing-covid-19s-impact-on-air-traffic/.*

CHAPTER 13. THE MARKET

350.org. "About 350." Accessed August 23, 2020. *https://350.org/about/.*

Alaska Oil and Gas Association (AOGA). "Permanent Fund Dividend." Accessed August 22, 2020. *https://www.aoga.org/facts-and-figures/permanent-fund-dividend.*

Aronoff, Kate. "The Fossil Fuel Industry Spent $100 Million to Kill Green Ballot Measures in Three States—and Won." *The Intercept,* November 7, 2018. *https://theintercept.com/2018/11/07/midterm-elections-green-ballot-measures-fossil-fuel/.*

Arrhenius, Svante. "On the Influence of Carbonic Acid in the Air upon the Temperature of the Ground." *Philosophical Magazine and Journal of Science* 41, no. 251 (April 1896): 237–276. *https://www.rsc.org/images/Arrhenius1896_tcm18-173546.pdf.*

BBC News. "Norway's $1 Trillion Fund to Cut Oil and Gas Investments." *BBC News,* March 8, 2019. *https://www.bbc.com/news/business-47494239.*

Climate Policy Info Hub. "The EU Emissions Trading System: an Introduction." Accessed September 29, 2020. *https://climatepolicyinfohub.eu/eu-emissions-trading-system-introduction.*

Collinson, Patrick and Jillian Ambrose. "UK's Biggest Pension Fund Begins Fossil Fuels Divestment." *The Guardian,* July 29, 2020. *https://www.theguardian.com/environment/2020/jul/29/national-employment-savings-trust-uks-biggest-pension-fund-divests-from-fossil-fuels.*

Colman, Zack. "Democrats Split from Obama Playbook with Aggressive Climate Plans." *Politico,* September 4, 2019. *https://www.politico.com/story/2019/09/04/democrats-2020-obama-climate-change-1705031.*

Colman, Zack. "Europe Threatens U.S. with Carbon Tariffs to Combat Climate Change." *Politico,* December 13, 2019. *https://www.politico.com/news/2019/12/13/europe-carbon-tariff-climate-change-084892.*

Delwiche, Theodore R. and Mariel A. Klein. "Judge Dismisses Divestment Lawsuit." *The Harvard Crimson,* March 24, 2015. *https://www.thecrimson.com/article/2015/3/24/judge-dismisses-divestment-lawsuit/.*

DeMarban, Alex. "This Year's Alaska Permanent Fund Dividend: $1,606." September 28, 2019. *https://www.adn.com/alaska-news/2019/09/27/this-years-alaska-permanent-fund-dividend-1606/.*

Drum, Kevin. "Lead: America's Real Criminal Element." *Mother Jones,* January/February 2013. *https://www.motherjones.com/environment/2016/02/lead-exposure-gasoline-crime-increase-children-health/.*

European Commission. "EU Emissions Trading System (EU ETS)." Accessed September 29, 2020. *https://ec.europa.eu/clima/policies/ets_en.*

Friedman, Zack. "Student Loan Debt Statistics in 2020: A Record $1.6 Trillion." *Forbes,* February 3, 2020. *https://www.forbes.com/sites/zackfriedman/2020/02/03/student-loan-debt-statistics/#572e7271281f.*

Fuast, Drew Gilpin. "Fossil Fuel Divestment Statement." *Harvard University,* October 3, 2013. *https://www.harvard.edu/president/news/2013/fossil-fuel-divestment-statement.*

Gould, Elise. "State of Working America Wages 2019: A Story of Slow, Uneven, and Unequal Wage Growth over the Last 40 Years." *Economic Policy Institute,* February 20, 2020. *https://www.epi.org/publication/swa-wages-2019/.*

Greenpeace. "Exxon's Climate Denial History: A Timeline." Accessed October 6, 2020. *https://www.greenpeace.org/usa/global-warming/exxon-and-the-oil-industry-knew-about-climate-change/exxons-climate-denial-history-a-timeline/.*

Grose, Thomas K. "Europe's Carbon Market Crisis: Why Does it Matter?" *National Geographic,* April 20, 2013. *https://www.nationalgeographic.com/news/energy/2013/04/130418-europe-carbon-market-crisis/.*

Hall, Shannon. "Exxon Knew about Climate Change almost 40 Years Ago." *Scientific American,* October 26, 2015. *https://www.scientificamerican.com/article/exxon-knew-about-climate-change-almost-40-years-ago/.*

Henning, Peter J. "Guilty Pleas and Heavy Fines Seem to Be Cost of Business for Wall St." *The New York Times,* May 20, 2015. *https://www.nytimes.com/2015/05/21/business/dealbook/guilty-pleas-and-heavy-fines-seem-to-be-cost-of-business-for-wall-st.html.*

Javed, Umair. "Lessons from Kerala." *Dawn,* May 18, 2020. *https://www.dawn.com/news/1557940.*

Keidan, Maiya and Carolyn Cohn. "British Pension Schemes Warn on Cost of Fossil Fuel Divestment." *Reuters,* January 20, 2020. *https://www.reuters.com/article/us-britain-pensions-divestment/british-pension-schemes-warn-on-cost-of-fossil-fuel-divestment-idUSKBN1ZJ1EK.*

Kiel, Paul and Jesse Eisinger. "How the IRS Was Gutted." *ProPublica*, December 11, 2018. *https://www.propublica.org/article/how-the-irs-was-gutted*.

Kitman, Jamie Lincoln. "The Secret History of Lead." *The Nation*, March 2, 2000. *https://www.thenation.com/article/archive/secret-history-lead/*.

Lund, Dorothy S. and Natasha Sarin. "Corporate Crime and Punishment: An Empirical Study." University of Pennsylvania Institute for Law and Economics Research Paper No. 20-13, February 17, 2020. *https://dx.doi.org/10.2139/ssrn.3537245*.

Marlon, Jennifer, Xinran Wang, Abel Gustafson, Matthew Ballew, Matthew Goldberg, Seth Rosenthal, and Anthony Leiserowitz. "Majority of Americans Think Fossil Fuel Companies are Responsible for the Damages Caused by Global Warming." *Yale Program on Climate Change Communication*, June 19, 2019. *https://climatecommunication.yale.edu/publications/majority-of-americans-think-fossil-fuel-companies-are-responsible-for-the-damages-caused-by-global-warming/*.

Martin, Nick. "Why are Democratic Governors Still Doing Favors for the Oil Industry?" *The New Republic*, November 22, 2019. *https://newrepublic.com/article/155823/democratic-governors-still-favors-oil-industry*.

Meredith, Sam. "A Contentious Russian-Led Gas Pipeline in Europe Will Soon Exist—Here's why It Matters." *CNBC*, October 31, 2019. *https://www.cnbc.com/2019/10/31/nord-stream-2-a-russian-led-gas-pipeline-in-europe-will-soon-exist.html*.

Michaels, Dave. "Wall Street Fines Peaked in 2020, Driven by Sums from Big Cases." *The Wall Street Journal*, November 2, 2020. *https://www.wsj.com/articles/wall-street-fines-peaked-in-2020-driven-by-sums-from-big-cases-11604340887*.

Michaels, David. *The Triumph of Doubt: Dark Money and the Science of Deception*. Oxford: Oxford University Press, 2020.

Milman, Oliver. "Microsoft Joins Group Seeking to Kill off Historic Climate Change Lawsuits." *The Guardian*, May 2, 2019. *https://www.theguardian.com/technology/2019/may/01/microsoft-joins-group-seeking-to-avoid-climate-change-lawsuit*.

Mufson, Steven. "Harvard Says Fighting Climate Change is a Top Priority. But it still Won't Divest from Fossil Fuels." *The Washington Post*,

July 7, 2019. *https://www.washingtonpost.com/climate-environment/harvard-says-fighting-climate-change-is-a-top-priority-but-it-still-wont-divest-from-fossil-fuels/2019/07/02/b6547684-9d03-11e9-9ed4-c9089972ad5a_story.html.*

Nova, Annie. "Why Millennials May Shrug at the Stock Market's Troubles." *CNBC*, updated March 11, 2020. *https://www.cnbc.com/2020/03/11/why-millennials-might-not-care-that-the-stock-market-is-crashing.html.*

OpenSecrets.org. "Politicians & Elections." Accessed December 23, 2020. *https://www.opensecrets.org/elections/.*

Roberts, David. "Meet the Fossil Fuel All-Stars Trump as Appointed to his Administration." *Vox*, June 14, 2017. *https://www.vox.com/policy-and-politics/2017/6/13/15789772/trumps-fossil-fuel-all-stars.*

Rodney and Otamatea Times, Waitemata and Kaipara Gazette. "Coal Consumption Affecting Climate." August 14, 1912. *https://paperspast.natlib.govt.nz/newspapers/ROTWKG19120814.2.56.5.*

Rust, Susanne. "California Communities Suing Big Oil over Climate Change Face a Key Hearing Wednesday." *Los Angeles Times*, February 5, 2020. *https://www.latimes.com/california/story/2020-02-05/california-counties-suing-oil-companies-over-climate-change-face-key-hearing-wednesday.*

Sönnichsen, N. "Natural Gas Consumption in the EU in Cubic Meters 1998-2018." *Statista*, June 23, 2020. *https://www.statista.com/statistics/265406/natural-gas-consumption-in-the-eu-in-cubic-meters/.*

The Economist Intelligence Unit. "Europe Coal Use on a Downward Spiral." *The Economist*, February 14, 2020. *http://www.eiu.com/industry/article/589070442/europe-coal-use-on-a-downward-spiral/2020-02-14.*

The New York Times "No Peril to Public Seen in Ethyl Gas; Bureau of Imtes Reports after Long Experiments with Motor Exhausts. More Deaths Are Unlikely All the 34-at Reconstruction Hospital Are Believed to Be out of Danger. Little Used in the City Tetra-ethyl Compound Sold to Only Two Firms, which Are Experimenting, Says Standard Oil." *The New York Times*, November 1, 1924. *https://www.nytimes.com/1924/11/01/archives/no-peril-to-public-seen-in-ethyl-gas-bureau-of-mines-reports-after.html.*

Tyler-Davies, Monica. "A New Fossil Free Milestone: $11 Trillion Has Been Committed to Divest from Fossil Fuels." *350.org*, September 8, 2019. *https://350.org/11-trillion-divested/*.

U.S. Census Bureau. "2019 U.S. Population Estimates Continue to Show the Nation's Growth is Slowing." December 30, 2019. *https://www.census.gov/newsroom/press-releases/2019/popest-nation.html*.

Watts, Jonathan, Gary Blight, Lydia McMullan, Pablo Gutiérrez. "Half a Century of Dither and Denial—A Climate Crisis Timeline." *The Guardian*, October 9, 2019. *https://www.theguardian.com/environment/ng-interactive/2019/oct/09/half-century-dither-denial-climate-crisis-timeline*.

World Resources Institute. "Leading U.S. Businesses Call on Congress to Enact a Market-Based Approach to Climate Change." May 15, 2019. *https://www.wri.org/news/2019/05/release-leading-us-businesses-call-congress-enact-market-based-approach-climate-change*.

Yoder, Kate. "Republicans Are Backing a 'Carbon Dividend.' What the Heck is that?" *Grist*, June 21, 2018. *https://grist.org/article/republicans-are-backing-a-carbon-dividend-what-the-heck-is-that/*.

Zou, Jie Jenny. "How Washington Unleashed Fossil-Fuel Exports and Sold out on Climate." *The Texas Tribune*, October 16, 2018. *https://www.texastribune.org/2018/10/16/how-washington-unleashed-fossil-fuel-exports-and-sold-out-climate/*.

CHAPTER 14. THE CONGRESS

Almukhtar, Sarah and Rod Nordland. "What did the U.S. Get for $2 Trillion in Afghanistan?" *The New York Times*, December 9, 2019. *https://www.nytimes.com/interactive/2019/12/09/world/middleeast/afghanistan-war-cost.html*.

American Public Power Association (APPA). "Public Power." Accessed October 18, 2020. *https://www.publicpower.org/public-power*.

Appalachian Voices. "Mountaintop Removal 101." Accessed September 16, 2020. *https://appvoices.org/end-mountaintop-removal/mtr101/*.

Best, Ryan. "Confederate Statues Were Never Really about Preserving History." *FiveThirtyEight*, July 8, 2020. *https://projects.fivethirtyeight.com/confederate-statues/*.

Brodkin, Jon. "City-Owned Internet Services Offer Cheaper and more Transparent Pricing." *Ars Technica*, January 15, 2018. *https://arstechnica.com/tech-policy/2018/01/city-owned-internet-services-offer-cheaper-and-more-transparent-pricing/.*

Budget Control Act of 2011, Pub. L. 112-25, 125 Stat. 239. *https://uslaw.link/citation/us-law/public/112/25.*

Carney, Jordain. "Senate GOP Votes to Permanently Ban Earmarks." *The Hill*, May 23, 2019. *https://thehill.com/homenews/senate/445338-senate-finance-senate-gop-votes-to-permanently-ban-earmarks.*

Chamberlain, Kendra. "Municipal Broadband Is Roadblocked or Outlawed in 22 States." *BroadbandNow Research*, May 13, 2020. *https://broadbandnow.com/report/municipal-broadband-roadblocks/.*

Channell, Jason, Elizabeth Curmi, Phuc Nguyen, Elaine Prior, Alastair R. Syme, Heath R. Jansen, Ebrahim Rahbari, Edward L. Morse, Seth M. Kleinman, and Time Kruger. "Energy Darwinism II: Why a Low Carbon Future Doesn't Have to Cost the Earth." *Citi Global Perspectives and Solutions*, August 2015. *https://ir.citi.com/hsq32Jl1m4aIzic-MqH8sBkPnbsqfnwy4Jgb1J2kIPYWIw5eM8yD3FY9VbGpK%2Baax.*

Chevron. "The Energy Transition: We Accept Science and Are Part of the Energy Future." Accessed September 24, 2020. *https://www.chevron.com/sustainability/environment/the-energy-transition.*

Crowley, Kevin. "All Eyes on Exxon and Chevron after BP Pledges to Go Carbon Neutral." *Los Angeles Times*, February 12, 2020. *https://www.latimes.com/business/story/2020-02-12/attention-on-exxon-chevron-after-bp-pledges-carbon-neutral.*

Davis, Jeff. "The Rule that Broke the Senate." *Politico Magazine*, October 15, 2017. *https://www.politico.com/magazine/story/2017/10/15/how-budget-reconciliation-broke-congress-215706.*

Dayen, David. "Nancy Pelosi Rams Austerity Provision into House Rules Package over Objections of Progressives." *The Intercept*, January 2, 2019. *https://theintercept.com/2019/01/02/nancy-pelosi-pay-go-rule/.*

Dunn, Amina. "Few Trump or Biden Supporters Have Close Friends who Back the Opposing Candidate." *Pew Research Center*, September 18, 2020. *https://www.pewresearch.org/fact-tank/2020/09/18/few-trump-or-biden-supporters-have-close-friends-who-back-the-opposing-candidate/.*

Ebrahimji, Alisha, Artemis Moshtaghian, and Lauren M. Johnson. "Confederate Statues Are Coming down following George Floyd's Death. Here's what we Know." *CNN*, updated July 1, 2020. *https://www.cnn. com/2020/06/09/us/confederate-statues-removed-george-floyd-trnd/ index.html.*

Eller, Donnelle. "Grassley Pushes Trump, EPA to Make Changes that Will Restore Biofuels Demand." *The Des Moines Register*, November 20, 2019. *https://www.desmoinesregister.com/story/money/agriculture/2019/11/20/grassley-lobbies-trump-epa-restore-ethanol-gallons-lost-waivers/4249785002/.*

Energy Policy Act of 2005, Pub. L. 109–58, 119 Stat. 594. *http://www.gpo. gov/fdsys/pkg/STATUTE-119/pdf/STATUTE-119-Pg594.pdf.*

Environmental and Energy Study Institute (EESI). "Fact Sheet: Fossil Fuel Subsidies: a Closer Look at Tax Breaks and Societal Costs." July 29, 2019. *https://www.eesi.org/papers/view/fact-sheet-fossil-fuel-subsidies-a-closer-look-at-tax-breaks-and-societal-costs.*

Grassley, Chuck. "Ethanol Is a Critical Piece of America's Energy Strategy." *CNBC*, May 11, 2018. *https://www.cnbc.com/2018/05/11/ethanol-is-critical-for-americas-energy-strategy-sen-grassley.html.*

Hanna, Thomas. "A History of Nationalization in the United States: 1917–2009." *The Next System Project*, November 4, 2019. *https://thenextsystem.org/history-of-nationalization-in-the-us.*

Hayes, Adam. "Why Didn't Quantitative Easing Lead to Hyperinflation." *Investopedia*, updated December 10, 2020. *https://www.investopedia. com/articles/investing/022615/why-didnt-quantitative-easing-lead-hyperinflation.asp.*

Holtz-Eakin, Doug. "How Much Will the Green New Deal Cost?" *Aspen Institute*, June 11, 2019. *https://www.aspeninstitute.org/blog-posts/how-much-will-the-green-new-deal-cost/.*

Horton, Emily. "The Legacy of the 2001 and 2003 "Bush" Tax Cuts." *Center on Budget and Policy Priorities*, October 23, 2017. *https://www. cbpp.org/research/federal-tax/the-legacy-of-the-2001-and-2003-bush-tax-cuts.*

Insinna, Valerie. "Inside America's Dysfunctional Trillion-Dollar Fighter-Jet Program." *The New York Times*, August 21, 2019. *https://www.*

nytimes.com/2019/08/21/magazine/f35-joint-strike-fighter-program.
html.

Kane, Paul. "Reid, Democrats Trigger 'Nuclear' Option; Eliminate most
Filibuster on Nominees." *The Washington Post*, November 21, 2013.
https://www.washingtonpost.com/politics/senate-poised-to-limit-
filibusters-in-party-line-vote-that-would-alter-centuries-of-prece-
dent/2013/11/21/d065cfe8-52b6-11e3-9fe0-fd2ca728e67c_story.html.

Khan, Rina Saeed. "As a 'Green Stimulus' Pakistan sets Virus-Idled to
Work Planting Trees." *Reuters*, April 28, 2020. *https://www.reuters.*
com/article/us-health-coronavirus-pakistan-trees-fea/as-a-green-
stimulus-pakistan-sets-virus-idled-to-work-planting-trees-idUSKC-
N22A369.

Klein, Ezra. "Bernie Sanders's Plan to Blow up the Filibuster and Pass
Medicare-for-all, Explained." *Vox*, April 11, 2019. *https://www.vox.*
com/policy-and-politics/2019/4/11/18306132/bernie-sanders-filibus-
ter-budget-reconciliation-medicare-60-votes.

Levitan, Dave. "The Green New Deal Costs Less than Doing Nothing."
The New Republic, May 3, 2019. *https://newrepublic.com/article/153702/*
green-new-deal-costs-less-nothing.

Matthews, Dylan. "Budget Reconciliation, Explained." *Vox*, November
23, 2016. *https://www.vox.com/policy-and-politics/2016/11/23/13709518/*
budget-reconciliation-explained.

McGreal, Chris. "Why Joe Lieberman Is Holding Barack Obama to Ran-
som over Healthcare." *The Guardian*, December 16, 2009. *https://www.*
theguardian.com/world/2009/dec/16/joe-lieberman-barack-obama-
us-healthcare.

Price, Asher. "'An Electrical Island': Texas Has Dodged Federal Regu-
lation for Years by Having its own Power Grid." *USA Today*, February 17, 2021. *https://www.usatoday.com/story/news/nation/2021/02/17/*
texas-power-grid-why-state-has-its-own-operated-ercot/6782380002/.

Pritchard, Justin. "How PACE Loans Work." *The Balance*, updated October 1, 2020. *https://www.thebalance.com/pace-loans-financing-for-*
upgrades-4124071.

Reynolds, Molly E. "What Is the Senate Filibuster, and what would it
Take to Eliminate it?" *Brookings*, September 9, 2020. *https://www.*

brookings.edu/policy2020/votervital/what-is-the-senate-filibuster-and-what-would-it-take-to-eliminate-it/.

Roberts, David. "On Climate Change, Oil and Gas Companies Have a Long Way to Go." *Vox*, September 25, 2020. *https://www.vox.com/energy-and-environment/2020/9/25/21452055/climate-change-exxon-bp-shell-total-chevron-oil-gas.*

Schiffman, Richard. "A Troubling Look at the Human Toll of Mountaintop Removal Mining." *Yale Environment 360*, November 21, 2017. *https://e360.yale.edu/features/a-troubling-look-at-the-human-toll-of-mountaintop-removal-mining.*

Stamp, Elizabeth. "Billionaire Bunkers: How the 1% Are Preparing for the Apocalypse." *CNN*, August 7, 2019 *https://www.cnn.com/style/article/doomsday-luxury-bunkers/index.html.*

Tausanovitch, Alex and Sam Berger. "The Impact of the Filibuster on Federal Policymaking." *Center for American Progress*, December 5, 2019. *https://www.americanprogress.org/issues/democracy/reports/2019/12/05/478199/impact-filibuster-federal-policymaking/.*

U.S. Constitution, 14th Amendment, Section 4. *https://www.law.cornell.edu/constitution/amendmentxiv.*

U.S. Department of Energy (USDOE). "Property Assessed Clean Energy Programs." Accessed September 16, 2020. *https://www.energy.gov/eere/slsc/property-assessed-clean-energy-programs.*

U.S. Energy Information Administration (USEIA). "U.S. Electric System is Made up of Interconnections and Balancing Authorities." July 20, 2016. *https://www.eia.gov/todayinenergy/detail.php?id=27152.*

U.S. Environmental Protection Agency (USEPA). "U.S. Electricity Grid & Markets." Accessed September 16, 2020. *https://www.epa.gov/greenpower/us-electricity-grid-markets.*

United States Senate. "Filibuster and Cloture." Accessed September 18, 2020. *https://www.senate.gov/artandhistory/history/common/briefing/Filibuster_Cloture.htm.*

USA Facts. "Federal Farm Subsidies: What the Data Says." January 20, 2020. *https://usafacts.org/articles/federal-farm-subsidies-what-data-says/.*

Waterson, Jim. "Guardian to Ban Advertising from Fossil Fuel Firms." *The Guardian*, January 29, 2020. *https://www.theguardian.com/*

media/2020/jan/29/guardian-to-ban-advertising-from-fossil-fuel-firms-climate-crisis.

Zukowski, Keith. "These Red and Blue States Are Tackling Climate Change since Trump Won't." *Environmental Defense Fund*, November 1, 2018. *https://www.edf.org/blog/2018/11/01/these-red-and-blue-states-are-tackling-climate-change-trump-wont.*

CHAPTER 15. THE EXECUTIVE

Atkin, Emily. "'I'm Not a Scientist': a Complete Guide to Politicians who Plead Ignorance on Climate Change." *Think Progress*, October 3, 2014. *https://archive.thinkprogress.org/im-not-a-scientist-a-complete-guide-to-politicians-who-plead-ignorance-on-climate-change-54de3a31644d/.*

Brown v. Board of Education, 347 U.S. 483, 1954. *https://tile.loc.gov/storage-services/service/ll/usrep/usrep347/usrep347483/usrep347483.pdf.*

Caldwell, Leigh Ann and Sahil Kapur. "McConnell Reaches Milestone on Judges by Filling Final Circuit Court Vacancy." *NBC News*, June 24, 2020. *https://www.nbcnews.com/politics/congress/mcconnell-reaches-milestone-judges-filling-final-circuit-court-vacancy-n1232011.*

Chappell, Bill. "California Gives Final OK to Require Solar Panels on New Houses." *NPR*, December 6, 2018. *https://www.npr.org/2018/12/06/674075032/california-gives-final-ok-to-requiring-solar-panels-on-new-houses.*

Colman, Zack. "Europe Threatens U.S. with Carbon Tariffs to Combat Climate Change." *Politico*, December 13, 2019. *https://www.politico.com/news/2019/12/13/europe-carbon-tariff-climate-change-084892.*

Darby, Luke. "What is Eco-Fascism, the Ideology Behind Attacks in El Paso and Christchurch?" *GQ*, August 7, 2019. *https://www.gq.com/story/what-is-eco-fascism.*

Ivanova, Irina. "Cities are Banning Natural Gas in New Homes, Citing Climate Change." *CBS News*, updated December 6, 2019. *https://www.cbsnews.com/news/cities-are-banning-natural-gas-in-new-homes-because-of-climate-change/.*

Kelemen, Michele. "Under Trump, More Big Donors Are Named Ambassadors—and Controversies Have Followed." *NPR*, August 18, 2020. *https://www.npr.org/2020/08/18/903199848/under-trump-more-big-donors-are-named-ambassadors-and-controversies-have-followe.*

Leuchtenburg, William E. "When Franklin Roosevelt Clashed with the Supreme Court—and Lost." *Smithsonian Magazine*, May 2005. *https:// www.smithsonianmag.com/history/when-franklin-roosevelt-clashed- with-the-supreme-court-and-lost-78497994/.*

Levinthal, Dave and Chris Zubak-Skees. "Barack Obama's Ambassador Legacy: Plum Postings for Big Donors." *The Center for Public Integrity,* January 4, 2017. *https://publicintegrity.org/politics/barack-obamas- ambassador-legacy-plum-postings-for-big-donors/.*

Marbury v. Madison, 5 U.S. 137, 1803. *http://cdn.loc.gov/service/ll/usrep/ usrep005/usrep005137/usrep005137.pdf.*

Moffitt, Benjamin. "The Trouble with Anti-populism: Why the Champions of Civility Keep Losing." *The Guardian*, February 14, 2020. *https://www.theguardian.com/politics/2020/feb/14/anti-populism-pol- itics-why-champions-of-civility-keep-losing.*

Mogensen, Jackie Flynn. "What Could Happen if a Democratic President Declared a National Climate Emergency." *Bulletin of the Atomic Scientists,* March 9, 2019. *https://thebulletin.org/2019/03/ what-could-happen-if-a-democratic-president-declared-a-nation- al-climate-emergency/.*

National Conference of State Legislature (NCSL). "State Renewable Portfolio Standards and Goals." April 17, 2020. *https://www.ncsl.org/ research/energy/renewable-portfolio-standards.aspx.*

Office of the United States Trade Representative (OUSTR). "Agreement between the United States of America, the United Mexican States, and Canada Text." Accessed September 20, 2020. *https://ustr.gov/ trade-agreements/free-trade-agreements/united-states-mexico-can- ada-agreement/agreement-between.*

Plessy v. Ferguson, 163 U.S. 537, 1896. *https://supreme.justia.com/cases/ federal/us/163/537/.*

Reuters Staff. "France Says Won't Support Mercosur Given Brazil President's Climate Comments." *Reuters*, August 23, 2019. *https://www. reuters.com/article/us-brazil-politics-france/france-says-wont-sup- port-mercosur-given-brazil-presidents-climate-comments-idUSKCN- 1VD1A3.*

Savell, Stephanie and 5W Infographics. "This Map Shows where in the World the U.S. Military Is Combatting Terrorism." *Smithsonian Mag-*

azine, January/February 2019. *https://www.smithsonianmag.com/history/map-shows-places-world-where-us-military-operates-180970997/*.

Shapiro, Walter. "The Case Against Court-Packing." *Brennan Center for Justice*, June 24, 2019. *https://www.brennancenter.org/our-work/analysis-opinion/case-against-court-packing*.

The National Emergencies Act of 1976, Pub. Law 94-412, 90 Stat. 1255. *https://www.govinfo.gov/content/pkg/STATUTE-90/pdf/STATUTE-90-Pg1255.pdf*.

Treyz, Catherine. "Lindsey Graham Jokes about how to Get away with Murdering Ted Cruz." *CNN Politics*, February 26, 2016. *https://www.cnn.com/2016/02/26/politics/lindsey-graham-ted-cruz-dinner/index.html*.

U.S. Constitution, Article II section 2. *https://www.law.cornell.edu/constitution/articleii#section2*.

Union of Concerned Scientists (UCS). "Each Country's Share of CO2 Emissions." Updated August 12, 2020. *https://www.ucsusa.org/resources/each-countrys-share-co2-emissions*.

Walker, Shaun. "Migration v Climate: Europe's New Political Divide." *The Guardian*, December 2, 2019. *https://www.theguardian.com/environment/2019/dec/02/migration-v-climate-europes-new-political-divide*.

Windustry. "How Much to Wind Turbines Cost?" Accessed September 20, 2020. *http://www.windustry.org/how_much_do_wind_turbines_cost*.

CHAPTER 16. YOU

Cole, Devan. "Progressive House Democrats Rebuke DCCC 'Blacklist' of Companies Working with Primary Challengers to Incumbent Democrats." *CNN Politics*, April 1, 2019. *https://www.cnn.com/2019/03/31/politics/dccc-primary-challenger-rule/index.html*.

Colman, Zach. "Gaetz Drafting 'Green Real Deal' Climate Resolution." *Politico*, March 3, 2019. *https://www.politico.com/story/2019/03/22/gaetz-green-real-deal-1290463*.

Forgey, Quint. "AOC: 'In any other Country, Joe Biden and I would not Be in the Same Party'." *Politico*, updated January 6, 2020. *https://www.politico.com/news/2020/01/06/alexandria-ocasio-cortez-joe-biden-not-same-party-094642*.

Murray, Stephanie. "Markey Overcomes Kennedy Challenge in Massachusetts." *Politico*, September 1, 2020. *https://www.politico.com/news/2020/09/01/massachusetts-primary-markey-kennedy-407078*.

Mutnick, Ally. "Rep. Dan Lipinski Falls in Democratic Primary." *Politico*, April 18, 2020. *https://www.politico.com/news/2020/03/18/rep-dan-lipinski-falls-in-democratic-primary-135175*.

Nawaguna, Elvina. "Young Republicans Push Party to Act on Climate Change." *Roll Call*, February 13, 2020. *https://www.rollcall.com/2020/02/13/young-republicans-push-party-to-act-on-climate-change/*.

Nguyen, Daisy. "Approvals for New Oil and Gas Wells up in California." *AP News*, September 2, 2020. *https://apnews.com/d04910d29539d39e24eaa725bcf4545f*.

OpenSecrets.org. "Politicians & Elections." Accessed December 23, 2020. *https://www.opensecrets.org/elections/*.

Rainey, James. "Bob Inglis, a Republican Believe in Climate Change, Is out to Convert his Party." *NBC News*, September 30, 2018. *https://www.nbcnews.com/news/us-news/bob-inglis-republican-believer-climate-change-out-convert-his-party-n912066*.

Roberts, David. "This One Weird Trick Can Help any State or City Pass Clean Energy Policy." *Vox*, December 26, 2019. *https://www.vox.com/energy-and-environment/2019/5/15/18624294/renewable-energy-policy-cities-states*.

Schwarz, Jon. "Barack Obama Never Said Money Wasn't Corrupting; in Fact, he Said the Opposite." *The Intercept*, April 15, 2016. *https://theintercept.com/2016/04/15/barack-obama-never-said-money-wasnt-corrupting-in-fact-he-said-the-opposite/*.

Silver, Nate. "The Invisible Undecided Voter." *FiveThirtyEight*, January 23, 2017. *https://fivethirtyeight.com/features/the-invisible-undecided-voter/*.

Smith-Schoenwalder, Cecelia. "Poll: Young Republicans Break with Party on Climate Change." *U.S. News & World Report*, November 25, 2019. *https://www.usnews.com/news/politics/articles/2019-11-25/poll-young-republicans-break-with-party-on-climate-change*.

Stone, Jon. "Anti-Corbyn Labour Officials Worked to Lose General Election to Oust Leader, Leaked Dossier Finds." *The Independent*, April

13, 2020. *https://www.independent.co.uk/news/uk/politics/labour-leak-report-corbyn-election-whatsapp-antisemitism-tories-yougov-poll-a9462456.html*.

Taibbi, Matt. "Far too many House Seats Have Been Uncontested for too Long." *Rolling Stone*, November 6, 2018. *https://www.rollingstone.com/politics/politics-features/uncontested-house-seats-history-752658/*.

Villarreal, Alexandra. "Meet the Doomers: Why some Young US Voters Have Given up Hope on Climate." *The Guardian*, September 21, 2020. *https://www.theguardian.com/environment/2020/sep/21/meet-the-doomers-some-young-us-voters-have-given-up-hope-on-climate*.

Made in the USA
Middletown, DE
12 May 2021